T0201814

Geometric and Topological Inference

Geometric and topological inference deals with the retrieval of information about a geometric object using only a finite set of possibly noisy sample points. It has connections to manifold learning and provides the mathematical and algorithmic foundations of the rapidly evolving field of topological data analysis. Building on a rigorous treatment of simplicial complexes and distance functions, this self-contained book covers key aspects of the field, from data representation and combinatorial questions to manifold reconstruction and persistent homology. It can serve as a textbook for graduate students or researchers in mathematics, computer science and engineering interested in a geometric approach to data science.

JEAN-DANIEL BOISSONNAT is a Research Director at INRIA, France. His research interests are in Computational Geometry and Topology. He has published several books and more than 180 research papers, and is on the editorial board of the *Journal of the ACM* and of *Discrete and Computational Geometry*. He received the IBM award in Computer Science in 1987, the EADS award in Information Sciences in 2006 and was awarded an advanced grant from the European Research Council in 2014. He has taught at several universities in Paris and at the Collège de France.

FRÉDÉRIC CHAZAL is a Research Director at INRIA, France, where he is heading the DataShape team, a pioneering and world leading group in computational geometry and topological data analysis. His current primary research is on topological data analysis and its connections with statistics and machine learning, and he has authored several reference papers in this domain. He is an associate editor of four international journals and he teaches topological data analysis in various universities and engineering schools in the Paris area.

MARIETTE YVINEC was a researcher at INRIA, France. She is a specialist in the field of shape reconstruction and meshing, and taught master's courses on the subject in various universities in Paris. She coauthored a reference book on computational geometry with Jean-Daniel Boissonnat, and played an active role in the design and development of the software library CGAL.

Cambridge Texts in Applied Mathematics

All titles listed below can be obtained from good booksellers or from Cambridge University Press. For a complete series listing, visit www.cambridge.org/mathematics.

Geometric and Topological Inference

JEAN-DANIEL BOISSONNAT
INRIA Sophia Antipolis

FRÉDÉRIC CHAZAL
INRIA Saclay – Ile-de-France

MARIETTE YVINEC
INRIA Sophia Antipolis

CAMBRIDGE
UNIVERSITY PRESS

CAMBRIDGE
UNIVERSITY PRESS

University Printing House, Cambridge CB2 8BS, United Kingdom

One Liberty Plaza, 20th Floor, New York, NY 10006, USA

477 Williamstown Road, Port Melbourne, VIC 3207, Australia

314–321, 3rd Floor, Plot 3, Splendor Forum, Jasola District Centre, New Delhi – 110025, India

79 Anson Road, #06–04/06, Singapore 079906

Cambridge University Press is part of the University of Cambridge.

It furthers the University's mission by disseminating knowledge in the pursuit of education, learning, and research at the highest international levels of excellence.

www.cambridge.org
Information on this title: www.cambridge.org/9781108419390
DOI: 10.1017/9781108297806

© Jean-Daniel Boissonnat, Frédéric Chazal and Mariette Yvinec 2018

First published 2018

Printed in the United States of America by Sheridan Books, Inc.

A catalogue record for this publication is available from the British Library.

Library of Congress Cataloging-in-Publication Data
Names: Boissonnat, J.-D. (Jean-Daniel), 1953– author. | Chazal, Frédéric, 1971– author. | Yvinec, Mariette, 1953– author.
Title: Geometric and topological inference / Jean-Daniel Boissonnat, INRIA Sophia Antipolis, Frédéric Chazal, Inria Saclay – Ile-de-France, Mariette Yvinec, INRIA Sophia Antipolis.
Description: New York, NY, USA : Cambridge University Press, 2018. | Includes bibliographical references and index.
Identifiers: LCCN 2018015875 | ISBN 9781108419390 (Hardback) | ISBN 9781108410892 (Paperback)
Subjects: LCSH: Shapes–Mathematical models. | Geometric analysis. | Pattern perception. | Topology.
Classification: LCC QA491 .B5995 2018 | DDC 514/.2–dc23
LC record available at https://lccn.loc.gov/2018015875

ISBN 978-1-108-41939-0 Hardback
ISBN 978-1-108-41089-2 Paperback

Contents

v

Introduction

Motivation and goals. In many practical situations, geometric objects are only known through a finite set of possibly noisy sample points. A natural question is then to recover the geometry and the topology of the unknown object from this information. The most classical example is probably surface reconstruction, where the points are measured on the surface of a real-world object. A perhaps more surprising example is the study of the large-scale structure formed by the galaxies, which cosmologists believe to be an interconnected network of walls and filaments. In other applications, the shape of interest may be a low-dimensional object embedded in a higher-dimensional space, which is the basic assumption in *manifold learning* [102]. This is for example the case in time series analysis, when the shape of study is the attractor of a dynamical system sampled by a sequence of observations. When these structures are highly nonlinear and have a nontrivial topology, as is often the case, simple dimensionality reduction techniques do not suffice and must be complemented with more geometric and topological techniques.

A lot of research was done in this direction, originating from several sources. A few contributions came from the field of *computational geometry*, where much effort was undertaken to elaborate provably correct surface reconstruction algorithms, under a suitable sampling condition. We refer to [65] for a thorough review of this approach. However, most of this research focused on the case of sampled smooth surfaces in $\mathbb{R}^3$, which is by now fairly well covered. Extending these results to higher-dimensional submanifolds and to nonsmooth objects is one of the objectives of this book. Such an extension requires new data structures to walk around the curse of dimensionality. Handling more general geometric shapes also requires concepts from topology and has provoked an interest in the subject of *computational topology*. Computational topology has recently gained a lot of momentum and has been very successful at providing qualitative invariants and efficient algorithms to compute them. Its application to data analysis led to the rapidly evolving field of *topological data analysis* that provides a general framework to analyze the shape of data and has been applied to various types of data across many fields.

This book. This book intends to cover various aspects of geometric and topological inference, from data representation and combinatorial questions to persistent homology, an adaptation of homology to point cloud data. The aim of this book is not to provide a comprehensive treatment of topological data analysis, but to describe the mathematical and algorithmic foundations of the subject.

Two main concepts will play a central role in this book: simplicial complexes and distance functions. *Simplicial complexes* generalize the notion of triangulation of a surface and are constructed by gluing together simplices: points, line segments, triangles, and their higher-dimensional counterparts. Simplicial complexes can be considered, at the same time, as continuous objects carrying topological and geometric information and as combinatorial data structures that can be efficiently implemented. Simplicial complexes can be used to produce fine meshes leading to faithful approximations well suited to scientific computing purposes, or much coarser approximations, still useful to infer important features of shapes such as their homology or some local geometric properties.

Simplicial complexes have been known and studied for a long time in mathematics but only used in low dimensions due to their high complexity. In this book, we will address the complexity issues by focusing on the inherent, usually unknown, structure in the data which we assume to be of relative low intrinsic dimension. We will put emphasis on output-sensitive algorithms, introduce new simplicial complexes with low complexity, and describe approximation algorithms that scale well with the dimension.

Another central concept in this book is the notion of *distance function*. All the simplicial complexes used in this book encode proximity relationships between the data points. A prominent role is taken by Voronoi diagrams, their dual Delaunay complexes and variants of those, but other simplicial complexes based on distances like the Čech, the Vietoris-Rips, or the witness complexes will also be considered.

This book is divided into four parts.

Part I contains two chapters that present background material on topological spaces and simplicial complexes.

Part II introduces Delaunay complexes and their variants. Since Delaunay complexes are closely related to polytopes, the main combinatorial and algorithmic properties of polytopes are presented first in Chapter 3.

Delaunay complexes, to be introduced in Chapter 4, are defined from Voronoi diagrams, which are natural space partitions induced by the distance function to a sample. Delaunay complexes appear as the underlying basic data structure for manifold reconstruction. The extensions of Voronoi diagrams and Delaunay complexes to weighted distances are also presented together with their relevant applications to kth-nearest neighbor search and Bregman divergences, which are used in information theory, image processing, and statistical analysis.

Although Delaunay triangulations have many beautiful properties, their size depends exponentially on the dimension of the space in the worst case. It is thus important to exhibit realistic assumptions under which the complexity of the Delaunay triangulation does not undergo such a bad behavior. This will be done through the notion of nets. Another issue comes from the fact that, in dimensions greater than 2, Delaunay simplices may have an arbitrarily small volume, even if their vertices are well distributed. Avoiding such bad simplices is a major issue and the importance of thick triangulations has been recognized since the early days of differential topology. They play a central role in numerical simulations to ensure the convergence of numerical methods solving partial differential equations. They also play a central role in the triangulation of manifolds and, in particular, the reconstruction of submanifolds of high-dimensional spaces as shown in Chapter 8. Chapter 5 defines thick triangulations and introduces a random perturbation technique to construct thick Delaunay triangulations in Euclidean space.

Chapter 6 introduces two filtrations of simplicial complexes. Filtrations are nested sequences of subcomplexes that allow to compute persistent homology as described in Chapter 11. We first introduce alpha-complexes and show that they provide natural filtrations of Delaunay and weighted Delaunay complexes. We then introduce witness complexes and their filtrations. The witness complex is a weak version of the Delaunay complex that can be constructed in general metric spaces using only pairwise distances between the points, without a need for coordinates. We will also introduce a filtration of the witness complex.

Part III is devoted to the problem of reconstructing a submanifold $\mathcal{M}$ of $\mathbb{R}^d$ from a finite point sample $P \in \mathcal{M}$. The ultimate goal is to compute a triangulation of $\mathcal{M}$, i.e., a simplicial complex that is homeomorphic to $\mathcal{M}$. This is a demanding quest and, in this part, we will restrict our attention to the case where $\mathcal{M}$ is a smooth submanifold of $\mathbb{R}^d$.

In Chapter 7, we introduce the basic concepts and results, and state a theorem that provides conditions for a simplicial complex $\hat{\mathcal{M}}$ with vertex set $P \subset \mathcal{M}$ to be both a triangulation and a good geometric approximation of $\mathcal{M}$.

Chapter 8 is devoted to the problem of reconstructing submanifolds from point samples. This problem is of primary importance when $\mathcal{M}$ is a surface of $\mathbb{R}^3$ (it is then known as the surface reconstruction problem). It also finds applications in higher dimensions in the context of data analysis where data are considered as points in some Euclidean space, of possibly high dimension. In this chapter, we first exhibit conditions under which the alpha-complex of $P \subset \mathcal{M}$ has the same homotopy type as $\mathcal{M}$, a weaker property than being homeomorphic to $\mathcal{M}$. We then consider the problem of reconstructing a smooth submanifold $\mathcal{M}$ embedded in a space of possibly high dimension d. We then cannot afford to triangulate the ambient space as is being routinely done when working in low dimensions. A way to walk around this difficulty is to assume, as is common practice in data analysis and machine learning, that the intrinsic dimension k of $\mathcal{M}$ is small, even if the dimension of the ambient space may be very large. Chapter 8 takes advantage of this assumption and presents a reconstruction algorithm whose complexity is linear in d and exponential only in k.

The assumptions made in Part III are very demanding: the geometric structures of the data should be smooth submanifolds, the amount of noise in the data should be small and the sampling density should be high. These assumptions may not be satisfied in practical situations. Part IV aims at weakening the assumptions. Chapter 9 studies the stability properties of the sublevel sets of distance functions and provide sampling conditions to infer the underlying geometry and topology of data.

Approximations in Chapter 9 are with respect to the Hausdorff distance. This is a too strong limitation when the data contain outliers that are far away from the underlying structure we want to infer. To overcome this problem, Chapter 10 introduces a new framework where data are no longer considered as points but as distributions of mass or, more precisely probability measures. It is shown that the distance function approach can be extended to this more general framework.

Although Chapters 9 and 10 provide strong results on the topology of the sublevel sets of distance functions, computing and manipulating such sublevel sets is limited in practice to low dimensions. To go beyond these limitations, we restrict our quest to the inference of some topological invariants of the level sets, namely their homology and the associated Betti numbers. Chapter 11 introduces persistent homology and provides tools to robustly infer the homology of sampled shapes.

Efficient implementations of most of the algorithms described in this book can be found in the CGAL library (www.cgal.org/) or in the GUDHI library (http://gudhi.gforge.inria.fr/).

Acknowledgments. This book results from long-standing joint research with several colleagues and collaborators and would not exist without their continuous support and unfailing friendship. We are especially indebted to David Cohen-Steiner, Ramsay Dyer, Vin de Silva, Arijit Ghosh, Marc Glisse, Leonidas Guibas, André Lieutier, Quentin Mérigot, Steve Oudot, and Mathijs Wintraecken who influenced this book in essential ways. This book also includes results obtained together with Clément Maria, Olivier Devillers, Kunal Dutta, and Frank Nielsen. We have been very lucky interacting with them. The book originates from a course that the authors gave at MPRI (*Master Parisien de Recherche en Informatique*). Many students and colleagues commented on parts of this book. We are particularly grateful to Ramsay Dyer, Arijit Ghosh, and Mathijs Wintraecken for helping shaping Part II, and to Claire Brécheteau for kindly reading Part III and suggesting improvements. We also thank Clément Maria, Mael Rouxel-Labbé, and Mathijs Wintraecken for some of the figures.

The research leading to this book has been partially supported by the Agence Nationale de la Recherche under the project TopData and by the European Research Council under the Advanced Grant GUDHI (Geometric Understanding in Higher Dimensions).

PART I

TOPOLOGICAL PRELIMINARIES

1

Topological Spaces

Basic mathematical notions useful in the rest of this book are given in this chapter. For conciseness, the definitions and results are not always given in full. They are restricted to the simplest version necessary to follow and understand the results and proofs in this book.

1.1 Topological Spaces

This section lists a few basic notions and definitions from general topology. Most of the topological objects encountered in this book are metric spaces whose definition is also recalled.

Definition 1.1 (Topological space) A *topology* on a set X is a family $\mathcal{O}$ of subsets of X that satisfies the three following conditions:

1. the empty set $\emptyset$ and X are elements of $\mathcal{O}$,
2. any union of elements of $\mathcal{O}$ is an element of $\mathcal{O}$,
3. any finite intersection of elements of $\mathcal{O}$ is an element of $\mathcal{O}$.

The set X together with the family $\mathcal{O}$, whose elements are called open sets, is a *topological space*. A subset C of X is *closed* if its complement is an open set. If $Y \subset X$ is a subset of X, then the family $\mathcal{O}_Y = \{O \cap Y : O \in \mathcal{O}\}$ is a topology on Y, called the *induced topology*.

Definition 1.2 (Closure, interior and boundary) Let S be a subset of a topological space X. The *closure* $\bar{S}$ of S is the smallest closed set containing S. The *interior* $\mathring{S}$ of S is the largest open set contained in S. The *boundary* ∂S of S is the set difference $\partial S = \bar{S} \setminus \mathring{S}$.

Definition 1.3 (Metric space) A *metric (or distance)* on a set X is a map $d : X \times X \to [0, +\infty)$ such that:

1. for any $x, y \in X$, $d(x, y) = d(y, x)$,
2. for any $x, y \in X$, $d(x, y) = 0$ if and only if $x = y$,
3. for any $x, y, z \in X$, $d(x, z) \le d(x, y) + d(y, z)$.

The set X together with d is a *metric space*. The smallest topology containing all the open balls $B(x, r) = \{y \in X : d(x, y) < r\}$ is called the *metric topology* on X induced by d.

Definition 1.4 (Continuous map) A map $f : X \to X'$ between two topological spaces X and X' is *continuous* if and only if the pre-image $f^{-1}(O') = \{x \in X : f(x) \in O'\}$ of any open set $O' \subset X'$ is an open set of X. Equivalently, f is continuous if and only if the pre-image of any closed set in X' is a closed set in X.

Definition 1.5 (Compact space) A topological space X is a *compact space* if any open cover of X admits a finite subcover, i.e. for any family $\{U_i\}_{i \in I}$ of open sets such that $X = \cup_{i \in I} U_i$ there exists a finite subset $J \subseteq I$ of the index set I such that $X = \cup_{j \in J} U_j$.

For metric spaces, compacity is characterized using sequences: a metric space X is compact if and only if any sequence in X has a convergent subsequence.

Definition 1.6 (Connected spaces) A topological space X is connected if it is not the union of two disjoint open sets: if O_1, O_2 are two disjoint open sets such that $X = O_1 \cup O_2$ then $O_1 = \emptyset$ or $O_2 = \emptyset$.

A topological space X is path-connected if for any $x, y \in X$ there exists a continuous map $\gamma : [0, 1] \to X$ such that $\gamma(0) = x$ and $\gamma(1) = y$.

A path-connected space is always connected, but the reverse is not true in general. See Exercise 1.1.

Euclidean spaces. The space $\mathbb{R}^d$, $d \ge 1$ and its subsets are examples of particular interest. Throughout the book, for $x = (x_1, \cdots, x_d) \in \mathbb{R}^d$

$$\|x\| = \sum_{i=1}^{d} x_i^2$$

denotes the *Euclidean norm* on $\mathbb{R}^d$. It induces the *Euclidean metric* on $\mathbb{R}^d$: $d(x, y) = \|x - y\|$. The standard topology on $\mathbb{R}^d$ is the one induced by the Euclidean metric.

A subset $K \subset \mathbb{R}^d$ (endowed with the topology induced from the Euclidean one) is compact if and only if it is closed and bounded (Heine–Borel theorem).

1.2 Comparing Topological Spaces

There are many ways of measuring how close two objects are. We distinguish between topological and geometric criteria.

1.2.1 Homeomorphism, Isotopy and Homotopy Equivalence

In topology, two topological spaces are considered to be the same when they are *homeomorphic*.

Definition 1.7 (Homeomorphism) Two topological spaces X and Y are homeomorphic if there exists a continuous bijective map $h : X \to Y$ such that its inverse h^{-1} is also continuous. The map h is called a homeomorphism.

As an example, a circle and a simple closed polygonal curve are homeomorphic. By contrast, a circle and a segment are not homeomorphic. See Exercise 1.6.

The continuity of the inverse map in the definition is automatic in some cases. If U is an open subset of $\mathbb{R}^d$ and $f : U \to \mathbb{R}^d$ is an injective continuous map, then $V = f(U)$ is open and f is a homeomorphism between U and V by Brower's invariance of domain.[1] The domain invariance theorem may be generalized to manifolds: If M and N are topological k-manifolds without boundary and $f : U \to N$ is an injective continuous map from an open subset of M to N, then f is open and is an homeomorphism between U and $f(U)$.

If X is homeomorphic to the standard unit ball of $\mathbb{R}^d$, X is called a *topological ball*.

The notions of compacity and connexity are preserved by homeomorphism. See Exercise 1.4.

Let h be a map between two topological spaces X and Y. If h is a homeomorphism onto its image, it is called an *embedding* of X in Y.

When the spaces X and Y are subspaces of $\mathbb{R}^d$, the notion of *isotopy* is stronger than the notion of homeomorphism to distinguish between spaces.

Definition 1.8 (Ambient isotopy) An ambient isotopy between $X \subset \mathbb{R}^d$ and $Y \subset \mathbb{R}^d$ is a map $F : \mathbb{R}^d \times [0, 1] \to \mathbb{R}^d$ such that $F(., 0)$ is the identity map on $\mathbb{R}^d$, $F(X, 1) = Y$ and for any $t \in [0, 1]$, F is a homeomorphism of $\mathbb{R}^d$.

---

[1] See T. Tao's blog https://terrytao.wordpress.com/2011/06/13/brouwers-fixed-point-and-invariance-of-domain-theorems-and-hilberts-fifth-problem/

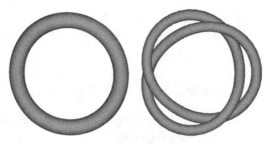

Figure 1.1 Two surfaces embedded in $\mathbb{R}^3$ homeomorphic to a torus that are not isotopic.

Intuitively, the previous definition means that X can be continuously deformed into Y without creating any self-intersection or topological changes. The notion of isotopy is stronger than the notion of homeomorphism in the sense that if X and Y are isotopic, then they are obviously homeomorphic. Conversely, two subspaces of $\mathbb{R}^d$ that are homeomorphic may not be isotopic. This is the case for a knotted and an unknotted torus embedded in $\mathbb{R}^3$ as the ones in Figure 1.1. Note that, although intuitively obvious, proving that these two surfaces are not isotopic is a nonobvious exercise that requires some background in algebraic topology.

In general, deciding whether two spaces are homeomorphic is a very difficult task. It is sometimes more convenient to work with a weaker notion of equivalence between spaces called *homotopy equivalence*.

Given two topological spaces X and Y, two maps $f_0, f_1 : X \to Y$ are *homotopic* if there exists a continuous map $H : [0,1] \times X \to Y$ such that for all $x \in X$, $H(0,x) = f_0(x)$ and $H(1,x) = f_1(x)$. Homotopy equivalence is defined in the following way.

Definition 1.9 (Homotopy equivalence) Two topological spaces X and Y have the same homotopy type (or are homotopy equivalent) if there exist two continuous maps $f : X \to Y$ and $g : Y \to X$ such that $g \circ f$ is homotopic to the identity map in X and $f \circ g$ is homotopic to the identity map in Y.

As an example, the unit ball in a Euclidean space and a point are homotopy equivalent but not homeomorphic. A circle and an annulus are also homotopy equivalent: see Figure 1.2 and Exercise 1.8.

Definition 1.10 (Contractible space) A contractible space is a space that has the same homotopy type as a single point.

For example, a segment or more generally any ball in a Euclidean space $\mathbb{R}^d$ is contractible: see Exercise 1.7.

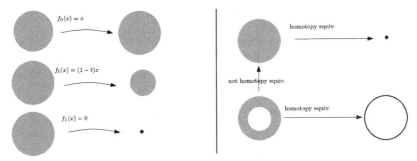

Figure 1.2 An example of two maps that are homotopic (left) and examples of spaces that are homotopy equivalent, but not homeomorphic (right).

It is often difficult to prove homotopy equivalence directly from the definition. When Y is a subset of X, the following criterion is useful to prove homotopy equivalence between X and Y.

Proposition 1.11 *If $Y \subset X$ and if there exists a continuous map $H : [0,1] \times X \to X$ such that:*

1. $\forall x \in X, H(0,x) = x,$
2. $\forall x \in X, H(1,x) \in Y,$
3. $\forall y \in Y, \quad \forall t \in [0,1], H(t,y) \in Y,$

then X and Y are homotopy equivalent.

Definition 1.12 (Deformation retract) If, in Proposition 1.11, the last property of H is replaced by the following stronger one

$$\forall y \in Y, \quad \forall t \in [0,1], \quad H(t,y) = y,$$

then H is called a *deformation retract* of X to Y.

A classical way to characterize and quantify topological properties and features of spaces is to consider their *topological invariants*. These are mathematical objects (numbers, groups, polynomials, ...) associated to each topological space that have the property of being the same for homeomorphic spaces. The homotopy type is clearly a topological invariant: two homeomorphic spaces are homotopy equivalent. The converse is false: for example, a point and a segment are homotopy equivalent but are not homeomorphic. See Exercise 1.7. Moreover, most of the topological invariants considered in the sequel are indeed homotopy invariants, i.e. they are the same for spaces that are homotopy equivalent.

1.2.2 Hausdorff Distance

The set of compact subsets of a metric space can be endowed with a metric, called the Hausdorff distance, that allows to measure how two compact subsets are from each other. We give the definition for compact subspaces of $\mathbb{R}^d$ here but this immediately adapts to the compact subsets of any metric space.

Definition 1.13 (Offset) Given a compact set X of $\mathbb{R}^d$, the *tubular neighborhood* or *offset* X^ε of X of radius ε, i.e., the set of all points at distance at most ε from X:

$$X^\varepsilon = \left\{ y \in \mathbb{R}^d : \inf_{x \in X} \|x - y\| \le \varepsilon \right\} = \bigcup_{x \in X} \bar{B}(x, \varepsilon) \right\}$$

where $\bar{B}(x, \varepsilon)$ denotes the closed ball $\{y \in \mathbb{R}^d : \|x - y\| \le \varepsilon\}$.

Definition 1.14 The *Hausdorff distance* $d_H(X, Y)$ between two closed subsets X and Y of $\mathbb{R}^d$ is the infimum of the $\varepsilon \ge 0$ such that $X \subset Y^\varepsilon$ and $Y \subset X^\varepsilon$. Equivalently,

$$d_H(X, Y) = \max \left(\sup_{y \in Y} (\inf_{x \in X} \|x - y\|), \sup_{x \in X} (\inf_{y \in Y} \|x - y\|) \right).$$

The Hausdorff distance defines a distance on the space of compact subsets of $\mathbb{R}^d$. See Exercise 1.10.

1.3 Exercises

Exercise 1.1 Let X be a path connected space. Show that X is connected. Let $X \subset \mathbb{R}^2$ be the union of the vertical closed segment $\{0\} \times [-1, 1]$ and the curve $\{(t, sin(\frac{1}{t})) \in \mathbb{R}^2 : t \in (0, 1]\}$. Show that X is compact and connected but not path-connected.

Exercise 1.2 Let S be a subset of a metric space X. Show that:

1. $x \in X \in \bar{S}$ if and only if for any $r > 0$, $B(x, r) \cap S \ne \emptyset$.
2. $x \in X \in \mathring{S}$ if and only if there exists $r > 0$ such that $B(x, r) \subset S$.

Exercise 1.3 Let X be a metric space. Given $x \in X$ and $r > 0$, show that the set $\bar{B}(x, r) = \{y \in X : d(x, y) \le r\}$ is a closed set which is indeed the closure of the open ball $B(x, r) = \{y \in X : d(x, y) < r\}$.

Exercise 1.4 Let X, Y two homeomorphic topological spaces. Prove the following equivalences:

1. X is compact if and only if Y is compact.
2. X is connected (resp. path-connected) if and only if Y is connected (resp. path-connected).

Exercise 1.5 Show that the Euclidean space is not compact (without using the Heine–Borel theorem).

Exercise 1.6 A continuous polygonal curve $P \subset \mathbb{R}^2$ with consecutive edges $e_1 = [p_1, p_2], e_2 = [p_2, p_3], \ldots, e_n = [p_n, p_{n+1}]$ is simple and closed if and only if $e_i \cap e_j = \emptyset$ whenever $2 \leq |i - j|$ mod (n), $e_i \cap e_{i+1} = p_{i+1}$ for $i = 1, \ldots, n - 1$ and $e_n \cap e_1 = p_1$. Show that P is homeomorphic to a circle. Show that a circle and a segment are not homeomorphic.

Exercise 1.7 Let X be a segment (i.e., a space homeomorphic to $[0, 1]$) and let Y be a point. Prove that X and Y are homotopy equivalent but not homeomorphic. More generally prove that any ball in $\mathbb{R}^d$ is contractible.

Exercise 1.8 Let X be the unit circle in $\mathbb{R}^2$ and let $Y \subset \mathbb{R}^2$ be the annulus of inner radius 1 and outer radius 2. Prove that X and Y are homotopy equivalent.

Exercise 1.9 Let X and Y be two topological spaces that are homotopy equivalent. Show that if X is path-connected, then Y is also path-connected.

Exercise 1.10 Show that the Hausdorff distance is a distance on the space of compact subsets of $\mathbb{R}^d$. Show that this is no longer true if we extend the definition to noncompact sets (give an example of two different sets that are at distance 0 from each other).

1.4 Bibliographical Notes

All the ideas introduced in this chapter are classical but fundamental, and presented with many details in the classical mathematical literature. For more details about basic topology, the reader may refer to any standard book on general topology such as, e.g. [111]. The geometry of metric spaces is a wide subject in mathematics. The reader interested in the topics may have a look at [30]. More details and results about the notions of homotopy and homotopy equivalence can be found in [86, pp. 171–172] or [110, p. 108].

2

Simplicial Complexes

Geometric shapes like curves, surfaces or their generalization in higher dimensions are "continuous" mathematical objects that cannot be directly encoded as a finite discrete structure usable by computers or computing devices. It is thus necessary to find representations of these shapes that are rich enough to capture their geometric structure and to comply with the constraints inherent to the discrete and finite nature of implementable data structures. By contrast, when the only available data are point clouds sampled around unknown shapes, it is necessary to be able to build some continuous space on top of the data that faithfully encode the topology and the geometry of the underlying shape. Simplicial complexes offer a classical and flexible solution to overcome these difficulties.

2.1 Geometric Simplicial Complexes

The points of a finite set $P = \{p_0, p_1, \cdots, p_k\}$ in $\mathbb{R}^d$ are said to be *affinely independent* if they are not contained in any affine subspace of dimension less than k.

Definition 2.1 (Simplex) Given a set $P = \{p_0, \ldots, p_k\} \subset \mathbb{R}^d$ of $k+1$ affinely independent points, the k-dimensional simplex σ, or k-*simplex* for short, spanned by P is the set of convex combinations

$$\sum_{i=0}^{k} \lambda_i p_i, \quad \text{with} \quad \sum_{i=0}^{k} \lambda_i = 1 \quad \text{and} \quad \lambda_i \geq 0.$$

The points $p_0, \ldots, p_k$ are called the vertices of σ.

Notice that σ is the convex hull of the points P, i.e., the smallest convex subset of $\mathbb{R}^d$ containing $p_0, p_1, \cdots, p_k$. A 0-simplex is a point, a 1-simplex is a line segment, a 2-simplex is a triangle, and a 3-simplex is a tetrahedron.

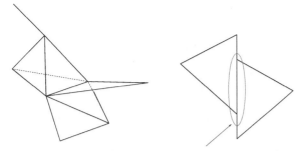

Figure 2.1 Left: an example of a simplicial complex. Right: a union of simplices
that is not a simplicial complex

The *faces* of the simplex σ whose vertex set is P are the simplices spanned
by the subsets of P. Any face different from σ is called a *proper face* of σ.

For example, the faces of a triangle spanned by three independent points
$\{p_0, p_1, p_2\} \in \mathbb{R}^d$ are the simplices $\emptyset, [p_0], [p_1], [p_0, p_1], [p_1, p_2], [p_2, p_0]$, and
$[p_0, p_1, p_2]$. Observe that, by convention, $\emptyset$ is usually added to the faces as the
simplex spanned by the empty subset of the vertices.

Definition 2.2 (Simplicial complex)   A (finite) simplicial complex K in $\mathbb{R}^d$
is a (finite) collection of simplices such that:

1. any face of a simplex of K is a simplex of K,
2. the intersection of any two simplices of K is either empty or a common face
    of both (see Figure 2.1).

All the simplicial complexes considered in this book are finite. The simplices
of K are called the *faces* of K. The *dimension* of K is the highest dimension of
its simplices. A complex of dimension k is also called a k-complex. A subset of
the simplices of K, which is itself a simplicial complex, is called a *subcomplex*
of K. The *j-skeleton* $\mathrm{Sk}_j(K)$ of K is the subcomplex of K consisting of the
simplices of dimension at most j.

For a simplicial complex K in $\mathbb{R}^d$, its *underlying space* $|K| \subset \mathbb{R}^d$ is the
union of the simplices of K. The *topology of K* is the topology induced on $|K|$
by the standard topology in $\mathbb{R}^d$. When there is no risk of confusion, we do not
clearly make the distinction between a complex in $\mathbb{R}^d$ and its underlying space.

2.2 Abstract Simplicial Complexes

Notice that when its vertex set is known, a simplicial complex in $\mathbb{R}^d$ is fully
characterized by the list of its simplices. This leads to the following notion.

Definition 2.3 (Abstract simplicial complex)   Let $V = \{v_1, \cdots v_n\}$ be a finite set. An abstract simplicial complex $\tilde{K}$ with vertex set V is a set of finite subsets of V satisfying the two conditions:

1. The elements of V belong to $\tilde{K}$.
2. If $\tau \in \tilde{K}$ and $\sigma \subseteq \tau$, then $\sigma \in \tilde{K}$.

The elements of $\tilde{K}$ are called the simplices or the faces of $\tilde{K}$. If $\sigma \in \tilde{K}$ has precisely $k + 1$ elements, the dimension of σ is k and we say that σ is a k-simplex. The dimension of $\tilde{K}$ is the maximal dimension of its simplices.

Any simplicial complex K in $\mathbb{R}^d$ naturally determines an abstract simplicial complex $\tilde{K}$, called the *vertex scheme* of K: K and $\tilde{K}$ have the same set of vertices and the simplices of $\tilde{K}$ are the sets of vertices of the simplices of K. Conversely, if an abstract complex $\tilde{K}$ is the vertex scheme of a complex K in $\mathbb{R}^d$, then K is called a *geometric realization* of $\tilde{K}$. Notice that any finite abstract simplicial complex $\tilde{K}$ has a geometric realization in a Euclidean space in the following way. Let $\{v_1, v_2, \cdots, v_n\}$ be the vertex set of $\tilde{K}$ where n is the number of vertices of $\tilde{K}$, and let $\sigma \subset \mathbb{R}^n$ be the simplex spanned by $\{e_1, e_2, \cdots, e_n\}$ where, for any $i = 1, \cdots, n$, e_i is the vector whose coordinates are all 0 except the *ith* one that is equal to 1. Then K is the subcomplex of σ defined by: $[e_{i_0}, \cdots, e_{i_k}]$ is a k-simplex of K if and only if $[v_{i_0}, \cdots, v_{i_k}]$ is a simplex of K. It can also be proven that any finite abstract simplicial complex of dimension d can be realized as a simplicial complex in $\mathbb{R}^{2d+1}$ (Exercice 2.3).

Definition 2.4 (Isomorphism of abstract simplicial complexes)   Two abstract simplicial complexes $\tilde{K}, \tilde{K}'$ with vertex sets V and V' are isomorphic if there exists a bijection $\phi : V \to V'$ such that $\{v_0, \cdots v_k\} \in \tilde{K}$ if and only if $\{\phi(v_0), \cdots \phi(v_k)\} \in \tilde{K}'$.

The relation of isomorphism between two abstract simplicial complexes induces homeomorphism between their geometric realizations.

Proposition 2.5   *If two simplicial complexes K, K' are the geometric realizations of two isomorphic abstract simplicial complexes $\tilde{K}, \tilde{K}'$, then $|K|$ and $|K'|$ are homeomorphic topological spaces. In particular, the underlying spaces of any two geometric realizations of an abstract simplicial complex are homeomorphic.*

In this book, we will often encounter abstract simplicial complexes whose vertices are points in $\mathbb{R}^d$. Let $\tilde{K}$ be an abstract complex with vertex set $V \subset \mathbb{R}^d$. If the convex hull of each k-simplex $\sigma = \{v_0, \cdots, v_k\} \in \tilde{K}$ is a geometric k-simplex in $\mathbb{R}^d$ and if the collection of these simplices defines a simplicial complex K, then we say that $\tilde{K}$ *naturally embeds* in $\mathbb{R}^d$ and that K is the *natural embedding* of $\tilde{K}$. When there is no ambiguity, the same notation is used for $\tilde{K}$ and K.

An important remark about terminology: As the underlying spaces of all geometric realizations of an abstract simplicial complex are homeomorphic to each other, it is usual to relate the topological properties of these underlying spaces to the complex itself. For example, when one claims that an abstract simplicial complex K is homeomorphic or homotopy equivalent to a topological space X, it is meant that the underlying space of any geometric realization of K is homeomorphic or homotopy equivalent to X.

2.3 Nerve

As noticed in previous the section, simplicial complexes can be seen at the same time as topological spaces and as purely combinatorial objects.

Definition 2.6 (Covers) An open cover of a topological space X is a collection $\mathcal{U} = (U_i)_{i \in I}$ of open subsets $U_i \subseteq X, i \in I$ where I is a set, such that $X = \cup_{i \in I} U_i$. Similarly, a closed cover of X is a collection of closed sets whose union is X.

Definition 2.7 (Nerve) Given a cover of a topological space X, $\mathcal{U} = (U_i)_{i \in I}$ we associate an abstract simplicial complex $C(\mathcal{U})$ whose vertex set is $\mathcal{U}$ and such that

$$\sigma = [U_{i_0}, U_{i_1}, \cdots, U_{i_k}] \in C(\mathcal{U}) \ \text{ if and only if } \ \cap_{j=0}^{k} U_{i_j} \neq \emptyset.$$

Such a simplicial complex is called *the nerve of the cover* $\mathcal{U}$.

When all the sets U_i are open and all their finite intersections are contractible, i.e., are homotopy equivalent to a point, the Nerve Theorem relates the topology of X and $C(\mathcal{U})$.

Theorem 2.8 (Nerve Theorem) *Let* $\mathcal{U} = (U_i)_{i \in I}$ *be a finite open cover of a subset* X *of* $\mathbb{R}^d$ *such that any intersection of the* U_i's *is either empty or contractible. Then* X *and* $C(\mathcal{U})$ *are homotopy equivalent.*

The nerve theorem also holds for closed covers under a slightly more restrictive assumption on X. The following version is general enough for our purpose.

Theorem 2.9 (Nerve Theorem for convex covers) *Let* $X \subset \mathbb{R}^d$ *be a finite union of closed convex sets* $\mathcal{F} = (F_i)_{i \in I}$ *in* $\mathbb{R}^d$. *Then* X *and* $C(\mathcal{F})$ *are homotopy equivalent.*

A cover satisfying the assumptions of the Nerve Theorem is sometimes called a *good cover*. The Nerve Theorem is of fundamental importance in computational topology and geometric inference: it provides a way to encode the homotopy type of continuous topological space X by a simplical complex describing the intersection pattern of a good cover. In particular, when X is a (finite) union of (closed or open) balls in $\mathbb{R}^d$, it is homotopy equivalent to the nerve of this union of balls.

2.4 Filtrations of Simplicial Complexes

Simplicial complexes often come with a specific ordering of their simplices that plays a fundamental role in geometry inference.

Definition 2.10 A filtration of a finite simplicial complex K is a nested sequence of sub-complexes $\emptyset = K^0 \subset K^1 \subset \cdots \subset K^m = K$ such that

$$K^{i+1} = K^i \cup \sigma^{i+1} \ \text{ where } \sigma^{i+1} \text{ is a simplex of } K.$$

Equivalently, a filtration of K can be seen as an ordering of the simplices such that for any $i \geq 0$, the collection of the first i simplices is a simplicial complex. To ensure this later condition, it is sufficient to know that every simplex σ^i appears in the filtration after all its faces.

As a filtration of K is just an ordering of the simplices, in some cases, it might be more natural to index the simplices by an increasing sequence $(\alpha_i)_{i=1}^m$ of real numbers: $\emptyset = K^{\alpha_0} \subset K^{\alpha_1} \subset \cdots \subset K^{\alpha_m} = K$. In this case, it is often convenient to extend the filtration to the whole set of real numbers by defining $K^\alpha = K^{\alpha^i}$ for $\alpha \in [\alpha_i, \alpha_{i+1})$, $K^\alpha = \emptyset$ for $\alpha < \alpha_0$ and $K^\alpha = K$ for $\alpha \geq K^{\alpha_m}$.

For example, when a function is defined on the vertices of K, on can define a sublevel set filtration in the following way.

Filtration associated to a function defined on the vertices of a complex.
Let K be a simplicial complex and let f be a real valued function defined on the vertices of K. For any simplex $\sigma = \{v_0, \cdots v_k\}$ one defines $f(\sigma)$ by

$$f(\sigma) = \max_{i=0 \cdots k} f(v_i)$$

Ordering the simplices of K according to the values of each simplex defines a filtration of K. Note that different simplices can have the same value. In this case, they are ordered according to increasing dimension and simplices of the same dimension with same value can be ordered arbitrarily. The filtration induced by f is the filtration by the sublevel sets $f^{-1}(]-\infty; t])$ of f.

2.5 Vietoris-Rips and Čech Filtrations

Filtrations are often built on top of finite sets of points to reveal the underlying topological structure of data (see Chapter 11). Let $P \subset \mathbb{R}^d$ be a (finite) set of points.

Definition 2.11 Given $\alpha > 0$, the Čech complex with vertex set P and parameter α is the nerve $\check{C}ech(P, \alpha)$ of the unions of balls centered on P with radius α. The simplices of $\check{C}ech(P, \alpha)$ are characterized by the following condition:

$$\{x_0, x_1, \ldots, x_k\} \in \check{C}ech(P, \alpha) \quad \Leftrightarrow \quad \bigcap_{i=0}^{k} B(x_i, \alpha) \neq \emptyset.$$

As α goes from 0 to $+\infty$, the nested sequence of complexes $\check{C}ech(P, \alpha)$ defines the Čech complex filtration (see Figure 2.2, left).

Given a k-dimensional face σ of the simplex of dimension $|P| - 1$, the smallest α such that $\sigma \in \check{C}ech(P, \alpha)$ is the radius of the smallest ball enclosing the vertices of σ. As a consequence, the k-dimensional skeleton of the Čech filtration can be computed by computing the $O(|P|^k)$ minimum enclosing balls of all the subsets of at most k points of P. Although the computation of the minimum ball enclosing a set of k points can be done in time $O(k)$ (see the Bibliographic Notes), the computation of the whole Čech filtration quickly becomes intractable in practice. Given $\alpha > 0$, the computation of the k-skeleton of $\check{C}ech(P, \alpha)$ can be done by first computing all the cliques of at most $(k + 1)$ vertices of the 1-skeleton of $\check{C}ech(P, \alpha)$ which is a graph, and second by selecting the cliques whose minimum enclosing ball has its radius upper bounded by α.

A simplicial complex that is closely related to the Čech filtration is the *Vietoris-Rips filtration*, Rips(P) (see Figure 2.2, right).

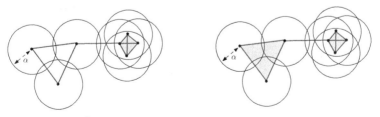

Figure 2.2 The Čech (left) and Vietoris-Rips (right) complexes built on top of a finite set of points in $\mathbb{R}^2$. Note that they both contain a 3-simplex and are thus not embedded in $\mathbb{R}^2$.

Definition 2.12   Given $\alpha > 0$, the Vietoris-Rips complex $\text{Rips}(P, \alpha)$ with vertext set P and parameter α is defined by the following condition

$$\{x_0, x_1, \cdots, x_k\} \in \text{Rips}(P, \alpha) \Leftrightarrow \|x_i - x_j\| \leq \alpha \quad \text{for all } i, j \in \{0, \ldots, k\}.$$

As α goes from 0 to $+\infty$, the nested sequence of complexes $\text{Rips}(P, \alpha)$ defines the Vietoris-Rips filtration.

The Vietoris-Rips complex is much simpler to compute than the Čech filtration as it just involves distance comparisons. The Vietoris-Rips complex is the largest simplicial complex that has the same 1-skeleton as the Čech complex. It is thus completely characterized by its 1-skeleton. The whole k-dimensional skeleton of the Vietoris-Rips filtration can be computed by computing the diameter of all the subsets of at most k points of P.

The Čech and the Vietoris-Rips filtrations are related by the following interleaving property that plays a fundamental role (see also Chapter 11).

Lemma 2.13   *Let P be a finite set of points in $\mathbb{R}^d$. for any $\alpha \geq 0$,*

$$\text{Rips}(P, \alpha) \subseteq \check{C}\text{ech}(P, \alpha) \subseteq \text{Rips}(P, 2\alpha)$$

Proof   If $\sigma = \{x_0, x_1, \cdots, x_k\} \in \text{Rips}(P, \alpha)$ then $x_0 \in \bigcap_{i=0}^{k} B(x_i, \alpha)$. So, $\sigma \in \check{C}\text{ech}(P, \alpha)$. This proves the first inclusion.

Now, if $\sigma = \{x_0, x_1, \cdots, x_k\} \in \check{C}\text{ech}(P, \alpha)$, there exists $y \in \mathbb{R}^d$ such that $y \in \bigcap_{i=0}^{k} B(x_i, \alpha)$, i.e. $\|x_i - y\| \leq \alpha$ for any $i = 0, \cdots k$. As a consequence, for all $i, j \in \{0, \ldots, k\}$, $\|x_i - x_j\| \leq 2\alpha$ and $\sigma \in \text{Rips}(P, 2\alpha)$. $\qquad \square$

Remark that the Čech and Vietoris-Rips filtrations can be defined for a set of points in any metric space and that the above interleaving property still holds. When the points P are in $\mathbb{R}^d$, the interleaving of Lemma 2.13 is not tight and can be slightly improved (see Exercise 11.3).

2.6 Combinatorial Manifolds Triangulations

Definition 2.14 (Star and link)   Let K be a simplicial complex with vertex set P. The star of $p \in P$ is the set of simplices of K that have p as a vertex. We denote it $\text{star}(p, K)$. The link of p is the set of simplices $\tau \subset \sigma$ such that $\sigma \in \text{star}(p, K)$ but $\tau \notin \text{star}(p, K)$. We denote it by $\text{link}(p, K)$.

Observe that the star of a simplex is *not* a complex, whereas the link is. We will use the name *closed star* of p in K to denote the subcomplex of K that consists of the simplices of $\text{star}(p, K)$ and their subfaces.

Definition 2.15 (Pure complex) A simplicial k-complex K is pure if every simplex in K is the face of a k-simplex.

Definition 2.16 (Boundary complex) Let K be a pure simplicial k-complex. The boundary of K, denoted ∂K is the $(k-1)$-subcomplex of K whose $(k-1)$-simplices are the $(k-1)$-simplices of K that are incident to only one face of dimension k.

Definition 2.17 (Combinatorial manifold) A simplicial complex K is a combinatorial k-manifold if

1. K is pure k complex
2. the link of any vertex of $K \setminus \partial K$ is a triangulated $(k-1)$-sphere
3. the link of any vertex of ∂K is a triangulated $(k-1)$-ball.

We define the *adjacency graph* of a combinatorial k-manifold K as the graph whose nodes are the k-simplices of K and two nodes are joined by an edge in the graph if the two simplices associated to the two nodes have a $(k-1)$-simplex in common.

An example of a combinatorial manifold is the boundary complex of a polytope (see Section 3.1).

Definition 2.18 (Triangulation of a point set) A triangulation of a finite point set $P \in \mathbb{R}^d$ is a geometric simplicial complex K whose vertex set is P and whose underlying space is the convex hull of P.

The triangulation of a finite point set $P \in \mathbb{R}^d$ is a combinatorial manifold whose boundary is the boundary complex of the convex hull of P (see Exercise 3.9).

Definition 2.19 (Triangulation of a topological space) A triangulation of a topological space X is a simplicial complex K and a homeomorphism $h : |K| \to X$.

2.7 Representation of Simplicial Complexes

To represent a simplicial complex K, we need a data structure that represents the simplices of the complex and is able to provide efficient implementations of elementary operations such as face and coface retrieval, and maintainance of the data structure upon elementary modifications of the complex, insertion or removal of a new simplex. In addition, we may want to attach a filtration to each simplex and iterate over the simplices of a filtered complex by increasing values of filtration. We present several data structures to represent simplicial complexes.

We say that two simplices σ and τ of a simplicial complex are *incident* if one is included in the other. We say that σ and τ are *adjacent* if they are incident and if their dimensions differ by exactly 1. The *Hasse diagram* of a simplicial complex K is a graph whose nodes represent the simplices (of all dimensions) and two nodes are joined by an arc if the associated simplices are adjacent.

The Hasse diagram provides an explicit representation of all the simplices of K. If the dimension of the complex is considered as a constant, it is easy to see that all elementary operations on K can be performed efficiently. However the size of the Hasse diagram may be problematic in practice when considering big complexes. A more compact data structure that still provides an explicit representation of all the simplices of K is the so-called *simplex tree* which is a minimal spanning tree of the Hasse diagram. The simplex tree is constructed as a prefix tree of the simplices considered as words on the alphabet $v_1, \ldots, v_n$ where $v_1, \ldots, v_n$ are the labels of the vertices of K (see Figure 2.3 and Exercise 2.1).

Both the Hasse diagram and the simplex tree are convenient to store and retrieve information attached to a simplex, e.g., a filtration value. Nevertheless, in some applications, we may content ourselves with less expressive but more compact representations. Instead of representing all simplices, one can represent only the maximal ones, i.e., the simplices that have no coface in the complex. This may lead to a dramatic saving in memory size as can be

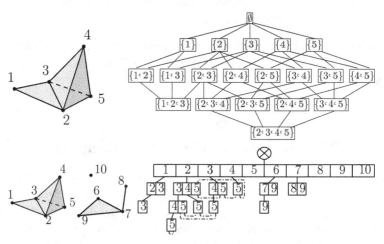

Figure 2.3 A Hasse diagram and a Simplex Tree with their associated simplicial complexes.

seen from the following simple example: the complex consisting of a unique simplex has one maximal simplex but 2^d simplices in total.

Representating only the maximal simplices is especially well suited for combinatorial manifold. A combinatorial manifold K can be represented by its maximal simplices, together with the adjacency graph of those maximal simplices. We will simply call this graph the *adjacency graph of the combinatorial manifold*. When K is of dimension d, the adjacency graph of the maximal simplices is a connected graph of degree $d+1$ that be efficiently traversed. Such a graph will be used in Section 3.4 when constructing convex hulls.

2.8 Exercises

Exercise 2.1   A simplicial complex C is said to be (path-)connected if for any pair of points $(x, y) \in C$ there exists a continuous path $\gamma : [0, 1] \to C$ such that $\gamma(0) = x$ and $\gamma(1) = y$. Prove that a simplicial complex C is connected if and only if its 1-skeleton is connected.

Exercise 2.2   Give examples of simplicial complexes in $\mathbb{R}^3$ that are homeomorphic to a ball, a sphere, and a torus.

Exercise 2.3   Prove that any abstract simplicial complex K of dimension d can be realized as a geometric simplicial complex in $\mathbb{R}^{2d+1}$. (Hint : map the vertices of K to points on the moment curve $C = \{(x, x^2, \ldots, x^{2d+1}) \in \mathbb{R}^{2d+1}, x \in \mathbb{R}\}$. Show that any subset of $2d + 2$ points on C are affinely independent and that the image of K is a realization of K in $\mathbb{R}^{2d+1}$. See also Exercise 3.12.)

Exercise 2.1 (Simplex Tree)   Let K be a d-simplicial complex whose vertices are labelled $1, \ldots, n$. Each simplex is represented by a word that is the sorted list of its labels. We then store all simplices of K as a prefix tree called the *simplex tree* of K. The simplex tree is characterized by the following properties:

1. The nodes of the simplex tree are in bijection with the simplices (of all dimensions) of the complex. The root is associated to the empty face.
2. Each node of the tree, except the root, stores the label of a vertex. Specifically, a node associated to a simplex σ stores the last label of σ.
3. The vertices whose labels are encountered along a path from the root to a node associated to a simplex σ are the vertices of σ. Along such a path, the labels are sorted by increasing order and each label appears no more than once.

Show that the simplex tree of K is a spanning tree of the Hasse diagram of K. Let σ be a i-simplex. Show that we can be decide whether σ is in K or insert σ in K (assuming all its subfaces are in K) in time $O(i \log n)$. Show also how to locate the faces and the cofaces of σ in the simplex tree and how to remove σ from K.

Exercise 2.2   Show how to compute the Vietoris-Rips filtration of a set of points P in some metric space using the simplex tree.

2.9 Bibliographical Notes

Our presentation of simplicial complexes follows the one in Munkres [109]. The nerve theorem and its variants are classical results in algebraic topology. A proof is given in Hatcher [96, Section 4G].

The computation of the Čech filtration of a finite set of points relies on the computation of minimum enclosing balls. Welzl has proposed an elegant randomized algorithm of linear complexity to compute the minimal ball enclosing a set of n points. The algorithm can be adapted to compute the minimal enclosing ellipsoid [129]. The Vietoris-Rips filtration can be obtained by computing the cliques in the 1-skeleton of the Vietoris-Rips complex. This is an NP-complete problem but efficient solutions exist for sparse graphs [78]. The Vietoris-Rips filtration can be constructed and stored using a simplex tree, a data structure proposed by Boissonnat and Maria [20]. The simplex tree is implemented in the GUDHI library [103]. More compact data structures can be found in [5, 11].

The problem of deciding if two abstract complexes are homeomorphic is undecidable Markov 1958. Deciding if a d-simplicial complex is a homeomorphic to a d-sphere is undecidable for $d \geq 5$ [Novikov]. It is trivial for $d = 2$ and decidable for $d = 3$. The question remains open $d = 4$.

PART II

DELAUNAY COMPLEXES

3

Convex Polytopes

Convex polytopes and convex polyhedra are fundamental structures that play an essential role in computational geometry, linear programming, optimisation and many other fields. In this book, they also play a central role because of their close relationship with Voronoi diagrams and Delaunay complexes, introduced in Chapter 4 and used throughout the book. This chapter presents here the combinatorial and algorithmic aspects of convex polyhedra to be used in the following chapters. For a more complete treatment of the rich theory of convex polytopes, the reader is referred to classical textbooks (see the Bibliographic Notes).

3.1 Definitions

3.1.1 Convex Polytopes

Definition 3.1   A *convex polytope* in $\mathbb{R}^d$ is the convex hull of a finite set of points. In this book, we only consider convex polytopes and the word polytope is used as a synonym for convex polytope.

Hence, a convex polytope is a closed bounded subset of $\mathbb{R}^d$. The *dimension* of a convex polytope is the dimension of the affine subspace spanned by the polytope. Simplices (see Section 2) are particular cases of polytopes.

3.1.2 Facial Structure of Polytopes

A hyperplane h of $\mathbb{R}^d$ is a subset of $\mathbb{R}^d$ defined by a linear equation:

$$h = \{x \in \mathbb{R}^d : h(x) = a \cdot x + b = 0\},$$

where $a \in \mathbb{R}^d, b \in \mathbb{R}$. A hyperplane h divides $\mathbb{R}^d$ in two half-spaces:

$$h^+ = \{x \in \mathbb{R}^d : h(x) = a \cdot x + b \geq 0\}$$
$$h^- = \{x \in \mathbb{R}^d : h(x) = a \cdot x + b \leq 0\}$$

Note the half-spaces h^+ and h^- are defined as closed subsets, so that h, h^+ and h^- do not form a partition of $\mathbb{R}^d$ but h, $h^+ \setminus h$ and $h^- \setminus h$ do.

Definition 3.2 A hyperplane h of $\mathbb{R}^d$ is *a supporting hyperplane* of the polytope $\mathcal{P}$ iff the intersection $\mathcal{P} \cap h$ is non empty and $\mathcal{P}$ is included in one of the two half-spaces defined by h.

The intersection of $\mathcal{P}$ with a supporting hyperplane h is called a *face* of $\mathcal{P}$.

Lemma 3.3 *A face of a polytope is a polytope.*

Proof Let $P = \{p_1, \ldots, p_n\}$ be a finite set of points in $\mathbb{R}^d$ and let $\mathcal{P} = \mathrm{conv}(P)$ be the polytope which is the convex hull of P. Any face f of $\mathcal{P}$ is the intersection of $\mathcal{P}$ with a supporting hyperplane h. We prove that the face $f = \mathcal{P} \cap h$ is the convex hull $\mathrm{conv}(P \cap h)$ of the subset of points of P included in h. The inclusion $\mathrm{conv}(P \cap h) \subset f$ comes from the convexity of f. Indeed, f is convex because it is the intersection of two convex sets. Furthermore f contains $P \cap h$, so it contains the convex hull $\mathrm{conv}(P \cap h)$. To prove the reverse inclusion, we assume without loss of generality that $\mathcal{P} \subset h^+$. Then we have $h(p_i) \geq 0$ for any $p_i \in P$. Any point p included in $\mathcal{P}$ is a convex combination $p = \sum_{i=1}^{n} \lambda_i p_i$ of points in P. If furthermore p belongs to f, $h(p_i) = \sum_{i=1}^{n} \lambda_i h(p_i)$ vanishes and this can happen only if $\lambda_i = 0$ for all points p_i that are not in h. Thus, if p belongs f, it belongs to $\mathrm{conv}(P \cap h)$.   □

The proof of the previous lemma, shows that the faces of the polytope $\mathcal{P}$ are the convex hulls of subsets of P. A polytope has therefore a finite number of faces. The boundary of the polytope $\mathcal{P}$ is the union of its faces. The faces of dimension 0 are called *vertices*. The faces of dimension 1 are called *edges*. If $\mathcal{P}$ has dimension d, the faces of dimension $d-1$ and $d-2$ are called respectively *facets* and *ridges*.

The vertices of the polytope $\mathcal{P} = \mathrm{conv}(P)$ are points of P. The following lemma, whose proof is left as an exercise (Exercise 3.1) is a well-known result of the theory of polytopes.

Lemma 3.4 *Any polytope is the convex hull of its vertices.*

The facial structure of a simplex can be easily described. Indeed, if σ is a simplex that is the convex hull of the set $S = \{p_1, \ldots, p_k\}$ of $k+1$ independent points, any subset of S is a set of independent points whose convex hull is a simplex and, except in the case of S itself, this simplex is a face of σ. Therefore, a k-simplex has $k+1$-vertices, and $\binom{k+1}{j+1}$ faces of dimension j, for $j = 0$ to $k - 1$.

Another fundamental result of the theory of polytopes is the following lemma, whose proof is also left as an exercise (see Exercises 3.4 and 3.5).

Lemma 3.5 *Any polytope is the intersection of a finite number of half-spaces. Reciprocally, any intersection of a finite number of half-spaces that is bounded, is a polytope.*

Therefore, any polytope can be described either as the convex hull of a finite set of points or as the intersection of a finite number of half-spaces. More precisely, the proof of Lemma 3.5 shows that the minimal set of half-spaces whose intersection is identical to the polytope $\mathcal{P}$ is the set of half-spaces bounded by the hyperplanes supporting $\mathcal{P}$ along its facets and containing $\mathcal{P}$.

3.1.3 Convex Polyhedra

In the sequel, we extend the notion of polytopes to describe unbounded intersections of half-spaces as well as polytopes.

Definition 3.6 A *convex polyhedron* is the intersection of a finite number of half-spaces.

A convex polyhedron may be bounded or not. From Lemma 3.5, a convex polytope is just a special case of convex polyhedron. The notion of supporting hyperplanes and faces introduced earlier for convex polytopes extend naturally to convex polyhedra. The faces of a convex polyhedron are themselves convex polyhedra and may be unbounded if the convex polyhedron is unbounded.

3.1.4 Simplicial Polytopes and Simple Convex Polyhedra

A point set P in $\mathbb{R}^d$ is said to be in *general position* when any subset of P with size at most $d + 1$ is a set of affinely independent points. When the points of P are in general position, any hyperplane h includes at most d points of P and the points in $P \cap h$ are affinely independent. Therefore all the faces of the polytope $\mathcal{P} = \text{conv}(P)$ are simplices and the polytope $\mathcal{P}$ is called a *simplicial polytope*.

A set of n hyperplanes in $\mathbb{R}^d$ is said to be *in general position* if the intersection of any subset of k of them is an affine subspace of dimension $d - k$. A convex polyhedron defined as the intersection of n half-spaces bounded by hyperplanes in general position is called *simple*.

3.1.5 The Boundary Complex

Let $\mathcal{P}$ be a convex polyhedron. Any face of a face of $\mathcal{P}$ is a face of $\mathcal{P}$ and the intersection of two faces of $\mathcal{P}$ is either empty or a common face of both faces.

Therefore, if $\mathcal{P}$ is simplicial polytope, its faces form a geometric simplicial complex (see Chapter 2). This complex is called the *boundary complex* of $\mathcal{P}$. It can be shown (see Exercise 3.9) that the boundary complex of a simplicial polytope is a combinatorial manifold (see Definition 2.17).

If $\mathcal{P}$ is not a simplicial polytope, its faces may not be simplices. Still, they are convex polyhedra and they form a cell complex as defined now.

Definition 3.7 (Cell complex)   A cell complex is a set C of convex polyhedra, called the faces of C, that satisfies the two following properties

– Any face of a face of C is a face of C.
– The intersection of any two faces of C is either empty or a common face of both faces.

The cell complex formed by the faces of a convex polyhedron $\mathcal{P}$ is still called the *boundary complex* of $\mathcal{P}$. We adapt to cell complexes and therefore to convex polyhedra the notions of incidence and adjacency defined in Section 2.7:

- Two faces of a convex polyhedron are said to be *incident* if one is included in the other.
- Two facets of a convex polyhedron are said to be *adjacent* if they share a $(d-2)$-subface.

3.2 Duality

3.2.1 Point-Hyperplane Duality

We introduce a duality between points and hyperplanes that makes use of the unit paraboloid of $\mathbb{R}^d$ and gives a special role to the last coordinate axis, called the *vertical axis*. We denote by $x(i), i = 1, \ldots, d$, the coordinates of a point $x \in \mathbb{R}^d$.

The unit paraboloid $\mathcal{Q}$ is defined as:

$$\mathcal{Q} = \left\{ x \in \mathbb{R}^d : x(d) = \sum_{i=1}^{d-1} x(i)^2 \right\}.$$

In the rest of this section, we write for short $\sum'$ for $\sum_{i=1}^{d-1}$.

Let p be a point of the paraboloid $\mathcal{Q}$. The duality associates to point p the hyperplane p^* tangent to $\mathcal{Q}$ at p:

$$p^* = \{x \in \mathbb{R}^d : x(d) = 2{\sum}' p(i)(x(i) - p(i)) + p(d)$$
$$= \{x \in \mathbb{R}^d : x(d) - 2{\sum}' p(i)x(i) + p(d) = 0\}.$$

More generally, duality associates to any point p of $\mathbb{R}^d$ the non vertical hyperplane p^* defined by:

$$p^* = \{x \in \mathbb{R}^d : x(d) - 2{\sum}' p(i)x(i) + p(d) = 0\}.$$

Conversely, let h be a nonvertical hyperplane of $\mathbb{R}^d$. The equation of h can be written in normal form:

$$h = \{x \in \mathbb{R}^d : x(d) + {\sum}' h(i)x(i) + h(d) = 0\},$$

and duality associates to h the point h^* with coordinates

$$\left(\frac{-h(1)}{2}, \ldots, \frac{-h(d-1)}{2}, h(d)\right).$$

Because $p^{**} = p$, duality is an involutive bijection between points of $\mathbb{R}^d$ and non vertical hyperplanes of $\mathbb{R}^d$. Duality preserves incidences of points and hyperplanes: if p and q are two points in $\mathbb{R}^d$ with dual hyperplanes p^* and q^* respectively, we have

$$q \in p^* \iff q(d) - 2{\sum}' p(d)q(d) + p(d) = 0 \iff p \in q^*.$$

Let h be a nonvertical hyperplane whose equation in normal form is $h(x) = 0$. We say that point p is above h or that h is below p if $h(p) > 0$. We say that point p is below h or that h is above p if $h(p) < 0$. For a nonvertical hyperplane h, we call *upper half-space* and denote by h^+ the half-space bounded by h that is above h. We call *lower half-space* and denote by h^- the half-space below h:

$$h^+ = \{x \in \mathbb{R}^d : h(x) > 0\}$$
$$h^- = \{x \in \mathbb{R}^d : h(x) < 0\}.$$

Duality reverses the above–below relations between points and hyperplanes: if p and q are two points in $\mathbb{R}^d$ with dual hyperplanes p^* and q^* respectively, we have:

$$q \in p^{*+} \iff q(d) - 2{\sum}' p(d)q(d) + p(d) > 0 \iff p \in q^{*+}$$
$$q \in p^{*-} \iff q(d) - 2{\sum}' p(d)q(d) + p(d) < 0 \iff p \in q^{*-}.$$

3.2.2 Lower Hulls and Upper Envelope

Let $P = \{p_1, \ldots, p_n\}$ be a set of n points in $\mathbb{R}^d$. The lower hull of P, denoted by lowerhull(P), is a subcomplex of the boundary complex of the polytope $\mathcal{P} = \text{conv}(P)$. Let $H(P)$ be the set of hyperplanes supporting the polytope $\mathcal{P}$. We distinguish the subset $H_+(P)$ of lower supporting hyperplanes where a hyperplane h of $H(P)$ is a lower supporting hyperplane if h is a nonvertical hyperplane and $\mathcal{P}$ is included in the upper half-space h^+. The *lower hull* of P is then defined as the subcomplex of the convex hull boundary, formed by faces of $\mathcal{P}$ included in lower supporting hyperplanes:

$$\text{lowerhull}(P) = \{\mathcal{P} \cap h : h \in H_+(P)\}$$

Consider now a set $H = \{h_1, \ldots, h_n\}$ of nonvertical hyperplanes in $\mathbb{R}^d$, and let $\mathcal{H}^+$ be the convex polyhedron, which is the intersection of the upper half-spaces bounded by the hyperplanes of H:

$$\mathcal{H}^+ = h_1^+ \cap h_2^+ \ldots \cap h_n^+.$$

The boundary complex of the convex polyhedron $\mathcal{H}^+$ is called the *upper envelope* of the set of hyperplanes H.

Two complexes K and K^* (simplicial or cellular complexes) of dimension d are said to be *dual complexes* if there is a bijective correspondence between the faces of K and the faces of K^* such that

- the k-faces of K correspond to the $(d-k)$-faces of K^*
- the correspondence preserves incidences and reverses inclusion relations, meaning that if if $f \subset g$ are incident faces of K, the corresponding faces f^* and g^* of K^* are incident and such that $g^* \subset f^*$.

Observe that the lower envelope of a set of points in $\mathbb{R}^d$, and the upper envelope of a set of hyperplanes are both $(d-1)$-complexes. The duality between points and hyperplanes of $\mathbb{R}^d$ introduced in Section 3.2.1 yields a duality between the lower hull of a set of points and the upper envelope of the set of dual hyperplanes.

Lemma 3.8 (Lower hull—upper enveloppe duality) *Let P be a set of points in $\mathbb{R}^d$ and let P^* be the set of dual hyperplanes. The lower hull of P and the upper envelope of P^* are dual $(d-1)$-complexes.*

Proof We assume here for simplicity that the points of P are in general position and leave the proof for the general case as an exercise (Exercise 3.10).

Let $\mathcal{P} = \text{conv}(P)$ be the convex hull of P and by $\mathcal{P}^{*+}$ be the convex polyhedron which is the intersection of the upper half-spaces bounded by the dual hyperplanes:

$$\mathcal{P}^{*+} = p_1^{*+} \cap p_2^{*+} \dots \cap p_n^{*+}.$$

Let f be a k-face of lowerhull(P). Face f is a k-face of the polytope $\mathcal{P}$ and, since general position is assumed, f includes $(k+1)$-vertices of $\mathcal{P}$ which are points of P. Let us assume, without loss of generality, that $\{p_1, \dots, p_{k+1}\}$ are included in f. We consider a lower supporting hyperplane h that intersects $\mathcal{P}$ along f. Hyperplane h includes $\{p_1, \dots, p_{k+1}\}$ and, because it is a lower supporting hyperplane, the other points of P are included in the upper half-space h^+. Let h^* be the point dual to h. Then, from the properties of the point hyperplane duality introduced earlier, we get:

$$p_i \in h^+ \Longleftrightarrow h^* \in p_i^{*+}, \quad \forall i = 1, \dots, n \tag{3.1}$$

$$p_i \in h \Longleftrightarrow h^* \in p_i^*, \quad \forall i = 1, \dots, k+1 \tag{3.2}$$

$$p_i \notin h \Longleftrightarrow h^* \notin p_i^*, \quad \forall i = k+2, \dots, n \tag{3.3}$$

Equations 3.1, 3.2 and 3.3 show that the point h^* belongs to the $(d-1-k)$-face f^* of $\mathcal{P}^{*+}$, which is the intersection of $\mathcal{P}^{*+}$ with the $k+1$ hyperplanes $\{p_i^*, i = 1, \dots k+1\}$. Therefore, duality maps the k-face $f = \text{conv}(\{p_1, \dots, p_{k+1}\})$ of lowerhull(P) to the $(d-1-k)$-face $f^* = p_1^* \cap p_2^* \cap \dots \cap p_{k+1}^* \cap \mathcal{P}^{*+}$ of $\mathcal{P}^{*+}$.

In the other way, any $(d-1-k)$-face of $\mathcal{P}^{*+}$ is the intersection of $\mathcal{P}^{*+}$ with $k+1$ hyperplanes in P^* (see Exercise 3.6). Let us consider a $(d-1-k)$-face f^* of $\mathcal{P}^{*+}$ and say that f^* is the intersection of $\mathcal{P}^{*+}$ with the k hyperplanes $\{p_i^*, i = 1, \dots k+1\}$. Equations 3.1, 3.2 and 3.3 show that any point h^* in f^* is the dual of a hyperplane h which supports $\mathcal{P}$ along the face $f = \text{conv}(\{p_1, \dots, p_{k+1}\})$. Moreover, h is a lower supporting hyperplane. Therefore, duality maps back f^* to f and the correspondence is bijective. $\square$

3.3 Combinatorial Bounds

The following theorem bounds the total number of faces of a convex polyhedron in $\mathbb{R}^d$, which is known to have either n facets or n vertices. The theorem is known as the *upper bound theorem*, although the bound is tight in the worst case.

Theorem 3.9 (Upper Bound Theorem) *The total number of faces of a convex polyhedron in $\mathbb{R}^d$, defined as the intersection of n half-spaces or as the convex hull of n points, is $\Theta\left(n^{\lfloor \frac{d}{2} \rfloor}\right)$.*

Proof We prove here the upper bound. The lower bound is the topic of Exercise 3.12.

Let $\mathcal{P}$ be a convex polyhedron defined as the intersection of n half-spaces of $\mathbb{R}^d$. To prove the upper bound on the number of faces of $\mathcal{P}$, we may assume that the hyperplanes bounding the half-spaces defining $\mathcal{P}$ are in general position. Indeed, otherwise, we can slightly perturb those hyperplanes to bring then in general position. During this process, the number of faces of $\mathcal{P}$ can only increase (see Exercise 3.11). Hence, any upper bound that is valid for hyperplanes in general position holds for any set of hyperplanes. We also assume that the polyhedron has at least one vertex. Indeed, otherwise the number of bounding hyperplanes is at most $d - 1$ and the total number of faces is at most 2^{d-1}. In addition, we may assume, without loss of generality, that two vertices of $\mathcal{P}$ do not have the same x_d coordinate.

We first bound the number of vertices of $\mathcal{P}$ and then extend this bound to faces of any dimension. Let p be one of the vertices of $\mathcal{P}$. Because general position is assumed, p, as any other vertex of $\mathcal{P}$, is included in exactly d of the bounding hyperplanes. Therefore p is incident to exactly d facets and d edges of $\mathcal{P}$. Thus at least $\lceil \frac{d}{2} \rceil$ edges incident to p are included in either in the half-space $h^+ : x_d \geq x_d(p)$ or in the half-space $h^- : x_d \leq x_d(p)$. Because the bounding hyperplanes are in general position, $\mathcal{P}$ is simple and the affine hull of any subset of $k < d$ edges incident to a vertex of $\mathcal{P}$ contains a k-face of $\mathcal{P}$ (Exercice 3.7). Therefore, each vertex p of $\mathcal{P}$ is a vertex with extremal x_d-coordinate for at least one face of dimension $\lceil \frac{d}{2} \rceil$. Because any face has at most one vertex of maximal x_d coordinate and one vertex of minimal x_d-coordinate, the number of vertices of $\mathcal{P}$ is at most twice the number of $\lceil \frac{d}{2} \rceil$-faces of $\mathcal{P}$.

From the general position assumption, a k-face of $\mathcal{P}$ is the intersection of $d - k$ of the bounding hyperplanes (see Exercise 3.6). We deduce that the number of k-faces is at most $\binom{n}{d-k} = O(n^{d-k})$, which is $O(n^{\lfloor \frac{d}{2} \rfloor})$ for $k = \lceil \frac{d}{2} \rceil$. From this discussion, we conclude that the number of vertices of $\mathcal{P}$ is $O(n^{\lfloor \frac{d}{2} \rfloor})$.

Let us bound now the number of k-faces for $k > 0$. The number of k-faces incident to any vertex of $\mathcal{P}$ is $\binom{d}{d-k}$, which is a constant for fixed d. Hence the upper bound $O(n^{\lfloor \frac{d}{2} \rfloor})$ holds also for the number of faces of any dimension.

The duality introduced in Section 3.2 immediately implies that the same upper bound holds for the lower hull of a set of n points and finally (by symmetry) to the number of faces of a polytope defined as the convex hull of n points.   □

3.4 Convex Hull Algorithms

We present here two algorithms to build the convex hull of a set of points P. Both algorithms are incremental, meaning that they insert the points of P one by one, while maintaining the convex hull of the currently subset of inserted points. Convex hulls are represented by the Hasse diagram of their boundary complexes (see Section 2.7). Incremental algorithms make also use of the adjacency graph of convex hull facets which, as noticed in Section 2.7), is encoded in the Hasse diagram. Both algorithms also work while maintaining only the adjacency graph of the facets of the convex hull. To make the description of the algorithms simple and to focus on the main ideas, we assume here that the input set of points P is in general position. However this is not a limitation of the presented convex hull algorithms.

3.4.1 An Incremental Algorithm

Assuming that points in P are added in the order $p_1, p_2, \ldots, p_n$, we denote by P_i the subset of the first i-points. Before presenting the whole algorithm and its analysis, we explain how the convex hull is updated when inserting point p_{i+1}.

From conv(P_i) to conv(P_{i+1})

When point p_{i+1} is considered, the faces of conv(P_i) may be classified in the following way (see Figure 3.1):

- A facet f of conv(P_i) is *red* if the hyperplane h_f supporting conv(P_i) along f *separates* p_{i+1} from conv(P_i) meaning that p_i belongs to the open half-space h_f^+ that does not intersect conv(P_i). Otherwise, as general position is assumed, p_i is included in the half-space h_f^- whose closure contains conv(P_i), and the facet f is said to be *blue*.
- A k-face with $k < d$ is said to be *red* if all its incident facets are red, *blue* if all its incident facets are blue, and *purple* if it is incident to both red and blue facets.

The incremental algorithm and its analysis relies on the three following facts, all related to the transformation of conv(P_i) into conv(P_{i+1}) when adding point p_{i+1}.

1. The set of red facets induces a connected subgraph of the adjacency graph of conv(P_i).
2. The set of faces of conv(P_{i+1}) includes the blue and purple faces of conv(P_i) together with additional *new faces* which are all incident to p_{i+1}.

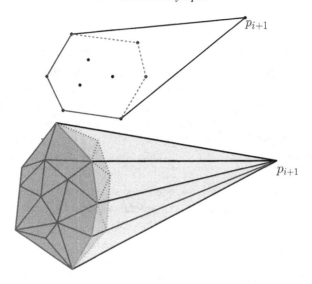

Figure 3.1 Incremental convex hull algorithm. Top: $d = 2$. Bottom: $d = 3$.

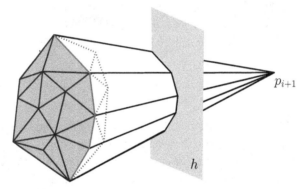

Figure 3.2 When adding point p_{i+1}, the set of purple facets of $\text{conv}(P_i)$ is isomorphic to a $(d-1)$-polytope with at most i vertices.

Each new face is formed by the convex hull $\text{conv}(g \cup p_{i+1})$ where g is a purple face of $\text{conv}(P_i)$. See Figure 3.1.

3. The set of purple faces of $\text{conv}(P_i)$ with their incidence relation is isomorphic to the set of new faces of $\text{conv}(P_{i+1})$. Both sets are isomorphic to the set of faces of a $(d-1)$-polytope with at most i vertices.

Fact 1 and Fact 2 are illustrated in Figure 3.1. Fact 3 is illustrated in Figure 3.2 showing that the purple faces of $\text{conv}(P_i)$ and the set of faces of $\text{conv}(P_{i+1})$ incident to p_{i+1} are both isomorphic to the set of faces of a $(d-1)$-polytope obtained as the intersection of $\mathrm{conv}(P_{i+1})$ with any hyperplane h that separates $\mathrm{conv}(P_i)$ from p_{i+1}.

In summary, updating $\mathrm{conv}(P_i)$ to $\mathrm{conv}(P_{i+1})$ requires to identify the red and purple faces of $\mathrm{conv}(P_i)$. The Hasse diagram of $\mathrm{conv}(P_{i+1})$ is then obtained form the Hasse diagram of $\mathrm{conv}(P_i)$ by removing red faces of $\mathrm{conv}(P_i)$ and creating a new face $\mathrm{conv}(g \cup p_{i+1})$ for each purple face g of $\mathrm{conv}(P_i)$. Incidence relations among new faces are deduced from incidence relations among purple faces in $\mathrm{conv}(P_i)$.

The Algorithm

The incremental convex hull algorithm is summarized in the pseudo-code of Algorithm 1.

Algorithm 1: Incremental convex hull algorithm

Input: A set P of n points in $\mathbb{R}^d$
Sort the points of P by lexicographic order of coordinates
Let $p_1, p_2 \ldots p_n$ be the points of P in lexicographic order
Let P_i be the subset of first i points
Build the Hasse diagram of $\mathrm{conv}(P_{d+1})$
for i = d + 1 **to** i = n − 1 **do**
    Find a red facet of $\mathrm{conv}(P_i)$ {with respect to p_{i+1}}
    Find all red and purple faces of $\mathrm{conv}(P_i)$
    Update the Hasse of $\mathrm{conv}(P_i)$ into the Hasse diagram of $\mathrm{conv}(P_{i+1})$.
Output: The Hasse diagram of the convex hull of P

The incremental algorithm sorts the points in P by lexicographic order of their coordinates and insert them in that order. Let $p_1, p_2, \ldots p_n$ be the sorted sequence of points in P and let P_i be the subset of first i points.

The lexicographic ordering ensures that when point p_{i+1} is inserted, at least one of the facet of $\mathrm{conv}(P_i)$ incident to p_i is red. Indeed, point p_{i+1} is separated from $\mathrm{conv}(P_i)$ by a hyperplane h through p_i. Let h^+ be the half-space bounded by h that does not contain $\mathrm{conv}(P_i)$. Let, in addition, H denote the set of hyperplanes that are the affine hulls of the facets of $\mathrm{conv}(P_i)$ incident to p_i. Write H^+ for the union of the half-spaces not containing $\mathrm{conv}(P_i)$ that are bounded by the hyperplanes in H. Since h^+ is included in H^+, p_{i+1} is separated from $\mathrm{conv}(P_i)$ by at least one of the hyperplanes of H. Thus to find a first red facet, the algorithm walks in the adjacency graph of the facets of $\mathrm{conv}(P_i)$, visiting only facets of $\mathrm{conv}(P_i)$ that are incident to p_i, until a red facet is encountered.

Then to find all red and purple faces, the algorithm traverses the adjacency graph visiting all red facets of $\mathrm{conv}(P_i)$ and, from each read facet, it traverses the Hasse diagram to identify all red and purple faces of conv(P_i). The Hasse diagram is then updated as explained in the previous paragraph.

Complexity Analysis

Theorem 3.10   *The incremental convex hull algorithm computes the convex hull of n points in $\mathbb{R}^d$ in $\Theta\left(n\log n + n^{\left\lfloor\frac{d+1}{2}\right\rfloor}\right)$ time.*

Proof   First notice that the only numerical predicates involved in Algorithm 1 are the *orientation predicates* called to decide if a facet of conv(P_i) is red or blue when inserting point p_{i+1}. The orientation predicate amounts to evaluate the sign of a $(d+1) \times (d+1)$ determinant (see Exercise 3.16).

To find the first red facet, the algorithm visits only facets of conv(P_i) incident to the last inserted point p_i. Therefore, each facet will be visited only once for this purpose during the whole algorithm.

Identifying red and purple faces is also clearly proportional to the number of these faces. As a red face disappears from the convex hull, each face is visited only once as a red face, and the cost of visiting a purple face g can be charged on the new face conv($g \cup p_{i+1}$).

Updating the Hasse diagram has a complexity proportional to the number of new and removed faces that are, respectively, the number of purple and red faces of conv(P_i).

In summary, the cost of step $i+1$ where point p_{i+1} is inserted is proportional to the number of new and removed faces. Because a face is created only once and removed at most once, the total cost of the incremental algorithm, except for the initial sorting of the points, is proportional to the total number of created faces.

From Fact 3 and the upper bound theorem (Theorem 3.9), the number of faces created when inserting p_{i+1} is $O\left(i^{\left\lfloor\frac{d-1}{2}\right\rfloor}\right)$ and the total cost of updating the Hasse diagram is:

$$\sum_{i=d+1}^{n-1} O\left(i^{\left\lfloor\frac{d-1}{2}\right\rfloor}\right) = O\left(n^{\left\lfloor\frac{d+1}{2}\right\rfloor}\right).$$

Taking into account the initial sorting of the points according to the lexicographic order, the complexity of the incremental algorithm is:

$$O\left(n\log n + n^{\left\lfloor\frac{d+1}{2}\right\rfloor}\right) = O(n\log n) \text{ if } d = 2$$
$$= O\left(n^{\left\lfloor\frac{d+1}{2}\right\rfloor}\right) \text{ if } d > 2$$

Furthermore, the complexity bound $O\left(n\log n + n^{\left\lfloor\frac{d+1}{2}\right\rfloor}\right)$ is tight for any incremental convex hull algorithm. See Exercise 3.14 for examples of points where the incremental convex hull requires $\Omega\left(n^{\left\lfloor\frac{d+1}{2}\right\rfloor}\right)$ times. □

The upper bound theorem gives a lower bound of $\Omega\left(n^{\left\lfloor\frac{d}{2}\right\rfloor}\right)$ for computing the convex hull of n points in $\mathbb{R}^d$.

Moreover, $\Omega(n\log n)$ is also a lower bound of complexity for computing the convex hull of n points because it is known that sorting n number reduces in linear time to the computation of the convex hull of n points (See Exercise 3.15).

We deduce that computing the convex hull of n points in $\mathbb{R}^d$ has a complexity which is at least $\Omega\left(n\log n + n^{\left\lfloor\frac{d}{2}\right\rfloor}\right)$. The incremental algorithm is therefore worst-case optimal in even dimensions. However, it is not optimal in odd dimensions.

3.4.2 A Randomized Algorithm

The Algorithm

The randomized incremental algorithm is quite similar to the above incremental algorithm: points are inserted one by one in the convex hull. At each insertion the set of red and purple faces of the current hull are identified and the convex hull is updated accordingly. The main difference with respect to the incremental algorithm of Section 3.4.1 is that the points are no longer introduced in lexicographic order but in random order. We will show that the expected complexity of the random algorithm matches the lower complexity bound for convex hull computation. Expectation here concerns only the random insertion order and assumes that, for an input set of n points, all the $n!$ possible insertion sequences occur with the same probability.

In the following, points in P are assumed to be indexed according to their insertion order. We denote by $P_i = \{p_1, \ldots, p_i\}$ the subset formed by the i first inserted points. As in the deterministic algorithm presented before, the randomized algorithm has to find a first red facet. However, we cannot rely now on the lexicographic order of the input points and restrict our attention to the faces incident to the lastly inserted point. To walk around this issue, we will use an additional data structure called the *conflict graph*.

A facet f of the current convex hull $\text{conv}(P_i)$ is said to be in *conflict* with the not yet inserted point p_j with $j > i$ iff the hyperplane h_f supporting conv(P_i) along f separates p_j from conv(P_i). The conflict graph maintained by the algorithm is a bipartite graph including for each not yet inserted point p_j an edge between this point and a facet of the current hull in conflict with p_j. Note that when a new point p_{i+1} is inserted, the current hull is conv(P_i) and the facets of conv(P_i) in conflict with p_{i+1} are precisely the red facets of conv(P_i). Therefore, when inserting point p_{i+1}, the conflict edge incident to p_{i+1} gives in constant time access to a red facet of conv(P_i). Then the algorithm finds all the red and purple faces of conv(P_i) and updates the Hasse diagram of the convex hull exactly as in the deterministic algorithm. The only difference is that now, after each insertion, the algorithm needs, in addition, to update the conflict graph. Before explaining how this is done, we summarize the randomized algorithm as Algorithm 2.

Algorithm 2: Randomized convex hull algorithm

Input: A set P of n points in $\mathbb{R}^d$
Choose randomly a subset P_{d+1} of $d + 1$ points in P
Build the Hasse diagram of conv(P_{d+1})
Initialize the conflict graph
for i = d + 1 **to** i = n − 1 **do**
    Choose randomly $p_{i+1} \in P \setminus P_i$
    $P_{i+1} = P_i \cup \{p_{i+1}\}$
    Follow the conflict edge of p_{i+1} to find a first red facet
    Find all red and purple faces of conv(P_i)
    Update the Hasse and compute the Hasse diagram of conv(P_{i+1}).
    Update the conflict graph
Output: The Hasse diagram of the convex hull of P

Updating the Conflict Graph

The algorithm needs to restore conflict edges between the facets of conv(P_{i+1}) and the points of $P \setminus P_{i+1}$. Nothing needs to be done for the points of $P \setminus P_{i+1}$ that were previously in conflict with a blue facet of conv(P_i) because such a facet is still a facet of conv(P_{i+1}). Let p_j be a point of $P \setminus P_{i+1}$ that was previously in conflict with a red facet f_j of conv(P_i). We need to find a facet of conv(P_{i+1}) in conflict with p_j. Let R denote the set of red facets of conv(P_i) and let R_j denote the set of facets of conv(P_i) in conflict with p_j. As noted previously, the set R induces a connected subgraph of the adjacency graph of conv(P_i). The same is true for R_j and for the subset $F_j = R \cap R_j$ of red facets in conflict with p_j. Note that the boundary of F_j includes red ridges which are

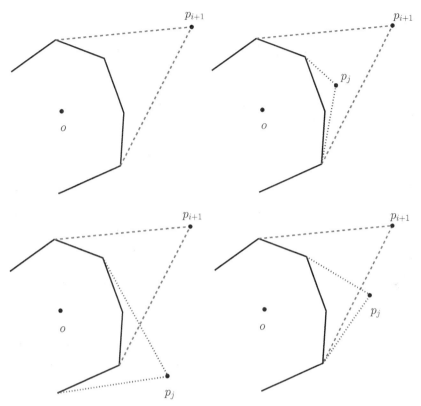

Figure 3.3 Randomized construction of the convex hull: updating the conflicting graph. The up left picture show the set of red facets when inserting p_{i+1}, the three other pictures show, in three different cases, the set of facets of $conv(P_i)$ in conflict with p_{i+1} and p_j. In upper right picture, p_j is internal to $conv(P_{i+1})$, in lower left picture, case 1 and case 2 both occur, in lower right picture only case 2 occurs.

on the boundary of R_j but not on the boundary of R and purple ridges which are on the boundary of R. See Figure 3.3 for an illustration in $\mathbb{R}^2$.

To find a facet of $conv(P_{i+1})$ in conflict with p_j, the algorithm starts at f_j, the facet that was in conflict with p_j before the insertion of p_{i+1}, and walk on the adjacency graph of $conv(P_i)$, visiting the facets of F_j. At each purple ridge h encountered on the boundary of F_j, the algorithm checks if one of the two following cases occurs:

Case 1: the blue facet g of $conv(P_i)$ incident on h is in conflict with p_{i+1},

Case 2: the new facet $f' = conv(h, p_{i+1})$ of $conv(P_{i+1})$, is in conflict with p_{i+1}.

In both cases, a facet of conv(P_{i+1}) in conflict with p_{i+1} has been found and the walk stops. If the walk traverses all facets of F_j without encountering one of the above two cases, p_j lies inside conv(P_{i+1}) and can be discarded. See Figure 3.3.

Analysis of the Randomized Algorithm

We insist that the randomized algorithm presented here always computes the actual convex hull of the set of input points. The random choices performed by the algorithm concern only the order in which the points are inserted and the performances of the algorithm. The analysis here will bound the expected complexity of the algorithm assuming that all insertion sequences occur with the same probability.

Theorem 3.11 *The randomized incremental algorithm computes the convex hull of n points in $\mathbb{R}^d$ in expected time $O\left(n \log n + n^{\lfloor \frac{d}{2} \rfloor}\right)$.*

Before we give the proof of the theorem, we recall an important result of Clarkson and Shor [59], known as the random sampling theorem.

The random sampling theorem. We call *configuration* a subset of d independent points in $\mathbb{R}^d$. A configuration σ is said to be defined on a set of points P if the points in σ belong to P. Let us choose as the origin a point o in conv(P). A configuration is said to be in conflict with a point p if the hyperplane which is the affine hull of σ separates o from p. A configuration is said to have j conflicts on P if it is in conflict with j points of P. We denote by $C(P)$ the set of configurations defined on P and by $C_j(P)$ (resp. $C_{\leq k}(P)$), the set of configurations defined on P and with j conflicts (resp. at most k conflicts) on P.

In the following, we consider random samples S of P and we denote by $\Gamma_0(s, P)$ the expected number of configurations defined on S and without conflict on S, where S is a random sample of size s of P.

Theorem 3.12 (The random sampling theorem) *Let P be a set of n points. The number $\left|C_{\leq k}(P)\right|$ of configurations defined on P and with at most k-conflicts on P is bounded as follows:*

$$\left|C_{\leq k}(P)\right| \leq 4(d + 1)^d \, k^d \, \Gamma_0\left(\left\lfloor \frac{n}{k} \right\rfloor, P\right). \tag{3.4}$$

In our context, a configuration that is defined on P and without conflict on P, is just the vertex set of a facet of conv(P) so that there is a bijection between $C_0(P)$ and the facets of conv(P). We then deduce from the upper bound theorem (Theorem 3.9) that the number of configurations defined and without conflict on a sample of size s of P is at most $O\left(s^{\lfloor \frac{d}{2} \rfloor}\right)$. Therefore:

$$\Gamma_0(s, P) = O\left(s^{\lfloor \frac{d}{2} \rfloor}\right). \tag{3.5}$$

Plugging Equation 3.5 into Equation 3.4, we get that for any set P of n points the number of configurations defined and with at most k conflicts over P is at most:

$$\left|C_{\leq k}(P)\right| = O\left(k^{\lceil \frac{d}{2} \rceil} n^{\lfloor \frac{d}{2} \rfloor}\right). \tag{3.6}$$

Proof of Theorem 3.11. We can now analyze the cost of updating the Hasse diagram of the convex hull and the cost of maintaining the conflict graph.

Cost of updating the Hasse diagram. As in the case of the incremental algorithm, the cost of updating the Hasse diagram is proportional to the total number of convex hull facets that are created by the algorithm.

Let us bound the expected number $n(i + 1)$ of facets that are created at Step $i + 1$ when point p_{i+1} is inserted. Because the algorithm inserts the points of P in random order, P_{i+1} is a random subset of P of size $i + 1$. Notice that a facet created at step $i + 1$ corresponds to a configuration of $C_0(P_{i+1})$. Given P_{i+1}, a configuration σ of $C_0(P_{i+1})$ corresponds to a facet created at step $i + 1$ iff one of the points in this configuration is the point p_{i+1} inserted at step i, which happens with probability $\frac{d}{i+1}$. Thus, we have

$$
\begin{aligned}
n(i + 1) &= \sum_{\sigma \in C(P)} \mathrm{proba}\,(\sigma \in C_0(P_{i+1})) \times \frac{d}{i + 1} \\
&= \frac{d}{i + 1}\,\Gamma_0(i + 1, P) \\
&= O\left((i + 1)^{\lfloor \frac{d}{2} \rfloor - 1}\right).
\end{aligned}
$$

By summing over all steps i and using linearity of expectation, we bound the expected total number of facets created by the algorithm and therefore the expected cost of updating the Hasse diagram by:

$$\sum_i^n n(i) = O\left(n^{\lfloor \frac{d}{2} \rfloor}\right). \tag{3.7}$$

Cost of updating the conflict graph. We now bound the cost of updating the conflict graph. As explained earlier, when inserting p_{i+1} at step $i + 1$, the algorithm has to restore a conflict edge for each point p_j with $j > i + 1$. This is done by traversing the incidence graph of $\mathrm{conv}(P_i)$, visiting the facets in conflict with both p_{i+1} and p_j. The cost of this procedure is proportional to the number of visited facets, which we analyze now.

For any $p_j \in P \setminus P_{i+1}$, the subset $S = P_{i+1} \cup \{p_j\}$ is a random sample of P of size $i + 2$. The facets visited to restore the conflict for p_j at step $i + 1$ correspond to configurations in $C_2(S)$. Assume that a subset S of P of size $i+2$ is given and that $S = P_{i+1} \cup \{p_j\}$. Then, any configuration σ in $C_2(S)$ is a facet of $\mathrm{conv}(P_i)$ in conflict with p_{i+1} and p_j iff p_{i+1} and p_j are the two elements of S in conflict with σ, which happens with probability $\frac{2}{(i+1)(i+2)}$. Given S, the expected number $n(i + 1, j, S)$ of facets visited to restore the conflict for p_j at step $i + 1$ is

$$n(i + 1, j, S) = \sum_{\sigma \in C(P)} \mathrm{proba}\,(\sigma \in C_2(S)) \times \frac{2}{(i + 1)(i + 2)}$$

$$\leq \frac{2}{(i + 1)(i + 2)} \left| C_{\leq 2}(S) \right|.$$

Then, using Equation 3.6,

$$n(i + 1, j, S) \leq O\!\left((i + 1)^{\left\lfloor \frac{d}{2} \right\rfloor - 2}\right).$$

Because this is true for any subset S of P of size $i+2$, we get that the expected number $n(i + 1, j)$ of facets visited to restore a conflict edge for p_j at step $i + 1$ is also $O\!\left((i+1)^{\left\lfloor \frac{d}{2} \right\rfloor - 2}\right)$. Then, the expected total cost for updating the conflict graph is

$$\sum_{i=1}^{n} \sum_{j=i+1}^{n} n(i, j) = \sum_{i=1}^{n} (n - i) O\!\left(i^{\left\lfloor \frac{d}{2} \right\rfloor - 2}\right) = O\!\left(n \log n + n^{\left\lfloor \frac{d}{2} \right\rfloor}\right). \qquad (3.8)$$

At each insertion, finding a first red facet takes constant time using the conflict graph. Finding all the red and purple faces then takes a time proportional to the number of red and purple faces and the total cost of this operation is thus also given by Equation 3.7. In summary, the expected combinatorial complexity of the randomized incremental construction of the convex hull is given by Equations 3.7 and 3.8, which achieves the proof of Theorem 3.11. □

The randomized version of the incremental construction of a convex hull has therefore an expected complexity which is better than the complexity of the deterministic incremental construction. Because this expected complexity matches the complexity of the convex hull, the randomized incremental construction of a convex hull is optimal.

3.5 Exercises

Exercise 3.1 Show that a convex polytope $\mathcal{P}$ is the convex hull ot its vertices.

Hint: One of the inclusion is trivial. To prove the other one, consider the minimal subset $P' \subseteq P$ such that $\mathcal{P} = \text{conv}(P) = \text{conv}(P')$ and prove that each point in P' is a vertex of $\mathcal{P}$.

Exercise 3.2 Show that the intersection of any finite set of faces of a polytope is also a face of the polytope.

Exercise 3.3 Show that any face of a convex polytope $\mathcal{P}$ is the intersection of facets of $\mathcal{P}$.

Show that a $(d-2)$-face of a polytope $\mathcal{P}$ is the intersection of two facets of $\mathcal{P}$.

Exercise 3.4 Let $\mathcal{P}$ be a convex polytope and let H be the set of hyperplanes that support $\mathcal{P}$ along its facets. To each hyperplane $h \in H$, we associate the half-space h^+ bounded by h that contains $\mathcal{P}$. Show that $\mathcal{P} = \cap_{h \in H} h^+$.

Exercise 3.5 (Polytopes and intersection of half-spaces) Show that, if it is bounded, the intersection of a finite set of half-spaces is a polytope.

Exercise 3.6 (Faces of a convex polyhedron) Let H be a set of n hyperplanes $h_1, \ldots, h_n$ and $\mathcal{P}$ be the polyhedron defined as the intersection of the n half-spaces $h_1^+, \ldots, h_n^+$ where h_i^+ is the half-space bounded by h_i that contains a given point o. Let I be any subset of the indices $1, \ldots, n$ and $F_I = \cap_{i \in I} h_i$. Show that, if it is nonempty, the intersection and $\mathcal{P} \cap F_I$ is a face of $\mathcal{P}$ and that all the faces of $\mathcal{P}$ can be obtained this way, i.e., as the intersection with $\mathcal{P}$ of the hyperplanes of a subset of H. Show, in addition, that, if H is in general position, $\mathcal{P} \cap F_I$ is a face of dimension $d-k$ if $|I| = k$.

Exercise 3.7 (Faces of a simple convex polyhedron) Prove that if $\mathcal{P}$ is a simple convex polyhedron and p is a vertex of $\mathcal{P}$, the affine hull of any subset of $k < d$ edges incident to p contains a face of P of dimension $d-k$. Hint: Use Exercise 3.2 and duality.

Exercise 3.8 (General position and duality) Show that n hyperplanes are in general position iff their dual points are in general position.

Exercise 3.9 Show that the boundary complex of a polytope is a combinatorial manifold.

Hint: Let p be a vertex of the d-polytope $\mathcal{P}$. We show that the link of p in the boundary complex of $\mathcal{P}$ is a $(d-2)$-topological sphere. Indeed, any hyperplane h that separates p from the other vertices of $\mathcal{P}$ (see Figure 3.2) intersects $\mathcal{P}$

along a polytope of dimension $(d-1)$ whose boundary complex is isomorphic to the link of p in the boundary complex of $\mathcal{P}$.

Exercise 3.10   Prove Lemma 3.8 in the general case.

Hint: Proves that if k' points in $\mathbb{R}^d$ span an affine hull of dimension $k < k'$, their dual hyperplanes intersect along a $(k-d)$-dimensional affine space.

Exercise 3.11   Let $\mathcal{P}$ be a convex polyhedron. Prove that perturbing the hyperplanes bounding the half-spaces that define $\mathcal{P}$ can only increase the number of faces of $\mathcal{P}$.

Exercise 3.12 (Cyclic polytopes)   A cyclic polytope is a polytope in $\mathbb{R}^d$ that is the convex hull of points lying on the moment curve $\mathcal{M}_d$ defined by the parametric representation

$$\mathcal{M}_d = \{x(t, t^2, \ldots t^d), t \in \mathbb{R}\}$$

Show that a cyclic polytope of $\mathbb{R}^d$ with n vertices has $\binom{n}{k}$ $(k-1)$-faces for any k such that $0 \le k \le d/2$.

Exercise 3.13 (Polarity)   Polarity has been introduced with the paraboloid $\mathcal{Q}$. A sphere could have been used instead as shown in this exercise. Let o be a point of $\mathbb{R}^d$. Polarity associates to any point p of $\mathbb{R}^d$ distinct of o the hyperplane $p^* = \{x : (x-o) \cdot (p-o) = 1\}$. Show that polarity is a bijection between points of $\mathbb{R}^d$ distinct de o and hyperplanes not passing through o. Let P be a set of point of $\mathbb{R}^d$ whose convex hull includes o. Show that polarity induces a duality between the boundary complex of the polytope $(P) = \text{conv}(P)$ and the boundary complex of the polytope $(P^{*+}) = \bigcap_{p \in P} p^{*+}$ where p^{*+} is the half-space bounded by p^* not containing o.

Exercise 3.14 (Lower bound for incremental convex hull computation)   Show that any incremental algorithm that constructs the convex hull of n points of $\mathbb{R}^d$ takes $\Omega(n^{\lfloor \frac{d+1}{2} \rfloor})$ time in the worst-case.

Hint: Take the points on the moment curve $\mathcal{M}_d$ (see Exercise 3.12) and insert them by increasing values of their first coordinate.

Exercise 3.15 (Lower bound for convex hull computation)   Show that sorting n number reduces in linear time to the computation of the convex hull of n points in $\mathbb{R}^2$.

Hint: Take n real numbers $x_1, \ldots, x_n$. We associate to each x_i the point $p_i = (x_i, x_i^2)$ on the unit parabola. If we know the convex hull of the p_i, we can deduce in linear time the list of the x_i sorted by increasing values.

Exercise 3.16 (Orientation predicate) Show that the numerical operation required to decide if a facet $f = \{p_{i_1}, \ldots, p_{i_d}\}$ of conv(P_i) is red or blue when inserting point p_{i+1} amounts to evaluate the sign of a $(d + 1) \times (d + 1)$-determinant

$$\begin{vmatrix} 1 & \cdots & 1 & 1 \\ p_{i_1} & \cdots & p_{i_d} & p_{i+1} \end{vmatrix}.$$

Exercise 3.17 (Vertical projection of a lower hull) Let P be a set of point in general position in $\mathbb{R}^d$. We call vertical projection the projection Π onto the hyperplane of equation $x(d) = 0$. Show that the restriction of the vertical projection to the lower hull of P is 1 to 1. Show that the vertical projection naturally embeds the lower hull of P as a triangulation of $\Pi(P')$, where P' is the vertex set of the lower hull of P.

Exercise 3.18 (Minkowski formula) Show that if $\mathcal{P}$ is a convex polytope and $f_j, j \in J$, are its facets, we have $\sum_{j \in J} \text{vol}(f_j)\, n_j = 0$, where n_j is the unit normal vector to f_j oriented toward the outside of $\mathcal{P}$).

Hint : Let $x \in \mathcal{P}$. Compute the volume of $\mathcal{P}$ by summing the volumes of the pyramids (x, f_j). The results follows by observing that the volume of $\mathcal{P}$ does not depend on x.

3.6 Bibliographical Notes

A modern introduction to the theory of polytopes can be found in Ziegler's book [132]. The original proof of the upper bound theorem has been established by McMullen in 1970. The simple asymptotic version given in Theorem 3.9 is due to Seidel [121].

The incremental convex hull algorithm is due to Seidel [127]. A complete description of this algorithm handling degenerated cases is given in Edelsbrunner's book [67]. The random sampling theorem is due to Clarkson and Shor [59]. The same paper proposes the first randomized algorithm to build convex hulls. This algorithm solves in fact the dual problem of computing the intersection of half-spaces. Chazelle [52] has proposed a *deterministic* algorithm to compute the convex hull of a finite point set that is worst case optimal in any dimension. Obtained through derandomization of the randomized algorithm this algorithm is, however, mostly of theoretical interest and no implementation is known.

The theory of randomized algorithms is well developed and finds applications in many areas of computer science. See the book by Motwani and Raghavan for a broad perspective [107], and the books of Boissonnat and Yvinec [25] and of Mulmuley [108] for a geometric viewpoint.

4

Delaunay Complexes

Delaunay complexes are fundamental data structures that have been extensively studied in computational geometry and used in many application areas.

The Delaunay complex of a finite set of points $P \in \mathbb{R}^d$ is defined as the nerve of the Voronoi diagram of P, which we define first. We prove Delaunay's theorem that states that, when the points of P are in general position, the Delaunay complex of P has a natural embedding in $\mathbb{R}^d$ called the Delaunay triangulation of P.

The proof relies on the so-called lifting map that associates to each point of $\mathbb{R}^d$ a point in $\mathbb{R}^{d+1}$. We show that the Delaunay triangulation of P is the projection onto $\mathbb{R}^d$ of the lower hull of the lifted points. Using then the results of Chapter 3, we will bound the combinatorial complexity of Delaunay complexes and Voronoi diagrams, and obtain optimal algorithms for their construction.

Voronoi diagrams and Delaunay complexes are a special case of more general structures called *weighted* Voronoi diagrams and Delaunay complexes. The class of weighted Voronoi diagrams includes the class of Voronoi diagrams and, as we will see, most of the properties of Voronoi diagrams still hold for weighted diagrams. Weighted Voronoi diagrams can be found under various disguises in various applications and the dual weighted Delaunay complexes will play an important role in Chapters 5 and 8.

4.1 Lower Envelopes and Minimization Diagrams

Let $\mathcal{F} = \{f_1, \ldots, f_n\}$ be a set of d-variate continuous functions defined over $\mathbb{R}^d$. The *lower envelope* of $\mathcal{F}$ is defined as

$$\mathcal{F}^- = \min_{1 \leq i \leq n} f_i.$$

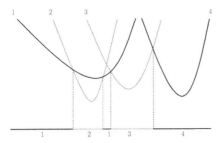

Figure 4.1 The lower envelope of a set of univariate functions. The minimization diagram is drawn on the horizontal line with the corresponding indices. The face of index $\{1\}$ consists of two components.

From $\mathcal{F}$ and $\mathcal{F}^-$, we define a partition of $\mathbb{R}^d$ called the *minimization diagram* of $\mathcal{F}$. For a point $x \in \mathbb{R}^d$, we define the *index set* $I(x)$ of x as the set of all indices i such that $\mathcal{F}^-(x) = f_i(x)$. An equivalence relation noted $\equiv$ can then be defined on the points of $\mathbb{R}^d$: two points are equivalent if they have the same index set:

$$x \equiv y \quad \Leftrightarrow \quad I(x) = I(y).$$

The equivalence classes are relatively open sets that cover $\mathbb{R}^d$. Their closures are called the *faces* of the minimization diagram of $\mathcal{F}$ and the collection of all those faces constitutes the minimization diagram of $\mathcal{F}$ (see Figure 4.1). The index set of a face is defined as the largest subset of indices common to all the points of the face. Conversely, the face of index set I is the set of all points x such that $I \subset I(x)$.

Upper envelopes and *maximization diagrams* can be defined analogously. Upper envelopes have been defined in a geometric way in Section 3.2.2 for sets of nonvertical hyperplanes. The two notions are in fact closely related. Let $H = \{h_1, \ldots, h_n\}$ be a set of nonvertical hyperplanes in $\mathbb{R}^{d+1}$. Each hyperplane h_i in H has an equation which in normal form reads $x(d+1) = f_i(x)$ where $x(d+1)$ is the last coordinate of a point in $\mathbb{R}^{d+1}$ and $f_i(x)$ is an affine function of the d first coordinates. Therefore h_i can be regarded as the graph of the affine function $f_i(x)$. Let $\mathcal{F}$ be the set of affine functions $\{f_1, \ldots, f_n\}$. The upper envelope defined in Section 3.2.2 for the set H is the graph of the upper envelope of the set $\mathcal{F}$, $\mathcal{F}^+ = \max_{1 \le i \le n} f_i$.

4.2 Voronoi Diagrams

Let $P = \{p_1, \ldots, p_n\}$ be a set of points of $\mathbb{R}^d$. To each p_i, we associate its *Voronoi cell* $V(p_i, P)$, or simply $V(p_i)$ when there is no ambiguity on the set P:

$$V(p_i, P) = \{x \in \mathbb{R}^d : \|x - p_i\| \le \|x - p_j\|, \forall p_j \in P\}.$$

The cell $V(p_i)$ is the intersection of the $n - 1$ half-spaces bounded by the bisecting hyperplanes of p_i and each of the other points of P. $V(p_i)$ is therefore a convex polyhedron, possibly unbounded, that contains p_i. The Voronoi cells of P have disjoint interiors and, because any point of $\mathbb{R}^d$ belongs to at least one Voronoi cell, they cover the entire space $\mathbb{R}^d$. The collection of the Voronoi cells and their faces constitute a *cell complex* called the Voronoi diagram of P and denoted by $\mathrm{Vor}(P)$.

The Voronoi diagram of P is the minimization diagram of the set of distance functions $\{\delta_i, \ldots, \delta_n\}$, where

$$\delta_i(x) = \|x - p_i\|.$$

An example of the Voronoi diagram of a set of 9 points is given in Figure 4.2. Because minimizing $\|x - p_i\|$ over i is the same as minimizing $(x - p_i)^2$, the Voronoi diagram of P can alternatively be defined as the minimization diagram of the smooth functions $(x - p_i)^2$. The graphs of those functions are translated copies of the vertical paraboloid of revolution of $\mathbb{R}^{d+1}$ of equation $x(d + 1) = x^2$.

Observing further that, for any x, $\arg\min_i(x - p_i)^2 = \arg\max_i(2p_i \cdot x - p_i^2)$, we obtain that the Voronoi diagram of P is the maximization diagram of a set of affine functions, namely, the functions

$$f_i(x) = 2p_i \cdot x - p_i^2.$$

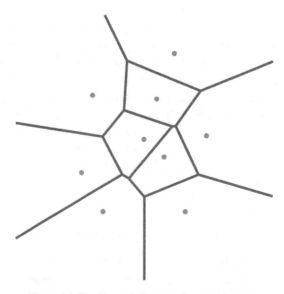

Figure 4.2 The Voronoi diagram of a set of 9 points.

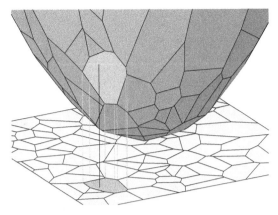

Figure 4.3 $\mathcal{V}(P)$, with one of its faces projected onto $\mathbb{R}^d$.

We can rewrite this construction in more geometric terms and establish a link with convex polyhedra. For $i = 1, \ldots, n$, let h_i be the hyperplane of $\mathbb{R}^{d+1}$ that is the graph of the affine function $f_i(x)$:

$$h_i = \{(x, x(d+1)) \in \mathbb{R}^d \times \mathbb{R}, \ x(d+1) = 2p_i \cdot x - p_i^2\}.$$

Let $H = \{h_1, \ldots, h_n\}$ and denote by $\mathcal{V}(P)$ the upper envelope of hyperplanes in H. By definition (see Section 3.2.2), the upper envelope $\mathcal{V}(P)$ is the boundary complex of the convex polyhedra $h_1^+ \cap h_2^+ \cdots \cap h_n^+$ which is the intersection of the upper half-spaces bounded by the hyperplanes in H. Since the Voronoi diagram Vor(P) is the maximization diagram of the set of functions $\{f_1, \ldots, f_n\}$, it is the projection onto the space $\mathbb{R}^d = \{x, x(d+1) = 0\}$ of the upper envelope $\mathcal{V}(P)$, see Figure 4.3.

We deduce that the combinatorial complexity of the Voronoi diagram of n points of $\mathbb{R}^d$ is at most the combinatorial complexity of a polyhedron defined as the intersection of n half-spaces of $\mathbb{R}^{d+1}$, which is $O\left(n^{\left\lceil \frac{d}{2} \right\rceil}\right)$ as shown in Section 3.3. This bound is tight (Exercise 4.3). Moreover, we can construct Vor(P) by constructing $\mathcal{V}(P) \subset \mathbb{R}^{d+1}$ and then projecting its faces onto $\mathbb{R}^d$. Thanks to Theorem 3.11, we conclude that Vor(P) can be constructed in time $\Theta\left(n \log n + n^{\left\lceil \frac{d}{2} \right\rceil}\right)$.

4.3 Delaunay Complexes

Let P be a finite set of points in $\mathbb{R}^d$ and write as before Vor(P) for its Voronoi diagram. The collection of all Voronoi cells of Vor(P) form a cover of $\mathbb{R}^d$ by

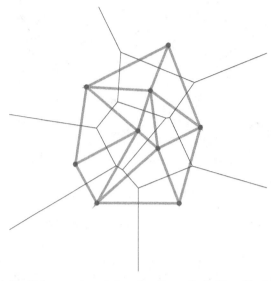

Figure 4.4 The Delaunay triangulation of a point set (in bold) and its dual Voronoi diagram (thin lines).

closed convex sets, and the nerve of this cover is an abstract simplicial complex called the *Delaunay complex* of P. Specifically, let f be a face of dimension k of Vor(P) and let int$f$ be the set of points of f that do not belong to any proper subface of f. All the points of int$f$ have the same subset σ of closest points in P and f is the intersection of the Voronoi cells of the points in σ. Accordingly, σ is a simplex in the Delaunay complex. See Figure 4.4. We denote by Del(P) the Delaunay complex of the set P.

This definition can be rephrased in terms of empty balls. A ball $B \in \mathbb{R}^d$ is said to be *empty* of points of P if the interior of B includes no points of P. We say that a d-ball circumscribes a finite subset of points if the sphere bounding B passes through all the points of the subset. The following lemma is just another view of the definition of the Delaunay complex.

Lemma 4.1 (The empty ball property) *Any subset $\sigma \subset P$ is a simplex of the Delaunay complex of P iff it has a circumscribing (open) ball empty of points of P. Such a ball is called a* Delaunay ball *(see Figure 4.5).*

The Delaunay complex cannot always be embedded in $\mathbb{R}^d$. Consider, for example, the case of a set P consisting of $m > d + 1$ points lying on a same hypersphere. The center of the hypersphere belongs to the Voronoi cells of all the m points, which implies that the Delaunay complex contains the

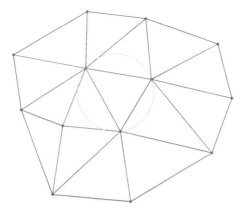

Figure 4.5 The empty ball property.

$(m - 1)$-simplex whose vertex set is P. This simplex cannot be embedded in $\mathbb{R}^d$ since its dimension $m - 1$ is greater than d.

However, as shown here, the Delaunay complex can be embedded in $\mathbb{R}^d$ when the points of P are in *general position wrt spheres*.

Definition 4.2 (General position wrt spheres) We say that a finite set of points P is in *general position wrt spheres* if no subset of $d + 2$ points of P lie on a same hypersphere.

We can now state Delaunay's fundamental result.

Theorem 4.3 (Delaunay triangulation) *If a finite set of points $P \in \mathbb{R}^d$ is in general position wrt spheres, then the Delaunay complex* $\mathrm{Del}(P)$ *has a natural embedding[1] in $\mathbb{R}^d$. This embedding is a triangulation of P called the Delaunay triangulation of P.*

Proof We identify $\mathbb{R}^d$ with the hyperplane of $\mathbb{R}^{d+1}$ of equation $x(d+1) = 0$ and introduce a lifting map ϕ that maps points and balls of $\mathbb{R}^d$ to points of $\mathbb{R}^{d+1}$. We then consider the lower hull of the set of lifted points $\phi(P)$ and show that the projection onto $\mathbb{R}^d$ embeds this lower hull as a geometric simplicial complex of $\mathbb{R}^d$. We will see that this complex is identical to the natural embedding of the Delaunay complex $\mathrm{Del}(P)$. Further, we will prove that it is a triangulation of P.

Let $b = b(c, r)$ be a d-ball of $\mathbb{R}^d$ with center c and radius r. The lifting map ϕ associates to b the point $\phi(b) = (c, c^2 - r^2)$ of $\mathbb{R}^{d+1}$. A point x of $\mathbb{R}^d$ can be

---

[1] Defined in Section 2.2.

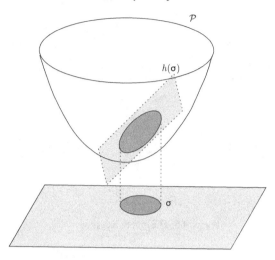

Figure 4.6 The polar hyperplane of a ball.

considered as a ball with null radius and is mapped to the point $\phi(x) = (x, x^2)$ of $\mathbb{R}^{d+1}$. Observe that the lift of a point lies on the paraboloid of revolution $Q = \{x \in \mathbb{R}^{d+1} : x(d + 1) = x^2\}$. We then use in $\mathbb{R}^{d+1}$ the point hyperplane duality defined in Section 3.2.1 and denote by $\phi(b)^*$ the hyperplane of $\mathbb{R}^{d+1}$ that is the dual of $\phi(b)$:

$$\phi(b)^* = \{x \in \mathbb{R}^{d+1} : x(d + 1) - 2cx + c^2 - r^2 = 0\}.$$

The sphere ∂b bounding $b(c, r)$ is the projection onto $\mathbb{R}^d$ of the intersection of Q with the hyperplan $\phi(b)^*$ (see Figure 4.6). Furthermore, the point x belongs to the (open) ball b iff $\phi(x)$ belongs to the halfspace $\phi(b)^{*-}$ below $\phi(b)^*$. Therefore, we have:

$$x \in \partial b \Longleftrightarrow \phi(x) \in \phi(b)^* \tag{4.1}$$

$$x \in b \Longleftrightarrow \phi(x) \in \phi(b)^{*-}. \tag{4.2}$$

Consider now a set P of n points in general position wrt spheres and let σ be a subset of $d + 1$ points of P. We write b for the ball that circumscribes σ. According to Lemma 4.1, σ is a Delaunay simplex iff the ball b is empty of points of P. Then, from Equations 4.1 and 4.2, the hyperplane $\phi(b)^*$ contains $\phi(\sigma)$ and the halfspace $\phi(b)^{*-}$ does not contain any point of $\phi(P)$. We conclude that σ is a Delaunay simplex iff the convex hull of $\phi(\sigma)$ is a facet of the lower hull $\mathcal{D}(P)$ of the lifted points $\phi(P)$.

Because P is in general position wrt spheres, $\phi(P)$ is in general position wrt hyperplanes (i.e., in the usual sense). It follows that $\mathcal{D}(P)$ is a simplicial complex embedded in $\mathbb{R}^{d+1}$. Consider now the projection onto $\mathbb{R}^d$, called the vertical projection. The restriction of the vertical projection to $\mathcal{D}(P)$ is 1-1 (see Exercise 3.17), and therefore the vertical projection of $\mathcal{D}(P)$ is a simplicial complex embedded in $\mathbb{R}^d$. From the previous paragraph, the facets of $\mathcal{D}(P)$ are in bijective correspondence with the Delaunay simplices of Del(P). Furthermore, for each simplex σ of Del(P), the corresponding facet of $\mathcal{D}(P)$ is the convex hull of the lift $\phi(\sigma)$ of σ so that its vertical projection is the convex hull of σ. It follows that the projection of the lower hull $\mathcal{D}(P)$ is the natural embedding of the Delaunay complex Del(P).

Let us further show that the natural embedding of Del(P) is a triangulation of P. By definition, the set of vertices of Del(P) is P. Furthermore, since $\mathcal{D}(P)$ is the lower hull of $\phi(P)$, its vertical projection coincides with the vertical projection of the convex hull of $\phi(P)$, which is just the convex hull of P. It follows that the natural embedding of Del(P) is a triangulation of P. This concludes the proof of Delaunay triangulation theorem. $\qquad\Box$

Since the Delaunay complex Del(P) is defined as the nerve of the cell complex Vor(P), there is a dual correspondence between the faces of these two complexes, i.e., a bijective correspondence between their faces that preserves incidences and reverses inclusions. The duality between lower hulls and upper envelopes introduced in Section 3.2 yields another dual correspondence between Vor(P) and Del(P). Indeed, notice that the set of hyperplanes $\{h_1, h_2, \ldots h_n\}$ defining the upper envelope $\mathcal{V}(P)$ are the duals $\{\phi(p_1)^*, \phi(p_2)^*, \ldots \phi(p_n)^*\}$ of the lifted points $\phi(P)$. Therefore, by the results of Section 3.2, the upper envelope $\mathcal{V}(P)$ and the lower hull $\mathcal{D}(P)$ are dual complexes. Because the vertical projection induces a bijection between the cellular complexes $\mathcal{V}(P)$ and Vor(P), and because the lifting map induces another bijection between the complexes $\mathcal{D}(P)$ and Del(P), we get a dual correspondence between Vor(P) and Del(P) through the duality between $\mathcal{V}(P)$ and $\mathcal{D}(P)$. In fact, the proof of the Delaunay triangulation theorem shows that the two correspondences between Vor(P) and Del(P) coincide, so that the following diagram commutes:

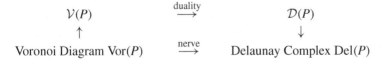

It follows that the combinatorial complexity of the Delaunay complex of n points is the same as the combinatorial complexity of its dual Voronoi diagram. Moreover, the Delaunay complex of n points of $\mathbb{R}^d$ can be deduced from the dual Voronoi diagram and vice versa in time proportional to their size. We also deduce from what precedes that computing the Delaunay complex of n points of $\mathbb{R}^d$ reduces to constructing the convex hull of n points of $\mathbb{R}^{d+1}$. The following theorem is then a direct consequence of Theorems 3.9 and 3.11.

Theorem 4.4 *The combinatorial complexity of the Voronoi diagram of a set of n points of $\mathbb{R}^d$ and of its Delaunay complex is $\Theta\left(n^{\left\lceil \frac{d}{2} \right\rceil}\right)$. Both structures can be computed in optimal time $\Theta\left(n \log n + n^{\left\lceil \frac{d}{2} \right\rceil}\right)$.*

The bounds in this theorem are tight in the worst case. In particular, the Voronoi diagram of n points of $\mathbb{R}^3$ may be quadratic (see Exercise 4.3). However, under some assumptions on the point distribution, better bounds can be obtained (see Section 5.1).

If the points of P are not in general position wrt spheres, the Delaunay complex may be of dimension greater than the dimension d of the embedding space and therefore cannot be embedded in $\mathbb{R}^d$. Accordingly, the hyperplane set $\phi(P)^*$ and the point set $\phi(P)$ are not in general position. Hence, $\mathcal{V}(P)$ is not simple and $\mathcal{D}(P)$ is not simplicial. The diagram won't commute.

Nevertheless, the projection of $\mathcal{D}(P)$ will still be a cell complex. Let f be a j-face of $\mathcal{D}(P)$ that is not a simplex. Its projection is no longer a simplex but is still a convex j-polytope we denote by f'. Moreover, f' is still the convex hull of the vertices of a k-simplex σ of the nerve of Vor(P) with $k > j$. We say that f' is the *shadow* of σ. An embedded triangulation can then be obtained by triangulating the shadows that are not simplices (see Exercise 4.6). Any such triangulation is called *a* Delaunay triangulation. Since there are several ways of triangulating the faces of a polytope, P admits several Delaunay triangulations.

4.4 Weighted Delaunay Complexes

4.4.1 Weighted Points and Weighted Distance

A weighted point $\hat{p} = (p, w)$ is an element of $\mathbb{R}^d \times \mathbb{R}$ where the point $p \in \mathbb{R}^d$ is called the *center* of $\hat{p}$ and $w \in \mathbb{R}$ is called its *weight*. A point is identified with a weighted point of weight 0. When w is non-negative, $\hat{p}$ can be considered as the ball $b(p, \sqrt{w})$ centered at p and of squared radius w. Because considering negative weights will cause no problem in our developments, we favor the name of weighted point.

We define the weighted distance between two weighted points $\hat{p}_1 = (p_1, w_1)$ and $\hat{p}_2 = (p_2, w_2)$ as

$$D(\hat{p}_1, \hat{p}_2) = (p_1 - p_2)^2 - w_1 - w_2.$$

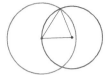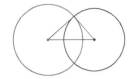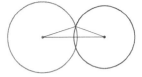

Figure 4.7 The weighted distance: two weighted points with a negative (left), null (middle) and positive (right) weighted distance respectively.

Note that the weighted distance is not a distance in the usual sense since it is not positive and does not satisfy the triangular inequality. Two weighted points are said to be *orthogonal* if their distance is zero. The term orthogonal comes from the observation that, when the weights are non-negative, two weighted points are orthogonal iff the spheres bounding the associated balls are orthogonal spheres (see Figure 4.7). The weighted distance $D(x, \hat{p})$ from an unweighted point x to a weighted point $\hat{p} = (p, w)$ whose weight w is non-negative is also called the *power* of point x with respect to the sphere bounding the ball $b(p, \sqrt{w})$.

4.4.2 Weighted Voronoi Diagrams

Let $\hat{P} = \{\hat{p}_1, \ldots, \hat{p}_n\}$ be a set of weighted points of $\mathbb{R}^d \times \mathbb{R}$. To each $\hat{p}_i = (p_i, w_i)$, we associate the cell $V(\hat{p}_i) \subset \mathbb{R}^d$ consisting of the points x of $\mathbb{R}^d$ whose weighted distance to $\hat{p}_i$ is not larger than its weighted distance to any other weighted points of $\hat{P}$:

$$V(\hat{p}_i) = \{x \in \mathbb{R}^d : D(x, \hat{p}_i) \le D(x, \hat{p}_j), \forall \hat{p}_j \in \hat{P}\}.$$

The set of points of $\mathbb{R}^d$ that are at equal distance from two weighted points $\hat{p}_i$ and $\hat{p}_j$ is a hyperplane called the bisecting hyperplane of $\hat{p}_i$ and $\hat{p}_j$. This hyperplane is orthogonal to the line joining the centers of $\hat{p}_i$ and $\hat{p}_j$. The cell $V(\hat{p}_i)$ is the intersection of the $n - 1$ half-spaces bounded by the bisecting hyperplanes of $\hat{p}_i$ and each of the other weighted points of $\hat{P}$. If this intersection is not empty, it is a convex polyhedron, possibly unbounded. We call *weighted Voronoi cells* the non empty cells $V(\hat{p}_i)$, $i \in [1 : n]$.

We define the *weighted Voronoi diagram* of $\hat{P}$, noted $\text{Vor}(\hat{P})$, as the cell complex whose faces are the weighted Voronoi cells and their faces. Note that the set of weighted Voronoi diagrams includes Voronoi diagrams. Indeed, when all weighted points have the same weight, their weighted Voronoi diagram is identical to the Voronoi diagram of their centers.

Equivalently, the weighted Voronoi diagram of $\hat{P}$ can be defined as the minimization diagram of the set of functions $\{D(x, \hat{p}_i), \ldots, D(x, \hat{p}_n)\}$. Observing

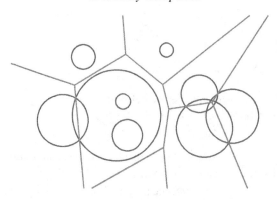

Figure 4.8 A weighted Voronoi diagram.

that, for any x, $\arg\min_i D(x, \hat{p}_i) = \arg\max_i(2p_i \cdot x - p_i^2 + w_i)$, we obtain that the weighted Voronoi diagram of $\hat{P}$ is the maximization diagram of the set of affine functions $\mathcal{F} = \{f_1, \ldots, f_n\}$, where

$$f_i(x) = 2p_i \cdot x - p_i^2 + w_i.$$

The graph of $f_i(x)$ is a nonvertical hyperplane of $\mathbb{R}^{d+1}$ that we denote by h_i:

$$h_i = \{(x, x(d+1)) \in \mathbb{R}^d \times \mathbb{R},\ x(d+1) = 2p_i \cdot x - p_i^2 + w_i\}.$$

Let $H = \{h_1, \ldots, h_n\}$ and let us denote by $\mathcal{V}(\hat{P})$ the upper envelope of the hyperplanes of H. The maximization diagram of $\mathcal{F}$ is obtained by projecting vertically the faces of the upper envelope $\mathcal{V}(\hat{P})$.

Hence, the faces of the weighted Voronoi diagram $\mathrm{Vor}(\hat{P})$ are the vertical projections of the faces of $\mathcal{V}(\hat{P})$.

Weighted Voronoi diagrams are very similar to Voronoi diagrams: the main difference is that some weighted point $\hat{p}_i$ in $\hat{P}$ may have an empty Voronoi cell in $\mathrm{Vor}(\hat{P})$ (see the small circle in the upper left corner of Figure 4.8). Equivalently, the corresponding hyperplane h_i does not contribute to a face of the upper envelope $\mathcal{V}(\hat{P})$. Notice, however, that if the weights are non-negative and small enough so that the weighted points in $\hat{P}$ correspond to disjoint balls, then all the weighted points have a nonempty Voronoi cell, (Exercise 4.13).

4.4.3 Weighted Delaunay Complexes

Let $\hat{P}$ be a finite set of weighted points of $\mathbb{R}^d$ and write as before $\mathrm{Vor}(\hat{P})$ for its Voronoi diagram. The nerve of the collection of all cells of $\mathrm{Vor}(\hat{P})$ is an abstract simplicial complex denoted by $\mathrm{Del}(\hat{P})$ and called the *weighted*

Delaunay complex of $\hat{P}$. Specifically, let f be a face of dimension k of $\text{Vor}(\hat{P})$ and let $\text{int}f$ be the set of points of f that do not belong to any proper subface of f. All the points of $\text{int}f$ have the same subset $\hat{\sigma}$ of closest weighted points in $\hat{P}$ (for the weighted distance), and f is the intersection of the weighted Voronoi cells of the weighted points in $\hat{\sigma}$. Accordingly, $\hat{\sigma}$ is a simplex in the weighted Delaunay complex.

Recall that two weighted points are said to be *orthogonal* if their weighted distance is zero. A weighted point $\hat{x}$ is said to be orthogonal to a finite set $\hat{\sigma}$ of weighted points if $\hat{x}$ is orthogonal to all the weighted points of $\hat{\sigma}$.

We say that the set $\hat{P}$ of weighted points is in *general position* when no weighted point of $\mathbb{R}^d \times \mathbb{R}$ is at equal weighted distance from more than $d+1$ weighted points of $\hat{P}$. In the following, we assume that the set $\hat{P}$ of weighted points is in general position.

Then, if $\hat{\sigma} = \{\hat{p}_0, \ldots, \hat{p}_d\}$ is a subset of $d+1$ weighted points in $\hat{P}$, there exists a unique weighted point $\hat{c}$ in $\mathbb{R}^d \times \mathbb{R}$ orthogonal to $\hat{\sigma}$. The center $c(\sigma)$ of $\hat{c}$ is called the weighted center of $\hat{\sigma}$, and the square root of the weight of $\hat{c}$, denoted by $r(\hat{\sigma})$, is called the weighted radius of $\hat{\sigma}$. Observe that the weighted radius may be imaginary which causes no problem.

A weighted point $\hat{x}$ is said to be *free* of weighted points of $\hat{P}$ if no point of $\hat{P}$ has a negative weighted distance to $\hat{x}$. Observe that the notion of free weighted points generalizes the notion of empty balls (see Lemma 4.1). Indeed, when the weights of points in $\hat{P}$ are 0 and the weight of $\hat{x}$ is positive, the ball corresponding to $\hat{x}$ is an empty ball for P.

Let v be a vertex of $\text{Vor}(\hat{P})$. The weighted Delaunay simplex $\hat{\sigma}$ associated to v is a d-simplex. The vertex v is at equal weighted distance w from all the weighted points of $\hat{\sigma}$, and this distance is smaller than the weighted distance from v to all other weighted points in $\hat{P} \setminus \hat{\sigma}$. Therefore the weighted point (v, w) is orthogonal to $\hat{\sigma}$ and free of points of $\hat{P}$. This property generalizes to faces of $\text{Vor}(\hat{P})$ of any dimension and the following lemma is just another view of the definition of the weighted Delaunay complex.

Lemma 4.5 (The free weighted point property) *Any subset $\hat{\sigma} \subset \hat{P}$ is a simplex of the weighted Delaunay complex $\text{Del}(\hat{P})$ iff there is a weighted point orthogonal to $\hat{\sigma}$ and free of weighted points of $\hat{P}$.*

We proceed now as in Section 4.3 and prove the weighted version of Delaunay's triangulation theorem. With a slight abuse of language, we call natural embedding of $\text{Del}(\hat{P})$ in $\mathbb{R}^d$, a geometric realization of $\text{Del}(\hat{P})$ in which each simplex $\hat{\sigma}$ of $\text{Del}(\hat{P})$ is embedded as the convex hull of the set σ of the centers of the weighted points in $\hat{\sigma}$.

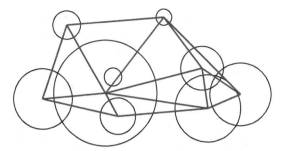

Figure 4.9 The weighted delaunay triangulation associated to the weighted Voronoi diagram of Figure 4.8.

Theorem 4.6 (Weighted Delaunay triangulation)   *If a finite set of weighted points $\hat{P} \in \mathbb{R}^d \times \mathbb{R}$ is in general position, then the weighted Delaunay complex $\mathrm{Del}(\hat{P})$ has a natural embedding in $\mathbb{R}^d$ which is a triangulation of a subset P' of P. P' is the set of centers of the weighted points in $\hat{P}$ that have a non empty cell in $\mathrm{Vor}(\hat{P})$ (see Figure 4.9).*

Proof   We first define the lifting map for weighted points as follows: to a weighted point $\hat{p} = (p, w)$ of $\mathbb{R}^d$, we associate the point $\phi(\hat{p}) = (p, p^2 - w)$ of $\mathbb{R}^{d+1}$. Then we consider the lower hull of points of $\phi(\hat{P})$, denoted by $\mathcal{D}(\hat{P})$. Arguing as in Section 4.3, we get that the lower hull $\mathcal{D}(\hat{P})$ is a geometric simplicial complex embedded in $\mathbb{R}^{d+1}$ whose vertical projection onto $\mathbb{R}^d$ is the natural embedding of $\mathrm{Del}(\hat{P})$. Let $\hat{P}'$ be the subset of weighted points in $\hat{P}$ that have non empty cells in $\mathrm{Vor}(\hat{P})$. The vertex set of $\mathcal{D}(\hat{P})$ is the set $\phi(\hat{P}') \subseteq \phi(\hat{P})$ and the vertical projection of $\mathcal{D}(\hat{P})$ is a triangulation of P', the set of centers of the weighted points of $\hat{P}'$.   □

Observe that the hyperplanes $h_i, i = 1, \ldots, n$ defined in Section 4.4.2 are the hyperplanes dual to the points in $\phi(\hat{P})$. Therefore, by the results of Section 3.2, the upper envelope $\mathcal{V}(\hat{P})$ and the lower hull $\mathcal{D}(\hat{P})$ are dual complexes. Arguing once more as in Section 4.3, we get the following diagram which commutes when the weighted points are in general position :

$$
\begin{array}{ccc}
\mathcal{V}(\hat{P}) & \xrightarrow{\text{duality}} & \mathcal{D}(\hat{P}) \\
\uparrow & & \downarrow \\
\mathrm{Vor}(\hat{P}) & \xrightarrow{\text{nerve}} & \mathrm{Del}(\hat{P})
\end{array}
$$

If the weighted points are not in general position, we can triangulate the non simplicial faces $\mathcal{D}(\hat{P})$ as described in Section 4.3. The vertical projection of $\mathcal{D}(\hat{P})$ will then be a triangulation of P'.

4.4.4 Complexity of weighted Delaunay complexes

The following theorem states that computing the weighted Voronoi diagram of n weighted points of $\mathbb{R}^d \times \mathbb{R}$ (or equivalently its dual weighted Delaunay triangulation) has the same asymptotic complexity as computing the Euclidean Voronoi diagram or the Delaunay triangulation of n points of $\mathbb{R}^d$. The theorem is a direct consequence of Section 4.4.3 and of results on convex hulls (Theorems 3.9 and 3.11).

Theorem 4.7 *The combinatorial complexity of the weighted Voronoi diagram of n weighted points of $\mathbb{R}^d \times \mathbb{R}$ and of its dual weighted Delaunay triangulation are* $\Theta\left(n^{\left\lceil \frac{d}{2} \right\rceil}\right)$. *Both structures can be computed in optimal time* $\Theta\left(n \log n + n^{\left\lceil \frac{d}{2} \right\rceil}\right)$.

4.5 Examples of Weighted Voronoi Diagrams

We have seen that the weighted Voronoi diagram of n weighted points is the maximization diagram of n affine functions. The converse is also true (see Exercise 4.14). We give in this section two examples of weighted Voronoi diagrams that are of interest in the context of data analysis.

4.5.1 *k*-order Voronoi Diagrams

Let P be a set of n points of $\mathbb{R}^d$ and let P_k be the set of all subsets of k points of P for some fixed $k \in [1 : n-1]$. We define the Voronoi cell of a subset $K \in P_k$ as the set of points of $\mathbb{R}^d$ that are closer to all the sites in K than to any other site in $P \setminus K$:

$$V_k(K) = \{x \in \mathbb{R}^d : \forall p_i \in K, \forall p_j \in P \setminus K, \|x - p_i\| \leq \|x - p_j\|\}.$$

Let us consider the subsets of P_k whose Voronoi cells are not empty. These cells are convex polyhedra and form a cell complex whose domain is $\mathbb{R}^d$ called the *k-order diagram* of P (see Figure 4.10). For $k = 1$, we obtain the usual Voronoi diagram.

Theorem 4.8 *The k-order diagram of P is the weighted Voronoi diagram of a set of $\binom{n}{k}$ weighted points of $\mathbb{R}^d$.*

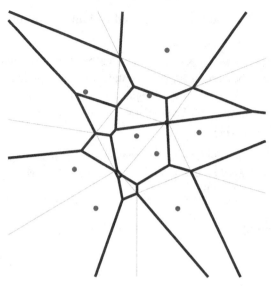

Figure 4.10 The 2-order Voronoi diagram of a set of points (in bold line) and the corresponding 1-order Voronoi diagram (in thin line).

Proof Let $K_1, \ldots, K_s$ be the $s = \begin{pmatrix} n \\ k \end{pmatrix}$ subsets of k points of P. For any point $x \in \mathbb{R}^d$, we have

$$x \in V_k(K_i) \iff \frac{1}{k} \sum_{p \in K_i} (x - p)^2 \leq \frac{1}{k} \sum_{q \in K_j} (x - q)^2 \qquad \forall j, 1 \leq j \leq s$$

$$\iff x^2 - 2 \left(\frac{1}{k} \sum_{p \in K_i} p \right) \cdot x + \frac{1}{k} \sum_{p \in K_i} p^2$$

$$\leq x^2 - 2 \left(\frac{1}{k} \sum_{q \in K_j} q \right) \cdot x + \frac{1}{k} \sum_{q \in K_j} q^2$$

$$\iff D(x, \hat{p}_i) \leq D(x, \hat{p}_j)$$

where $\hat{p}_i = (c_i, w_i)$ is the weighted point centered at the center of mass $c_i = \frac{1}{k} \sum_{p \in K_i} p$ of K_i of weight $w_i = c_i^2 - \rho_i^2$ with $\rho_i^2 = \frac{1}{k} \sum_{p \in K_i^k} p^2$. Hence, $x \in V_k(K_i)$ iff x lies in the weighted Voronoi cell of $\hat{p}_i$. $\qquad \square$

It follows that the k-order Voronoi diagram of a finite set of points P of $\mathbb{R}^d$ is a cell complex of $\mathbb{R}^d$ whose nerve is a triangulation of $\mathbb{R}^d$ under a general position assumption.

The k-order Voronoi diagram of P can be used as a data structure to compute in sublinear time the k points of P that are closest to a query point x. The query can be answered by identifying the cell of the k-order Voronoi diagram that contains x and reading the associated k-nearest points of P.

4.5.2 Bregman Diagrams

Let Ω be a convex domain of $\mathbb{R}^d$ and F a strictly convex and differentiable function F (called the *generator function* of the divergence) defined over Ω. For any two points $p = (p(1), \ldots, p(d))$ and $q = (q(1), \ldots, q(d))$ of Ω, the Bregman divergence $D_F(p\|q) : \Omega \times \Omega \mapsto \mathbb{R}$ associated to F is defined as

$$D_F(p\|q) = F(p) - F(q) - \nabla F(q) \cdot (p - q) \tag{4.3}$$

where $\nabla F = \left[\frac{\partial F}{\partial x_1} \ \cdots \ \frac{\partial F}{\partial x_d} \right]^T$ denotes the gradient operator.

Informally speaking, Bregman divergence D_F is the *tail* of the Taylor expansion of F. Geometrically, the Bregman divergence $D_F(p\|q)$ is measured as the vertical distance (i.e., along the $(d + 1)$-axis) between $\hat{p} = (p, F(p))$ and the hyperplane H_q tangent to the graph $\mathcal{F}$ of F at point $\hat{q}$: $D_F(p\|q) = F(p) - H_q(p)$. See Figure 4.11.

We now give some basic properties of Bregman divergences. First, observe that, for most functions F, the associated Bregman divergence is *not* symmetric, i.e., $D_F(p\|q) \neq D_F(q\|p)$ (the symbol $\|$ is put to emphasize this point). Hence, it is not a distance. Nevertheless, the strict convexity of the generator

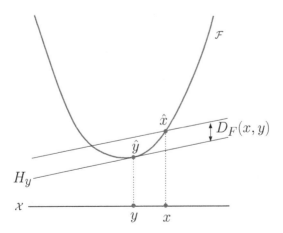

Figure 4.11 The Bregman divergence.

function F implies that, for any p and q in Ω, $D_F(p||q) \geq 0$, with $D_F(p||q) = 0$ if and only if $p = q$.

Examples of Bregman Divergences

Examples of Bregman divergences are the squared Euclidean distance, obtained with $F(x) = x^2$, and the quadratic distance function $D_F(x||y) = \frac{1}{2}(x-y)^T Q(x-y)$ (also known as the squared Mahalanobis distance extensively used in Computer Vision and Data Mining), obtained with $F(x) = \frac{1}{2}x^T Qx$ where Q is a symmetric positive definite matrix. See Exercise 4.16 for other examples.

The notion of Bregman divergence encapsulates various information measures based on entropic functions such as the Kullback-Leibler divergence based on the Shannon entropy, which is widely used in information theory, image processing and various fields. Let p be a discrete probability distribution so that $\sum_{i=1}^{d} p(i) = 1$. The Shannon entropy is defined as $F(p) = \sum_i p(i) \log_2 p(i)$. F is a convex function and the associated Bregman divergence between two probability distributions p and q is easily shown to be

$$D_F(p||q) = \sum_{i=1}^{d} p(i) \log_2 p(i) - \sum_{i=1}^{d} q(i) \log_2 q(i) - (p - q) \cdot \nabla F(q)$$

$$= \sum_{i=1}^{d} p(i) \log_2 \left(\frac{p(i)}{q(i)} \right) \quad \left(\text{since } \sum_{i=1}^{d} p(i) = \sum_{i=1}^{d} q(i) = 1 \right)$$

$$\overset{\text{def}}{=} KL(p||q).$$

$KL(p||q)$ is called the *Kullback-Leibler divergence* or the relative entropy of the two probability distributions p and q.

Bregman Diagrams

Let $P = \{p_1, \ldots, p_n\}$ be a finite point set of $\Omega \subset \mathbb{R}^d$. We associate to each site p_i the distance function, $D_i(x) = D_F(x||p_i)$. The *minimization diagram* of the $D_i, i = 1, \ldots, n$, is called the Bregman Voronoi diagram of P, which we denote by $\text{Vor}_F(P)$. The d-dimensional cells of this diagram are in *1-1 correspondence* with the sites p_i and the d-dimensional cell of p_i is defined as

$$V_F(p_i) \overset{\text{def}}{=} \{x \in \Omega \mid D_F(x||p_i) \leq D_F(x||p_j) \; \forall p_j \in P\}.$$

It is easy to see that the minimization diagram of the n functions $D_F(x||p_i)$ $i = 1, \ldots, n$, is the maximization of the n affine functions

$$h_i(x) = (x - p_i) \cdot \nabla F(p_i) + F(p_i), \quad i = 1, \ldots, n.$$

Hence, Bregman diagrams are weighted Voronoi diagrams. More precisely, we have

Theorem 4.9 *The Bregman Voronoi diagram of n sites is identical to the restriction to Ω of the weighted Voronoi diagram of the n weighted points (p'_i, w_i), $i = 1, \ldots, n$, where $p'_i = \nabla F(p_i)$ and $w_i = p'^2_i + 2(F(p_i) - p_i \cdot p'_i)$.*

Proof $D_F(x||p_i) \leq D_F(x||p_j)$ iff

$$-F(p_i) - (x - p_i) \cdot p'_i \leq -F(p_j) - (x - p_j) \cdot p'_j.$$

Multiplying the two sides of the inequality by 2 and adding x^2 to both sides yields

$$x^2 - 2x \cdot p'_i - 2F(p_i) + 2p_i \cdot p'_i \leq x^2 - 2x \cdot p'_j - 2F(p_j) + 2p_j \cdot p'_j$$
$$\iff (x - p'_i) \cdot (x - p'_i) - w_i \leq (x - p'_j) \cdot (x - p'_j) - w_j,$$

where $w_i = p'^2_i + 2(F(p_i) - p_i \cdot p'_i)$ and $w_j = p'^2_j + 2(F(p_j) - p_j \cdot p'_j)$. The last inequality means that the weighted distance of x to the weighted point (p'_i, w_i) is no more than its weighted distance to the weighted point (p'_j, w_j). □

It is to be observed that not all weighted Voronoi diagrams are Bregman Voronoi diagrams. Indeed, in weighted Voronoi diagrams, some weighted points may have empty cells while each site has necessarily a nonempty cell in a Bregman Voronoi diagram.

Bregman Complexes

We define the Bregman complex of P as the nerve of the Bregman diagram of P, $\text{Vor}_F(P)$. We denote it by $\text{Del}_F(P)$. An analogue of Delaunay's triangulation theorem also exists in this context.

Let $\hat{P}$ be the lifted image of P on the graph $\mathcal{F}$ of F, i.e., $\hat{P} = \{(p, F(p)), p \in P\} \in \mathbb{R}^{d+1}$. Write $\mathcal{T}$ for the lower hull of $\hat{P}$. We assume in this section that P is in *general position*, meaning that there is no point $x \in \Omega$ whose divergences to $d+2$ points of P are equal. Equivalently, P is in general position if $\hat{P}$ contains no subset of $d + 2$ points on a same hyperplane.

Assume that P is in general position. Then, for the same reasons as for Delaunay triangulations (see Section 4.3), $\mathcal{T}$ is a simplicial complex and the vertical projection of $\mathcal{T}$ onto $\mathbb{R}^d$ is a triangulation that is equal to $\text{Del}_F(P)$ by the lifting map argument given in the beginning of Section 4.5.2 (see Figurefig:bregman-lift). In other words, $\text{Del}_F(P)$ naturally embeds in $\Omega \subseteq \mathbb{R}^d$. We call $\text{Del}_F(P)$ the *Bregman triangulation* of P. When $F(x) = x^2$ and $\Omega = \mathbb{R}^d$, $\text{Del}_F(P)$ is the Delaunay triangulation of P.

We now show that the empty ball property of Delaunay triangulations (Lemma 4.1) naturally extends to Bregman triangulations. We define the *Bregman ball* centered at c and of radius r as

$$b_F(c, r) = \{x \in \Omega \mid D_F(x||c) < r\}.$$

It is easy to see that any Bregman ball b_F is obtained as the vertical projection of the intersection of $\mathcal{F}$ with a halfspace below a nonvertical hyperplane (see Figure 4.6 for the case where $F = x^2$).

A Bregman ball is said to be *empty* if it does not contain any point of P. Let $\sigma = [p_0, \ldots, p_d]$ be a (geometric) d-simplex of $\mathrm{Breg}_F(P)$. The affine hull of the lifted points $\hat{p}_0, \ldots, \hat{p}_d$ is a hyperplane h_σ of $\mathbb{R}^{d+1}$ whose intersection with $\mathcal{F}$ projects vertically onto the boundary of the (unique) Bregman ball b_σ that circumscribes σ. Because, by construction, $\mathrm{conv}(\hat{p}_0, \ldots, \hat{p}_d) \in h_\sigma$ is a facet of the lower hull of $\hat{P}$, b_σ must be empty.

It also follows from the discussion that, under the general position assumption, Bregman complexes naturally embeds in $\mathbb{R}^d$. This is another extension of Delaunay's triangulation theorem.

Bregman Diagrams and Complexes of the Second Type

We have defined Bregman diagrams as the minimization diagram of the functions $D_F(x||p_i)$. A symmetric definition can be given when exchanging the variable x and the site p_i and considering $D_F(p_i||x)$. The bisectors are no longer hyperplanes and the diagram is no longer a weighted Voronoi diagram. Still, Legendre duality, an essential notion in convex analysis, allows to transform a diagram of the second type into a diagram of the first type as explained next (Lemma 4.11).

Legendre Duality

Let F be a strictly convex and differentiable real-valued function on Ω. The gradient of F, ∇F, is well defined as well as its inverse $\nabla^{-1}F$, and $\nabla F \circ \nabla^{-1}F = \nabla^{-1}F \circ \nabla F$ are identity maps. We write x' for $\nabla F(x)$ and Ω' for the *gradient space* $\{\nabla F(x) | x \in \Omega\}$.

The Legendre transformation associates to F a *convex conjugate* function $F^* : \Omega' \mapsto \mathbb{R}$ given by [119]:

$$F^*(x') = x \cdot x' - F(x). \tag{4.4}$$

Taking the derivative of Equation 4.4, we get

$$\nabla F^*(x') \cdot dx' = x \cdot dx' + x' \cdot dx - \nabla F(x) \cdot dx = x \cdot dx' = \nabla^{-1}F(x') \cdot dx',$$

from which we deduce that $\nabla F^* = \nabla^{-1}F$.

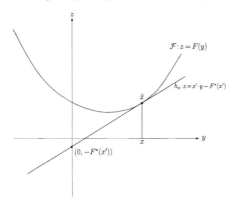

Figure 4.12 The z-intercept $(0, -F^*(x'))$ of the tangent hyperplane h_x of F at $\hat{x}$ defines the value of the Legendre transform F^* for the dual coordinate x'.

Figure 4.12 gives a geometric interpretation of the Legendre transformation. Consider the hyperplane h_x tangent to the graph $\mathcal{F}$ of F at $\hat{x}$. This hyperplane intersects the $(d + 1)$-axis at the point $(0, -F^*(x'))$. Indeed, the equation of h_x is $y(d + 1) = x' \cdot (y - x) + F(x) = x' \cdot y - F^*(x')$. Hence, the $(d + 1)$-axis intercept of h_x is equal to $-F^*(x')$. Any hyperplane passing through another point of $\mathcal{F}$ and parallel to h_x necessarily intersects the z-axis above $-F^*(x')$.

To ensure that D_{F^*} is a Bregman divergence, we need Ω' to be convex. This is trivial if Ω has no boundary and, in particular, when $\Omega = \mathbb{R}^d$. Otherwise, we will further require that F is a function of Legendre type, i.e., that the norm of the gradient of F goes to infinity whenever we approach the boundary of Ω (see [119]). Under the additional assumption that F is of Legendre type, we can associate to the conjugate function F^* a Bregman divergence D_{F^*}. We have the following remarkable result:

Lemma 4.10 $D_F(p\|q) = F(p) + F^*(q') - p \cdot q' = D_{F^*}(q'\|p')$

Proof   By Equation 4.3, $D_F(p\|q) = F(p) - F(q) - (p-q) \cdot q'$, and, according to Equation 4.4, we have $F(p) = p' \cdot p - F^*(p')$ and $F(q) = q' \cdot q - F^*(q')$. Hence,

$$
\begin{aligned}
D_F(p\|q) &= F(p) - F(q) - (p - q) \cdot q' \\
&= p' \cdot p - F^*(p') - p \cdot q' + F^*(q') \\
&= F^*(q') - F^*(p') - p \cdot (q' - p') \\
&= D_{F^*}(q'\|p')
\end{aligned}
$$

where the last equality holds since $p = \nabla F^{-1} \nabla F(p) = \nabla F^*(p')$.   □

Observe that, when D_F is symmetric, D_{F^*} is also symmetric.

The Legendre transform of the quadratic form $F(x) = \frac{1}{2}x^T Q x$, where Q is a symmetric invertible matrix, is $F^*(x') = \frac{1}{2}x'^T Q^{-1} x'$. We say that F is self dual. Observe that the corresponding divergences D_F and D_{F^*} are both generalized quadratic distances.

To compute F^*, we can use the fact that $\nabla F^* = \nabla F^{-1}$ (see above). However, integrating functions symbolically may be difficult or even not possible, and, in some cases, it will be required to approximate numerically the inverse gradient $\nabla^{-1} F(x)$.

We can now define Bregman diagrams of the second type where the cell of p_i is defined as

$$\tilde{V}_F(p_i) \stackrel{\text{def}}{=} \{x \in \Omega \mid D_F(p_i \| x)) \leq D_F(p_j \| x) \; \forall p_j \in P\}.$$

In contrast with the diagram of the first-type $\mathrm{Vor}_F(P)$, the diagram of the second type $\widetilde{\mathrm{Vor}}(P)$ has, in general, curved faces. From the Legendre duality between divergences, we deduce correspondences between the diagrams of the first and the second types. As usual, F^* denotes the convex conjugate of F.

Lemma 4.11 *We have*

$$\widetilde{\mathrm{Vor}}_F(P) = \nabla^{-1} F(\mathrm{Vor}_{F^*}(P')) \quad \text{and} \quad \mathrm{Vor}_F(P) = \nabla^{-1} F(\widetilde{\mathrm{Vor}}_{F^*}(P')).$$

Proof By Lemma 4.10, we have $D_F(x\|y) = D_{F^*}(y'\|x')$, which gives $V_F(p_i) = \{x \in \Omega \mid D_{F^*}(p_i'\|x') \leq D_{F^*}(p_j'\|x') \; \forall p_j' \in P'\} = \nabla^{-1} F(\tilde{V}_{F^*}(p_i'))$. This proves the second part of the lemma. The proof of the first part follows the same path. □

Hence, constructing $\widetilde{\mathrm{Vor}}_F(P)$, the (curved) Bregman diagram of the second-type, reduces to constructing an affine diagram in the gradient space Ω' (and mapping the cells by $\nabla^{-1} F$). The nerve of the Bregman diagram of the second-type is a simplicial complex called the Bregman triangulation of the second type. It follows from Lemma 4.11 that the Bregman triangulation of the second type of P can be realized as the (curved) image by $\nabla^{-1} F$ of the Bregman Delaunay triangulation of the first type of P'.

4.6 Exercises

Exercise 4.1 (Space of spheres) Let b be a d-ball of $\mathbb{R}^d$ of center c and radius r and let $s = c^2 - r^2$. We associate to b the point of $\mathbb{R}^{d+1}$ $\phi(\sigma) = (c, s)$. Show that the image by ϕ of a point, considered as a ball of radius 0, is a point of the paraboloid $\mathcal{Q}$ of equation $x_{d+1} = x^2$.

Show that the image by ϕ of the balls whose bounding spheres pass through a given point p of $\mathbb{R}^d$ is the *hyperplane* h_p of $\mathbb{R}^{d+1}$ of equation $x_{d+1} = 2p \cdot x - p^2$, which is tangent to $\mathcal{Q}$ at $\phi(p) = (p, p^2)$.

What are the preimages by ϕ of the points of $\mathbb{R}^{d+1}$ that lie above $\mathcal{Q}$, on a line? The same question can be asked about the image of the balls that contain p.

Exercise 4.2 (Farthest point diagram) Consider the diagram obtained by projecting the faces of $h^-_{p_1} \cap \cdots \cap h^-_{p_n}$ vertically, where the h_{p_i} are defined as in Exercise 4.1. Characterize the points that belong to a face of this diagram.

Dually, project vertically the faces of the *upper* convex hull of the $\phi(p_i) = (p_i, p_i^2)$, $i = 1, \ldots, n$. Show that we obtain a triangulation of the vertices of $\mathrm{conv}(P)$ such that each ball circumscribing a simplex contains all the points of P.

Exercise 4.3 (Upper bound) Consider first the case of a set of points P lying on two non coplanar lines of $\mathbb{R}^3$. Let $n_1 + 1$ and $n_2 + 1$ be the numbers of points on each of the lines. Show that the Delaunay complex of P has $n_1 n_2$ tetrahedra (or, equivalently, that their Voronoi diagram has $n_1 n_2$ vertices).

Show that the moment curve $\mathcal{M}_d \subset \mathbb{R}^d$ (defined in Exercise 3.12) can be drawn on the paraboloid $\mathcal{Q}$ of equation $x_{d+1} = x^2$. Deduce then from Exercise 3.12 that the bound in Theorem 4.4 is tight.

Exercise 4.4 (Triangulation of linear size) Prove that any set of n points of $\mathbb{R}^d$ in general position admits a triangulation of size $O(n)$.

Exercise 4.5 (in_ball predicate) Let B be a ball of $\mathbb{R}^d$ whose bounding sphere S passes through $d + 1$ points $p_0, \ldots, p_d$. Show that a point p_{d+1} of $\mathbb{R}^d$ lies on S, in the interior of B or outside B, depending whether the determinant of the $(d + 2) \times (d + 2)$ matrix

$$\mathrm{in\_sphere}(p_0, \ldots, p_{d+1}) = \begin{vmatrix} 1 & \cdots & 1 \\ p_0 & \cdots & p_{d+1} \\ p_0^2 & \cdots & p_{d+1}^2 \end{vmatrix}$$

is 0, negative or positive. Show that this predicate is the only numerical operation that is required to check if a triangulation is a Delaunay triangulation.

Show that the only numerical operation that is required to check if a triangulation is the weighted Delaunay triangulation of a set of weighted points $\hat{p}_1, \ldots, \hat{p}_n$ is the evaluation of signs of determinants of $(d+2) \times (d+2)$ matrices of the form

$$\texttt{power\_test}(\hat{p}_{i_1},\ldots,\hat{p}_{i_{d+2}}) = \begin{vmatrix} 1 & \cdots & 1 \\ p_{i_1} & \cdots & p_{i_{d+2}} \\ p_{i_0}^2 - w_{i_0} & \cdots & p_{i_{d+1}}^2 - w_{i_{d+1}} \end{vmatrix}$$

where p_i and w_i are, respectively, the center and the weight of $\hat{p}_i$. (Hint : use the lifting map and Exercise 3.16.)

Exercise 4.6 (Triangulation of a convex polytope)   Describe an algorithm to triangulate a convex polytope (Hint: Proceed by faces of increasing dimensions.)

Exercise 4.7 (Minimal spanning tree)   Let P be a finite set of points of $\mathbb{R}^d$. A spanning tree of P is a tree whose vertices are the points of P. A spanning tree is called a minimum spanning tree (MST) if the sum of the lengths of its edges is minimal among all spanning trees. Show that $MST(P) \subset Del(P)$.

Exercise 4.8 (Delaunay complexes contain a triangulation)   Let P be any finite set of points of $\mathbb{R}^d$. Show that there exists a subcomplex $K \subseteq Del(P)$ that is a triangulation of P.

Exercise 4.9 (Natural coordinates)   Let $P = \{p_1,\ldots,p_n\}$ be a finite set of points of $\mathbb{R}^d$. As usual, $Vor(P)$ denotes the Voronoi diagram of P and $V(p_i)$ the cell of p_i in $or(P)$. Given a point $x \in conv(P)$, we write $P^+ = P \cup \{x\}$, $V^+(x)$ for the Voronoi cell of x in $Vor(P^+)$, $V^+(x,p_i) = V^+(x) \cap V^+(p_i)$ and $W(x,p_i) = V^+(x) \cap V(p_i) = V(p_i) \setminus V^+(p_i)$. Now we define $v_i(x) = vol(V^+(x,p_i))$, $\bar{v}_i(x) = v_i(x)/\|x - p_i\|$ and $\bar{v}(x) = \sum_{i=1}^n \bar{v}_i(x)$. In addition, we define $w_i(x) = vol(W(x,p_i))$ and $w(x) = \sum_{i=1}^n w_i(x)$.

We call Laplace coordinates the n functions $\lambda_1,\ldots,\lambda_n$ defined by $\lambda_i(x) = \bar{v}_i(x)/\bar{v}(x)$ for $x \notin P$, and $\lambda_i(p_j) = \delta_{ij}$ otherwise, where δ_{ij} is the Kronecker delta. We call Sibson's coordinates the n functions $\varsigma_i(x) = w_i(x)/w(x)$, $i = 1,\ldots,n$. Show that the set of λ_i is a partition of unity, i.e. $x = \sum_i \lambda_i(x) p_i$. Same question for the set of ς_i.

(Hint: For Laplace coordinates, apply Exercise 3.18 to $V^+(x)$. For Sibson's coordinates, apply Exercise 3.18 to the polytope of $\mathbb{R}^{d+1}$ whose boundary is $\mathcal{V}(P^+) \setminus \mathcal{V}(P)$, where $\mathcal{V}(P)$ is defined in Section 4.3).

Exercise 4.10 (Conservation law)   Let $\hat{p}_i = (p_i, w_i)$, $i = 1,\ldots,n$, be weighted points. Prove the following conservation law for flows entering a weighted Voronoi cell $V(\hat{p}_i)$ normally to the facets of the cell: if $f_{ij}, j \in J$, are the facets of $V(\hat{p}_i)$, we have $\sum_{j \in J} vol(f_{ij}) \frac{p_j - p_i}{\|p_j - p_i\|} = 0$. This property makes Voronoi and weighted Voronoi diagrams useful when applying finite volume methods in fluid dynamics. (Hint: Use Exercise 3.18).

Exercise 4.11 (Section of a Voronoi diagram) Let H be a k-dimensional affine space of $\mathbb{R}^d$. Show that the intersection L_H of H with the weighted Voronoi diagram of n weighted points $\mathbb{R}^d$ is the weighted Voronoi diagram of n weighted points of H.

Exercise 4.12 (Union of balls) Show that the combinatorial complexity of the union of n balls of $\mathbb{R}^d$ is the same as the combinatorial complexity of their weighted Voronoi diagram. Design a worst-case optimal algorithm to compute such a union of balls. (Hint: Bound first the number of vertices.)

Exercise 4.13 (Centered triangulation) Let $\hat{P}$ be a finite set of weighted points with non-negative weights. Let P be the set of their centers and let $l = \min_{p,q \in P} \|p - q\|$ be the minimal distance between two centers. Prove that, if the weights are less than $\frac{l}{4}$, all weighted points of $\hat{P}$ have a non empty weighted Voronoi cell and each center belongs to the cell of its own weighted point.

Exercise 4.14 (Maximization diagrams) Show that the maximization diagram of n affine functions defined over $\mathbb{R}^d$ is the weighted Voronoi diagram of n weighted points of $\mathbb{R}^d$.

Exercise 4.15 (Complexity of k-order Voronoi diagrams) Use Theorems 3.12 and 3.9 to show that the combinatorial complexity of all $\leq k$-order Voronoi diagrams is $\Theta(k^{\lceil \frac{d+1}{2} \rceil} n^{\lfloor \frac{d+1}{2} \rfloor})$. Propose an efficient algorithm to compute all these diagrams.

Exercise 4.16 (Examples of divergences) The Itakura-Saito (or Burg) divergence is defined as

$$D_F(x\|y) = \sum_i \left(\frac{x_i}{y_i} - \log \frac{x_i}{y_i} - 1 \right).$$

The Itakura-Saito divergence is classical tool in speech recognition. Show that the Itakura-Saito divergence is the Bregman divergence associated to the convex function $F(x) = -\log x$ (Burg entropy). Show that the gradient and inverse gradient of F are identical, so that it is *self-dual*, i.e., $F = F^*$.

Show that, for the exponential function $F(x) = \exp x$, we have $F^*(y) = y \log y - y$ (the unnormalized Shannon entropy) and, for the dual bit entropy $F(x) = \log(1 + \exp x)$, we have $F^*(y) = y \log \frac{y}{1-y} + \log(1-y)$, the bit entropy.

Exercise 4.17 We define the Bregman ball of the second type centered at c and of radius r as

$$\tilde{b}_F = \{x \in \Omega | D_F(c\|x) < r\}.$$

Show that if, F is of Legendre type, $\tilde{b}_F$ is contractible.

Exercise 4.18 Define the α-Bregman complex as the restriction of the Bregman complex to the union of the Bregman balls of radius α. Consider the two types associated to the two types of balls. Show that, in both cases, the α-Bregman complex has the same homotopy type as the union of the Bregman balls.

4.7 Bibliographical Notes

Voronoi diagrams are very natural constructions that have been discovered several times and appear in the literature under various names like Dirichlet tesselations or Thiessen diagrams. The observation that Voronoi diagrams of $\mathbb{R}^d$ are projections of convex polyhedra of $\mathbb{R}^{d+1}$ goes back to Voronoi himself. Delaunay has defined the triangulations that bear his name and proved Theorem 4.3 in his seminal paper [64].

Voronoi diagrams and Delaunay triangulations are fundamental geometric structures that have received a lot a attention. Main results can be found in most textbooks on discrete and computational geometry [61, 25, 87] and more comprehensive treatments can be found in the books by Okabe et al. [113] and Aurenhammer et al. [7].

The space of spheres we referred to in Exercise 4.1 is fully developed in the books by Pedoe [115] and Berger [8].

Weighted Voronoi diagrams appear also in the literature under the names of Laguerre diagrams or power diagrams. Weighted Delaunay triangulations are also named regular triangulations. They were first studied in a systematic way by Aurenhammer [6] who proved Theorem 4.8. The solution to Exercise 4.15 is due to Clarkson and Shor [59]. Bregman Voronoi diagrams were introduced by Boissonnat, Nielsen, and Nock [21]. The fact that the α-Bregman complex has the same homotopy type as the union of the Bregman balls (Exercise 4.18) has been first observed by Edelsbrunner and Wagner [77]. A recent survey on affine and curved Voronoi diagrams can be found in [23].

Natural coordinates (Exercise 4.9) have been introduced by Sibson [124, 123].

The CGAL library [12] (www.cgal.org) offers fully reliable and efficient implementations of algorithms to construct Delaunay and weighted Delaunay triangulations in arbitrary dimensions.

5

Good Triangulations

In this chapter, we are interested in constructing simplicial complexes with a guaranteed quality. On the one hand, we would like to control the density of their vertices and, on the other hand, we would like to control the shape of the simplices and avoid simplices that are too flat.

In Section 5.1, we introduce ε-nets in order to capture a notion of *good* sample of a bounded subset $\Omega \subset \mathbb{R}^d$. We will see that, for fixed d, the complexity of Voronoi diagrams and Delaunay complexes of an ε-net of Ω of size n is linear in n. This is to be compared with the bound $\Theta(n^{\lceil \frac{d}{2} \rceil})$ given in Chapter 4 which is tight in the worst case.

Although Delaunay triangulations have many beautiful properties, their simplices, in dimension greater than 2, may have an arbitrarily small volume even if their vertices are well distributed. Avoiding such bad simplices is a major issue and the importance of thick triangulations, to be introduced in Section 5.2, has been recognized since the early days of differential topology. Thick triangulations play a central role in many works on the triangulation of manifolds (see Part III) and appear to be crucial in scientific computing to ensure the convergence of numerical methods.

In order to improve the quality of the simplices of a Delaunay complex, one can perturb the position of the vertices or the metric of the space. We introduce in Section 5.3 a perturbation scheme that associates to each point a weight and replaces the Delaunay complex by its weighted version. We show that the weight assigned to each point can be computed so that the resulting weighted Delaunay complex has some guaranteed thickness. The method is an algorithmic application of the Lovász local lemma, which is recalled in Section 5.3.4.

5.1 Nets

5.1.1 Nets in Euclidean Space

We consider a bounded subset Ω of $\mathbb{R}^d$ and denote by P a finite set of points in Ω. The Hausdorff distance $d_H(P, \Omega)$ is called the *sampling radius* of P and denoted by ε. We also say that P is an ε-*dense sample* of Ω. We further call $\eta = \min_{p,q \in P} \|p - q\|$ the *separation* of P and $\bar{\eta} = \eta/\varepsilon$ the *separation ratio* of P.

Any finite point set P of Ω whose sampling radius is ε and whose separation ratio is $\bar{\eta}$ is called an $(\varepsilon, \bar{\eta})$-*net* of Ω. Note that for *any* finite set of distinct points $P \subset \Omega$, there is some positive ε and $\bar{\eta}$ such that P is an $(\varepsilon, \bar{\eta})$-net for Ω. Thus ε and $\bar{\eta}$ are simply parameters that describe properties of P in Ω.

In the sequel, we will often consider the subset of $(\varepsilon, \bar{\eta})$-samples of Ω where $\bar{\eta}$ is lower bounded by a positive constant. Such point sets will be called ε-*nets* for short.

Lemma 5.1 *Let P be an $(\varepsilon, \bar{\eta})$-net of Ω. If the radius of the smallest ball enclosing any connected component of Ω is greater than ε, then for any point $p \in P$, the distance $L(p)$ from p to its nearest neighbor in $P \setminus \{p\}$ is at most 2ε. Therefore we must have $\bar{\eta} \leq 2$.*

Proof   Because P is ε-dense in Ω, the union of the balls $B(p, \varepsilon), p \in P$, covers Ω. Now let $r > \varepsilon$ and assume for a contradiction that there exists a point $p \in P$ such that $B(p, 2r)$ does not contain any point of P other than p. Then Ω intersects the spherical shell $B(p, r) \setminus B(p, \varepsilon)$ and this intersection is not covered by any ball $B(q, \varepsilon), q \in P$, violating the hypothesis that P is ε-dense in Ω.   □

The next lemma shows that nets exist.

Lemma 5.2 (Existence of ε-nets)   *Let Ω be a bounded subset of $\mathbb{R}^d$ and ε be any positive real. Then Ω admits an $(\varepsilon, 1)$-net.*

Proof   We apply the following procedure: while there exists a point $p \in \Omega$ at distance at least ε from P, insert p in P. Because the domain is compact and the algorithm inserts no point at distance less than ε from a previously inserted point, the algorithm terminates. Upon termination, any point of Ω is at distance less than ε from P.   □

Lemma 5.3 (Size of an ε-net)   *Let Ω be a bounded domain of $\mathbb{R}^d$. The number of points of an $(\varepsilon, \bar{\eta})$-net $n(\varepsilon, \bar{\eta})$ satisfies*

$$\frac{\mathrm{vol}_d(\Omega)}{\mathrm{vol}_d(B(\varepsilon))} \leq n(\varepsilon, \bar{\eta}) \leq \frac{\mathrm{vol}_d(\Omega^{\frac{\eta}{2}})}{\mathrm{vol}_d(B(\frac{\eta}{2}))}$$

where $B(r)$ denotes a d-ball of radius r, $\eta = \bar{\eta}\varepsilon$, and

$$\Omega^{\frac{\eta}{2}} = \left\{ x \in \mathbb{R}^d, d(x, \Omega) \le \frac{\eta}{2} \right\}.$$

If $\mathrm{vol}_d(\Omega) > 0$, then $n(\varepsilon, \bar{\eta}) = \Theta\left(\frac{1}{\varepsilon^d}\right)$ where the constant in the Θ depends on the geometry of Ω and on $\bar{\eta}^d$.

Proof The ball $B(p, \varepsilon)$ of radius ε that are centered at the points $p \in P$ cover Ω. This yields the left inequality. The balls $B(p, \frac{\eta}{2})$ of radius $\frac{\eta}{2}$ that are centered at the points $p \in P$ are disjoint and they are all contained in $\Omega^{\frac{\eta}{2}}$. This leads to the right inequality. $\qquad\qquad\square$

5.1.2 Delaunay Complex of a Net

Let Ω be a subset of $\mathbb{R}^d$ of positive d-volume and let P a finite set of points in Ω. The nerve of the covering of Ω by the Voronoi cells of P is called the *restriction* of $\mathrm{Del}(P)$ to Ω and denoted by $\mathrm{Del}_{|\Omega}(P)$. Equivalently, $\mathrm{Del}_{|\Omega}(P)$ is the subcomplex of $\mathrm{Del}(P)$ whose dual Voronoi faces intersect Ω.

We consider now the case in which P is an $(\varepsilon, \bar{\eta})$-net of Ω. We already observed that every simplex σ of $\mathrm{Del}_{|\Omega}(P)$ must have a circumradius not greater than ε.

Observe also that all Delaunay simplices with a vertex at distance greater than 2ε from the boundary of Ω belong to $\mathrm{Del}_{|\Omega}(P)$ (see Exercise 5.1).

Lemma 5.4 (Delaunay complex of a net) *Let Ω be a bounded subset of $\mathbb{R}^d$, P an $(\varepsilon, \bar{\eta})$-net of Ω, and assume that d and $\bar{\eta}$ are positive constants. The restriction of the Delaunay complex of P to Ω has size $2^{O(d^2)}|P|$ (i.e., the size is linear for fixed d).*

Proof Let p be a point of P. We first bound the number of neighbors of p, i.e., the vertices of the link of p in $\mathrm{Del}_{|\Omega}(P)$. Let σ be a simplex of $\mathrm{Del}_{|\Omega}(P)$ in the star of p. As observed above, the diameter of σ is at most 2ε. Moreover, all the open balls $B(q, \frac{\bar{\eta}\varepsilon}{2})$, $q \in P$, are disjoint by definition of the separation. Hence, the number of neighbors of p is at most

$$n_p = \frac{\mathrm{vol}_d\left(B(2\varepsilon + \frac{\bar{\eta}\varepsilon}{2})\right)}{\mathrm{vol}_d\left(B(\frac{\bar{\eta}\varepsilon}{2})\right)} = \left(1 + \frac{4}{\bar{\eta}}\right)^d$$

where $B(r)$ denotes a ball of radius r.

Assuming without real loss of generality that $n_p \geq d + 1$, we deduce that the number of simplices in the star of p is at most

$$\sum_{i=1}^{d+1} \binom{n_p}{i} = 2^{O(d^2)}.$$

$\square$

We will show now that the randomized incremental construction (see Theorems 4.4 and 3.11) constructs the Delaunay complex of any net P in time $O(n \log n)$ time where $n = |P|$. Remarkably, we don't need to modify the algorithm whose behaviour will automatically adapt to the fact that the input point set is a net. To analyze the complexity of the algorithm in this context, it is sufficient to show that the expected complexity of the Delaunay complex of a random sample S of P has linear size $O(|S|)$. Indeed, the expected number of simplices that appear in the Delaunay complex of a point set $P \in \mathbb{R}^d$ during the randomized incremental construction, is

$$O\left(\sum_{i=1}^{n} \frac{d}{i} \Gamma_0(i, P)\right),$$

where $\Gamma_0(i, P)$ is the expected size of the Delaunay complex of a random sample of size i, drawn from the point set P. It will then immediately follow from the analysis of the complexity of the randomized algorithm that the complexity of the algorithm is $O(n \log n)$ when P is a net.

Lemma 5.5 *A random subsample S of an $(\varepsilon, \bar{\eta})$-net P has a Delaunay complex of expected size $2^{O(d^2)}|S|$ (i.e. the expected size is linear for fixed d).*

Proof We first give the proof in the case in which S is a Bernoulli sample, i.e. it is obtained from P by picking every point $p \in P$ with probability ϖ. Without real loss of generality, we will take $\bar{\eta} = 1$ and, for convenience, we will write $\varpi = (\varepsilon/\delta)^d$.

Let us fix a point $p \in P$; we shall upper bound the size of $star(p, \text{Del}(S))$, i.e. the set of simplices of $\text{Del}(S)$ with vertex p. Let $I_k = [2^{k-1}\delta, 2^k\delta)$, $k \in \mathbb{N}$. Consider a d-tuple τ of points of P such that the d-simplex formed by the points in $\sigma = \tau \cup \{p\}$, has circumcentre c_σ and circumradius r_σ. Then, given that $p \in S$, the event $E^{(\tau)} = (\sigma \in \text{Del}(S))$ could occur only if the following two events occur:

(i) $E_1^{(\sigma)} = (\forall p' \in \sigma, \ p' \in S)$
(ii) $E_2^{(\sigma)} = (B(c_\sigma, r_\sigma) \cap S = \emptyset)$, where $B(x, r)$ is the open ball centered at x with radius r.

Given that $p \in S$, the probability that $\sigma \in \mathrm{Del}(S)$ can be therefore upper-bounded as follows. We write $n_\sigma = P \cap B(p, r_\sigma) \geq (r_\sigma/\varepsilon)^d$ (by a packing argument).

$$
\begin{aligned}
\mathrm{proba}[E^{(\tau)}] &= \mathrm{proba}[E_1^{(\sigma)} \wedge E_2^{(\sigma)}] \\
&= \varpi^d \, \mathrm{proba}[E_2^{(\sigma)}] \\
&\leq \varpi^d \, (1 - \varpi)^{n_\sigma} \\
&\leq \varpi^d \, e^{-\varpi \, n_\sigma} \\
&\leq \left(\frac{\varepsilon}{\delta}\right)^{d^2} e^{-(\varepsilon/\delta)^d (r_\sigma/\varepsilon)^d} \\
&\leq \left(\frac{\varepsilon}{\delta}\right)^{d^2} e^{-(r_\sigma/\delta)^d}
\end{aligned}
\tag{5.1}
$$

If σ has circumradius $r_\sigma \in I_k$, we get

$$
\mathrm{proba}[E^{(\tau)}] \leq (\varepsilon/\delta)^{d^2} e^{-2^{(k-1)d}}
$$

By the triangle inequality, if $\sigma \in \mathrm{Del}(S)$ has a circumradius r_σ, then all the points in σ must lie in the ball $B(p, 2r_\sigma)$. Therefore, the number of potential d-tuples which can contribute to $\mathrm{star}(p, \mathrm{Del}(S))$ is at most $((4r_\sigma/\varepsilon)^d)^d = (4r_\sigma/\varepsilon)^{d^2} \leq (2^{k+2}\delta/\varepsilon)^{d^2}$. Let

$$
Z_p(k) := \begin{cases} |\{\sigma \in \mathrm{Del}(S) \; : \; p \in \sigma, \; r_\sigma \in [2^{k-1}\delta, 2^k \delta)\}|, & p \in S, \\ 0, & \text{otherwise}, \end{cases}
$$

denote the number of Delaunay simplices that contain $p \in S$ and have circumradius $r_\sigma \in I_k$. Then we get

$$
\begin{aligned}
\mathbb{E}[Z_p(k)] &\leq \sum_{\tau \in (P \cap B(p, 2r))^d} \mathrm{proba}[E^{(\tau)}] \\
&\leq (2^{k+2}\delta/\varepsilon)^{d^2} (\varepsilon/\delta)^{d^2} e^{-2^{(k-1)d}} \\
&= 4^{d^2} 2^{kd^2} e^{-2^{(k-1)d}}
\end{aligned}
$$

Define $Y_p := \sum_{k=1}^{\infty} Z_p(k)$ to be the number of Delaunay simplices in $\mathrm{star}(p, \mathrm{Del}(S))$. Summing k over all allowed ranges of r, Summing over all allowed ranges of r, we get

$$
\begin{aligned}
\mathbb{E}[Y_p] &\leq \sum_{k=1}^{\infty} 4^{d^2} e^{-2^{(k-1)d}} \cdot 2^{kd^2} \\
&= 4^{d^2} \sum_{k'=1}^{\infty} e^{-k'} \cdot k'^d \cdot 2^{d^2} \qquad \text{(with } k' = 2^{(k-1)d})
\end{aligned}
$$

$$= 8^{d^2} \sum_{k'=1}^{\infty} e^{-k'} \cdot k'^d$$

$$\leq 8^{d^2} \int_{x=0}^{\infty} e^{-x} \cdot x^d dx = 8^{d^2} \Gamma(d+1)$$

$$= 2^{O(d^2)}.$$

where $\Gamma(t) := \int_0^{\infty} e^{-x} x^{t-1} dx$ denotes the *Gamma* function. Therefore, the expected size of Del(S) is given by

$$\mathbb{E}[|\mathrm{Del}(S)|] \leq \sum_{p \in P} \mathrm{proba}[p \in S] \, \mathbb{E}[Y_p] \leq n\varpi \cdot 2^{O(d^2)} = \mathbb{E}[|S|] \cdot 2^{O(d^2)}.$$

The previous result does not apply directly to the randomized construction of the Delaunay complex of P. When the points are inserted in a random order, the i-th point to be inserted is a random point in a uniform sample of size i of P. We thus consider now the case of a random subset $S \subseteq P$ of size s. Given that $p \in S$, choosing the rest of the random subsample S is equivalent to choosing a random sample of $s - 1$ elements from $P \setminus \{p\}$. Now from Equation 5.1 and Exercise 5.2, we get:

$$\mathrm{proba}[E^{(\tau)}] \leq \left(\frac{s-1}{n-1}\right)^d \left(1 - \frac{s-1}{n-1}\right)^{(r_\sigma/\varepsilon)^d}$$

$$\approx \left(\frac{s}{n}\right)^d \left(1 - \frac{s}{n}\right)^{(r_\sigma/\varepsilon)^d}$$

$$= \varpi^d (1 - \varpi)^{(r_\sigma/\varepsilon)^d},$$

where $\varpi = s/n$ is the probability for a point of P to belong to S. The rest of the computations follows as previously leading to the same asymptotic bound on $\mathbb{E}[|\mathrm{Del}(S)|]$. □

We conclude from this discussion and Lemma 5.5:

Theorem 5.6 *Let P be an ε-net in $\mathbb{R}^d$. The randomized incremental construction of a Delaunay complex of P requires on expectation $2^{O(d^2)}|P|$ memory space and $2^{O(d^2)}|P| \log |P|$ time.*

5.1.3 Nets in Discrete Metric Spaces

So far, we have considered nets in subsets of Euclidean spaces. However nets can be defined in more general metric spaces. In this section, we consider the case where Ω is a finite set of points that we rename W to emphasize the distinction. We do not assume that W is embedded in Euclidean space and the points are not given a location. Instead, we only assume to know the distance matrix of W, i.e., the $|W| \times |W|$ matrix M whose element $m_{i,j}$ is the distance between the points w_i and w_j. W together with M defines a *discrete metric space*. Nets can be defined in discrete metric spaces in very much the same way they have been defined in Euclidean space.

Extracting from W a coarser sample that is a net of W will allow to benefit from the nice properties of nets. It will also allow to represent data at various resolutions, to cluster data and to construct witness complexes, a weak variant of Delaunay complexes that can be defined and constructed in any discrete metric space (Section 6.2).

We first prove the existence of nets in the context of discrete metric spaces (see Lemma 5.2 for its analog in the Euclidean case).

Lemma 5.7 (Existence of nets) *Let W be a finite set of points such that the distance of any point $q \in W$ to $W \setminus \{q\}$ is at most ε and let $\lambda \geq \varepsilon$. One can extract from W a subsample L that is a $(\lambda, 1)$-net of W.*

In preparation for Section 6.2, we will often refer to the points of L as landmarks and to the points of W as witnesses.

Proof We construct the sample L by inserting points of W one by one. Initially $L := \emptyset$ and $W' := W$. At each step, we pick a point of W', say p, insert it in L, and remove p from W' as well as all the points of W' whose distance to p is less than λ. We stop when W' is empty. The algorithm necessarily terminates since W is finite. Upon termination, all the points of W are at distance at most λ from a point of L (since otherwise it would be inserted in L) and two points of L are at distance at least λ (since we never insert a point at distance less than λ from the current set L). It follows that L is a $(\lambda, 1)$-net of W. $\square$

We can improve the algorithm described in the proof of Lemma 5.7 by inserting, at each step, a point $p \in W$ that is farthest from the current set of landmarks L (see Algorithm 3 (Case 1)).

We maintain for each point w of W' its closest point $L(w)$ in L and, at each step, we select the point $w \in W'$ which is most distant from its closest landmark $L(w)$. The algorithm requires $O(|W|)$ storage and its time complexity is easily seen to be $O(|L| \times |W|)$.

The next lemma shows that this strategy implies that the separation ratio remains constant over the refinement.

For any $i > 0$, let L_i and λ_i denote, respectively, L and $\lambda^* = \max_{w \in W'} \|w - L(w)\|$ at the end of the i-th iteration of the main loop of the algorithm. If we label the points by their insertion order, we have $L_i = \{p_1, \ldots, p_i\}$ and

---

Algorithm 3: Farthest point insertion

Input: The distance matrix of a finite point set W and either a positive constant λ (Case 1) or an integer k (Case 2)

$L := \emptyset$

$W' := W$

$L(w) := p_\infty$ for all $w \in W'$ {p_∞ is a fake point at infinite distance from W}

$\lambda^* := \max_{w \in W'} \|w - L(w)\|$

$w^* :=$ a point $p \in W'$ such that $\|p - L(p)\| = \lambda^*$

while either $\lambda^* > \lambda$ (Case 1) or $|L| < k$ (Case 2) **do**

    add w^* to L and remove w^* from W'

    for each point w of W' such that $\|w - w^*\| < \|w - L(w)\|$ **do**

        $L(w) := w^*$

    update λ^* and w^*

Output: $L \subseteq W$, a $(\lambda, 1)$-net of W (Case 1), an approximate solution to the k-centers problem (Case 2)

$\lambda_i = d(p_i, L_{i-1})$. Because L_i grows with i, λ_i is a decreasing function of i. Moreover:

Lemma 5.8 *At each iteration $i > 0$, L_i is a $(\lambda_i, 1)$-net of W.*

Proof The fact that L_i is λ_i-dense in W follows directly from the definition of λ_i. Let us show that L_i is λ_i separated. Consider a closest pair of points $p_a p_b$ of L_i and assume that p_b has been inserted after p_a. Then $\|p_a - p_b\| = \lambda_b \geq \lambda_i$. This implies that L_i is λ_i-separated. $\square$

In some applications, we are interested in selecting a given number k of points. We are then interested in the following *k-centers problem* : select from W a subset L of k points that are as far apart from each other as possible. More precisely, we want to choose a subset L of k points of W in such a way as to maximize the separation of L, i.e., the minimum pairwise distance between the points of L. We can use Algorithm 3 (Case 2) for that purpose. Interestingly, this simple greedy algorithm provides a 2-approximation to the problem.

Lemma 5.9 (Approximation of the k-centers problem) *Algorithm 3 (Case 2) provides an approximation ratio of 2 for the k-centers problem.*

Proof Let $L_k = l_1, \ldots, l_k$ be the set of the k first selected points by the algorithm, labelled according to the order they have been selected. Let λ_k denote the distance of the k-th point from all previously selected points l_i, $i = 1, \ldots, k - 1$. Consider the set of balls $B(l_i, \lambda_k)$, $i, \ldots, k - 1$. Their union contains all the points of W and therefore all the points of any optimal solution L_{opt} to the k-centers problem. Since $|L_{opt}| = k$ and there are $k - 1$ balls, there must be two points of L_{opt} that fall in the same ball $B(l_i, \lambda_k)$ for some $i \leq k-1$. It follows that there exists a pair of points in L_{opt} that is at distance at most $2\lambda_k$ by the triangular inequality.

On the other hand, the distance between any two points of L_k is at least λ_k by Lemma 5.8. It follows that Algorithm 3 (Case 2) provides an approximation ratio of 2 for the k-centers problem. □

5.2 Thick Simplices

For a given set of points $P \in \mathbb{R}^2$, Del(P) maximizes, over all possible triangulations of P, the smallest angle of the triangles (Exercise 5.6) and it can be easily shown that, if P is a net, then the angles of the triangles are lower bounded by some positive constant (Exercise 5.5). However, the property does not hold for higher dimensional Delaunay triangulations and one cannot bound the dihedral angles of higher dimensional simplices as shown in Figure 5.1.

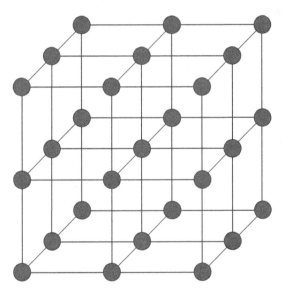

Figure 5.1 The four vertices of a squared face f of a uniform grid are cocircular and can be circumscribed by a sphere centered at the center of the face. This sphere does not enclose any other vertex of the grid. We can then slightly perturb the vertices of f so that the convex hull of the vertices of f is now a tetrahedron of positive volume whose circumscribing sphere does not include any other vertex of the grid. Hence, it is a tetrahedron in the Delaunay triangulation of the (perturbed) vertices of the grid.

For any vertex p of a simplex σ, the *face opposite* p, denoted by σ_p, is the convex hull of the other vertices of σ. The *altitude* of p in σ is the distance $D(p, \sigma) = d(p, \text{aff}(\sigma_p))$ from p to the affine space $\text{aff}(\sigma_p)$ spanned by σ_p. The altitude $D(\sigma)$ of σ is the minimum over all vertices p of σ of $D(p, \sigma)$. A poorly-shaped simplex can be characterized by the existence of a relatively small altitude. The *thickness* of a j-simplex σ is the dimensionless quantity

$$\Theta(\sigma) = \begin{cases} 1 & \text{if } j = 0 \\ \frac{D(\sigma)}{j\Delta(\sigma)} & \text{otherwise,} \end{cases}$$

where $\Delta(\sigma)$ denotes the *diameter* of σ, i.e. the length of its longest edge.

5.2.1 Thickness and Singular Value

We will show in the next lemma that the thickness of a simplex is related to the singular values of a matrix. Before stating the lemma, we recall some well known results on matrices and their singular values and refer the reader to the book of Trefethen and Bau [127] for an excellent introduction to singular values. If A is a $d \times j$ matrix with $j \leq d$, we assume that the singular values of A are ordered according to decreasing absolute values and we denote the ith singular value by $s_i(A)$. We have $s_1(A) = \|A\| = \sup_{\|x\|=1} \|Ax\|$ and $s_j(A) = \inf_{\|x\|=1} \|Ax\|$. We will employ the following standard observation:

Lemma 5.10 *If $\mu > 0$ is an upper bound on the norms of the columns of A, then $s_1(A) = \|A\| \leq \sqrt{j}\mu$.*

From the given definitions, one can verify that if A is an invertible $d \times d$ matrix, then $s_1(A^{-1}) = s_d(A)^{-1}$, but it is convenient to also accommodate non-square matrices, corresponding to simplices that are not full dimensional. If A is a $d \times j$ matrix of rank $j \leq d$, then the *pseudo-inverse* $A^\dagger = (A^\mathsf{T}A)^{-1}A^\mathsf{T}$ is the unique left inverse of A whose kernel is the orthogonal complement of the column space of A. We have the following general observation [127]:

Lemma 5.11 *Let A be a $d \times j$ matrix of rank $j \leq d$ and let $A^\dagger$ be its* pseudo inverse $= (A^\mathsf{T}A)^{-1}A^\mathsf{T}$. *We have*

$$s_i(A^\dagger) = s_{j-i+1}(A)^{-1}, \text{ for } i = 1, \ldots, j.$$

In particular, $s_j(A) = s_1(A^\dagger)^{-1}$.

The columns of A form a basis for the column space of A. The pseudo-inverse can also be described in terms of the *dual basis*. If we denote the

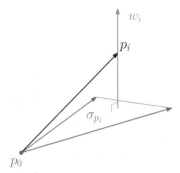

Figure 5.2 Choosing p_0 as the origin, the edges emanating from p_0 in $\sigma =$ $[p_0, \ldots, p_j]$ form a basis for aff(σ). The proof of Lemma 5.12 demonstrates that the dual basis $\{w_i\}$ consists of vectors that are orthogonal to the facets, and with magnitude equal to the inverse of the corresponding altitude.

columns of A by $\{a_i\}$, then the ith dual vector, w_i, is the unique vector in the column space of A such that $w_i^\mathsf{T} a_i = 1$ and $w_i^\mathsf{T} a_j = 0$ if $i \neq j$. Then $A^\dagger$ is the $j \times d$ matrix whose ith row is w_i^T.

By exploiting a close connection between the altitudes of a simplex and the vectors dual to a basis defined by the simplex, we obtain the following key lemma that relates the thickness of a simplex to the smallest singular value of an associated matrix (see Figure 5.2):

Lemma 5.12 (Thickness and singular value) *Let* $\sigma = \mathrm{conv}(p_0, \ldots, p_j)$ *be a non-degenerate j-simplex in $\mathbb{R}^d$, with $j > 0$, and let P be the $d \times j$ matrix whose ith column is $p_i - p_0$. Then*

$$s_j(\mathsf{P}) \geq D(\sigma)/\sqrt{j} = \sqrt{j}\,\Theta(\sigma)\Delta(\sigma).$$

Proof We first show that the ith row of $\mathsf{P}^\dagger$ is given by w_i^T, where w_i is orthogonal to aff(σ_{p_i}), and

$$\|w_i\| = D(p_i, \sigma)^{-1}.$$

Indeed, by the definition of $\mathsf{P}^\dagger$, it follows that w_i belongs to the column space of P, and it is orthogonal to all $(p_{i'} - p_0)$ for $i' \neq i$. Let $u_i = w_i/\|w_i\|$. By the definition of w_i, we have $w_i^\mathsf{T}(p_i - p_0) = 1 = \|w_i\|u_i^\mathsf{T}(p_i - p_0)$. By the definition of the altitude of a vertex, we have $u_i^\mathsf{T}(p_i - p_0) = D(p_i, \sigma)$. Thus $\|w_i\| = D(p_i, \sigma)^{-1}$. Since

$$\max_{1 \leq i \leq j} D(p_i, \sigma)^{-1} = \left(\min_{1 \leq i \leq j} D(p_i, \sigma)\right)^{-1} = (j\Theta(\sigma)\Delta(\sigma))^{-1},$$

Lemma 5.10, yields

$$s_1(\mathsf{P}^\dagger) \leq (\sqrt{j}\Theta(\sigma)\Delta(\sigma))^{-1}.$$

The stated bound on $s_j(\mathsf{P})$ follows from Lemma 5.11.   □

The proof of Lemma 5.12 shows that the pseudoinverse of P has a natural geometric interpretation in terms of the altitudes of σ, and thus the altitudes provide a convenient lower bound on $s_j(\mathsf{P})$. By Lemma 5.10, $s_1(\mathsf{P}) \leq \sqrt{j}\Delta(\sigma)$, and thus $\Theta(\sigma) \leq \frac{s_j(\mathsf{P})}{s_1(\mathsf{P})}$. In other words, $\Theta(\sigma)^{-1}$ provides a convenient upper bound on the *condition number* of P. Roughly speaking, thickness imparts a kind of stability on the geometric properties of a simplex. This is exactly what is required when we want to show that a small change in a simplex will not yield a large change in some geometric quantity of interest.

5.2.2 Whitney's Angle Bound

The following lemma is due to Whitney. It shows that, if the vertices of a simplex σ are at small relative distance from an affine space H, and if the thickness of the simplex is bounded away from 0, then the angle between the affine hull of σ and H is small. Before stating the lemma, we define angles between vector spaces.

Definition 5.13 (Angles between subspaces) If U and V are vector subspaces of $\mathbb{R}^d$, with $\dim U \leq \dim V$, the *angle* between them is defined by

$$\sin \angle(U, V) = \sup_{\substack{u \in U \\ \|u\|=1}} \|u - \pi_V u\|, \qquad (5.2)$$

where π_V is the orthogonal projection onto V.

Alternatively, the angle between vector subspaces U and V can be defined as:

$$\angle(U, V) = \max_{u \in U}\{\min_{v \in V} \angle(u, v)\} \qquad (5.3)$$

The angle between affine subspaces K and H is defined as the angle between the corresponding parallel vector subspaces.

Lemma 5.14 (Whitney's angle bound) *Suppose σ is a j-simplex of $\mathbb{R}^d$, $j < d$, whose vertices all lie within a distance δ from a k-dimensional affine space $h \subset \mathbb{R}^d$ with $k \geq j$. Then*

$$\sin \angle(\mathrm{aff}(\sigma), h) \leq \frac{2j\,\delta}{D(\sigma)} = \frac{2\delta}{\Theta(\sigma)\Delta(\sigma)}.$$

Proof Suppose $\sigma = \text{conv}(p_0, \ldots, p_j)$. Choose p_0 as the origin of $\mathbb{R}^d$ and let $\Pi_h : \mathbb{R}^d \to h$ be the orthogonal projection onto h. Let u be any unit vector in $\text{aff}(\sigma)$. Since the vectors $v_i = (p_i - p_0)$, $i \in \{1, \ldots, j\}$ form a basis for $\text{aff}(\sigma)$, we may write $u = \mathsf{P}a$, where P is the $d \times j$ matrix whose ith column is v_i, and $a \in \mathbb{R}^j$ is the vector of coefficients. Then, defining $X = \mathsf{P} - \Pi_h\mathsf{P}$, we get

$$\|u - \Pi_h u\| = \|Xa\| \leq \|X\| \, \|a\|.$$

Since $d(p_i, h) \leq h$ for all $0 \leq i \leq j$, $\|v_i - \Pi_h v_i\| \leq 2\delta$. It follows then from Lemma 5.10 that

$$\|X\| \leq 2\sqrt{j}\delta.$$

Observing that $1 = \|u\| = \|\mathsf{P}a\| \geq \|a\| \, \inf_{\|x\|=1} \|\mathsf{P}x\| = \|a\| \, s_j(\mathsf{P})$, we find

$$\|a\| \leq \frac{1}{s_j(\mathsf{P})},$$

and the result follows from Lemma 5.12. □

Whitney's angle bound will be especially useful in Chapter 8. There, h will be the tangent space T_p at a point p of a smooth manifold $\mathcal{M}$, and σ will be a thick simplex whose vertices are close (relatively to the diameter of the simplex) to T_p. Whitney's lemma asserts that the affine hull of σ makes a small angle with T_p. Thickness plays a crucial role here as the following example shows. The Schwarz lantern is a polyhedral surface inscribed in a cylinder as shown in Figure 5.3. By increasing the number of vertices of the lantern,

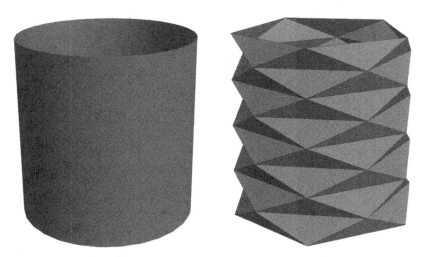

Figure 5.3 The Schwarz lantern.

we can make the Hausdorff distance between the lantern and the cylinder arbitrarily small but increasing the sampling density does not guarantee that the planes of the facets of the lantern provide a good approximation of the tangent planes of the cylinder. In fact, the angle between the normal to a facet and the normal to the cylinder at any of the vertices of the facet can be made arbitrarily close to $\pi/2$. Such a situation cannot happen if the facets have a bounded thickness as stated by Whitney's lemma.

5.3 Thick Triangulations via Weighting

The notion of thickness introduced in Section 5.2 is an important measure of the shape of a simplex. A simplicial complex is thick when all its simplices are thick. We have seen (Figure 5.1) that Delaunay triangulations are not necessarily thick even if the vertices form an $(\varepsilon, \bar{\eta})$-net. The goal of this section is to show that a thick simplicial complex can nevertheless be obtained from an $(\varepsilon, \bar{\eta})$-net by assigning (relatively small) weights to the points of the net and considering the weighted Delaunay triangulation of the resulting set of weighted points.

To keep the exposition simple, we depart from the rest of this book and will work in this section in the flat torus $\mathbb{T}^d = \mathbb{R}^d/\mathbb{Z}^d$ instead of $\mathbb{R}^d$. As a consequence, if P is a finite set of points in $\mathbb{T}^d$, the Delaunay complex and weighted Delaunay complexes of P have no boundary. Boundary issues obscure the central properties we want to develop. It is not difficult to extend the results to the case of a bounded domain of $\mathbb{R}^d$, provided that we only look sufficiently far away from the boundary of the domain.

5.3.1 Weighting Schemes

We consider a set of points P that is an $(\varepsilon, \bar{\eta})$-net in $\mathbb{T}^d$. A *weighting scheme* on P is a function w from P to $\mathbb{R}$, which assigns to each point $p \in P$ a weight $w(p) \in \mathbb{R}$. We denote by $\hat{P}$ the resulting set of weighted points, i. e. $\hat{P} = \{(p, w(p) : p \in P\}$, and by $\mathrm{Del}(\hat{P})$ the corresponding weighted Delaunay triangulation.

We restrict the weighting scheme to non-negative weights. The relative amplitude $\tilde{w}$ of the weighting scheme w is defined as

$$\tilde{w} = \max_{p \in P} \frac{w(p)}{L^2(p)},$$

where $L(p)$ is the distance from p to its nearest neighbor in $P \setminus p$. We also wish that each point of P appears as a vertex of $\mathrm{Del}(\hat{P})$. As shown in Section 4.4.3, this condition is ensured if, for each $p \in P$, $w(p) < \frac{L^2(p)}{4}$. From now on, we will only consider weighting schemes that have a relative amplitude smaller than $\frac{1}{4}$, that is $\tilde{w} \leq \tilde{w}_0$ where $\tilde{w}_0$ is a constant smaller than $\frac{1}{4}$.

The main result of this section is that, for any $(\varepsilon, \bar{\eta})$-net P of $\mathbb{T}^d$, given a small enough constant Θ_0, there are weighting schemes with relative amplitude smaller than $\tilde{w}_0 < \frac{1}{4}$ and such that the weighted Delaunay triangulation $\mathrm{Del}(\hat{P})$ has no j-simplex with thickness less than Θ_0^j, for $j = 1, \ldots, d$. Moreover, as we will see in Section 5.3, such weighting schemes can be computed by a simple randomized algorithm.

In the rest of this section, we use the same notation σ for a geometric simplex with vertices in P and for its abstract counterpart, which is just the subset of P formed by the vertices of σ. Given a weighting scheme w defined on P, each simplex $\sigma \subset P$ corresponds to a subset $\hat{\sigma}$ of $\hat{P}$: $\hat{\sigma} = \{(p, w(p)) : p \in \sigma\}$. Two weighted points are said to be *orthogonal* if their weighted distance is zero.

A weighted point orthogonal to all the weighted points of $\hat{\sigma}$ is said to be orthogonal to $\hat{\sigma}$. If σ is a simplex of dimension j, the weighted points orthogonal to $\hat{\sigma}$ are centered on an affine subspace of dimension $d - j$ orthogonal to the affine subspace $\mathrm{aff}(\sigma)$. The intersection point of these two subspaces is denoted by $c(\hat{\sigma})$. Let $(c(\hat{\sigma}), R^2(\hat{\sigma}))$ be the weighted point centered on $c(\hat{\sigma})$ and orthogonal to $\hat{\sigma}$. The weighted point $(c(\hat{\sigma}), R^2(\hat{\sigma}))$ is the weighted point with minimal weight among all the weighted points orthogonal to $\hat{\sigma}$. The point $c(\hat{\sigma})$ is called the *weighted center* of the simplex σ and $R(\hat{\sigma})$ is called *the weighted radius* of σ.

Note that weighted center $c(\hat{\sigma})$ and the weighted radius $R(\hat{\sigma})$ depend on the weights assigned to the vertices of σ and are different from the center $c(\sigma)$ and circumradius $R(\sigma)$ of σ. We will make use of the following lemma that bounds the weighted radii and the diameters of the simplexes in $\mathrm{Del}(\hat{P})$.

Lemma 5.15 (Weighted radii and diameters of simplices in $\mathrm{Del}(\hat{P})$) *Let P be an $(\varepsilon, \bar{\eta})$-net of $\mathbb{T}^d$ and assume that a non-negative weighting scheme with relative amplitude smaller than $\tilde{w}_0 < \frac{1}{4}$ has been defined on P. Then, any simplex σ of $\mathrm{Del}(\hat{P})$ has a weighted radius $R(\hat{\sigma})$ that is at most ϵ and a diameter $\Delta(\tau)$ that is at most $2\sqrt{2}\varepsilon$.*

Proof Let σ be a simplex of $\mathrm{Del}(\hat{P})$. The simplex σ being included in some d-simplex τ of $\mathrm{Del}(\hat{P})$, the weighted radius $R(\hat{\sigma})$ of σ is at most the weighted radius $R(\hat{\tau})$ of τ. We now prove that $R(\hat{\tau})$ is at most ϵ. Indeed otherwise, since P is ε-dense, the ball $B(c(\hat{\tau}), R(\hat{\tau}))$ associated to the weighted center $(c(\hat{\tau}), R^2(\hat{\tau}))$ of τ would include a point q of P. Then the weighted distance from q to $(c(\hat{\tau}), R^2(\hat{\tau}))$ is negative, and this contradicts the fact that σ belongs to $\mathrm{Del}(\hat{P})$.

Let us consider now the Euclidean distance $d(c(\hat{\sigma}), p)$ from the weighted circumcenter $c(\hat{\sigma})$ to any vertex p of σ. We have:

$$d(c(\hat{\sigma}), p)^2 = R(\hat{\sigma})^2 + w(p)$$
$$\leq \varepsilon^2 + \tilde{w}_0 L(p)^2.$$

where $L(p)$ is the distance from p to its nearest neighbor in $P \setminus \{p\}$. From Lemma 5.1, we have $Ł(p) \leq 2\varepsilon$ and thus $d(c(\hat{\sigma}), p) \leq \varepsilon\sqrt{1 + 4\tilde{w}_0} \leq \sqrt{2}\varepsilon$. Since this bound holds for any vertex p of σ, we conclude that the diameter $\Delta(\sigma)$ of σ is at most $2\sqrt{2}\varepsilon$. $\qquad\qquad\square$

5.3.2 Θ_0-thickness and Flakes

A simplex that is not thick has a relatively small altitude. We focus here on a special class of nonthick simplices, called *flakes* in which *all* the altitudes are relatively small. Let Θ_0 be a constant smaller than 1.

Definition 5.16 (Θ_0-flakes) A j-simplex σ is Θ_0-*thick* if $\Theta(\sigma) \geq \Theta_0^j$. A Θ_0-*flake* is a simplex that is not Θ_0-*thick* but whose proper faces are all Θ_0-thick.

Observe that a flake must have dimension at least 2, as $\Theta(\sigma) = 1$ for any simplex σ with dimension $j < 2$.

A simplicial complex whose simplices are all Θ_0-thick is said to be Θ_0-thick. Observe that a simplicial complex is Θ_0-thick iff it includes no Θ_0-flake. Indeed, if σ is not Θ_0-thick, then either it is a Θ_0-flake or it has a proper j-face $\sigma_j \subset \sigma$ that is not Θ_0-thick. By considering such a face with minimal dimension, we arrive at the following observation:

Lemma 5.17 *A simplex is not Θ_0-thick if and only if it has a face that is a Θ_0-flake.*

In Lemma 5.19, we show an upper bound on the altitudes of a Θ_0-flake. First, we provide a general relationship between the altitudes of a simplex:

Lemma 5.18 *Let σ be a j-simplex with $j \geq 2$. If p and q are two vertices of σ, we note σ_p the subface $\sigma \setminus \{p\}$ of σ and σ_q the subface $\sigma \setminus \{q\}$. The altitudes $D(p, \sigma)$ and $D(p, \sigma_q)$ of p within, respectively, σ and σ_q and the altitudes $D(q, \sigma)$ and $D(q, \sigma_p)$ of q within, respectively, σ and σ_p satisfy the following relation:*

$$\frac{D(p, \sigma)}{D(p, \sigma_q)} = \frac{D(q, \sigma)}{D(q, \sigma_p)}.$$

Proof   The proof follows from a volume computation. Let $vol_j(\sigma)$, $vol_{j-1}(\sigma_p)$ and $vol_{j-2}(\sigma_{pq})$ be the volumes of the simplices σ, σ_p and $\sigma_{pq} = \sigma \setminus \{p, q\}$ respectively. We have

$$vol_j(\sigma) = \frac{1}{j} D(p, \sigma) vol_{j-1}(\sigma_p) = \frac{1}{j(j-1)} D(p, \sigma) D(q, \sigma_p) vol_{j-2}(\sigma_{pq}).$$

The similar relation, obtained replacing p by q, obviously holds and both relations together prove the lemma. $\qquad\Box$

We arrive at the following important observation about flake simplices:

Lemma 5.19 (Flakes have small altitudes)   *If a k-simplex σ is a Θ_0-flake, then for every vertex $p \in \sigma$, the altitude $D(p, \sigma)$ satisfies the bound*

$$D(p, \sigma) < \frac{k}{k-1} \frac{\Delta^2(\sigma)\Theta_0}{L(\sigma)} < 2\frac{\Delta^2(\sigma)\Theta_0}{L(\sigma)},$$

where $\Delta(\sigma)$ and $L(\sigma)$ are the lengths of the longest and shortest edges of σ.

Proof   Recalling Lemma 5.18, we have

$$D(p, \sigma) = \frac{D(q, \sigma)D(p, \sigma_q)}{D(q, \sigma_p)}, \tag{5.4}$$

and taking q to be a vertex with minimal altitude in σ, we have

$$D(q, \sigma) = k\Theta(\sigma)\Delta(\sigma) < k\Theta_0^k\Delta(\sigma). \tag{5.5}$$

Moreover, since σ_p is Θ_0-thick, we have:

$$D(q, \sigma_p) \geq (k-1)\Theta(\sigma_p)\Delta(\sigma_p) \geq (k-1)\Theta_0^{k-1}L(\sigma). \tag{5.6}$$

Furthermore:

$$D(p, \sigma_q) \leq \Delta(\sigma_q) \leq \Delta(\sigma). \tag{5.7}$$

Plugging Equations 5.5, 5.6 and 5.7 into Equation 5.4 yields the claimed bound. $\qquad\Box$

5.3.3 The Weight Range of a Flake with Small Radius

Let σ be a Θ_0 flake of dimension j. If we assign weights to the vertices of σ, the weighted radius $R(\hat{\sigma})$ of σ depends on the weights of its vertices. We show here that to keep the weighted radius $R(\hat{\sigma})$ smaller than a given ε we have to choose the weight of each vertex of σ within a small interval whose measure is linear in Θ_0.

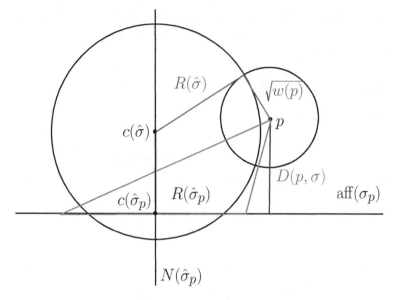

Figure 5.4 For the proof of Lemma 5.20.

Lemma 5.20 *Let σ be a Θ_0-flake and assume that we are given a weighting scheme with non-negative weights on the vertices of σ. If the weighted radius $R(\hat{\sigma})$ of σ is smaller than ε, the weight $w(p)$ of any vertex p of σ belongs to an interval $I(\sigma, p)$ whose measure $|I(\sigma, p)|$ satisfies:*

$$|I(\sigma, p)| \leq 8 \frac{\Delta(\sigma)^2}{L(\sigma)} \Theta_0 \varepsilon.$$

If furthermore the vertices of σ belongs to an $(\varepsilon, \bar{\eta})$-net, and the weighting scheme has a relative amplitude smaller than $\tilde{w}_0 < \frac{1}{4}$, the measure of $I(\sigma, p)$ satisfies:

$$|I(\sigma, p)| \leq |I| \overset{\text{def}}{=} 64 \, \Theta_0 \frac{\epsilon^2}{\bar{\eta}}.$$

Proof Let $c(\hat{\sigma})$ and $R(\hat{\sigma})$ be, respectively, the weighted center and weighted radius of σ. Likewise, we use $c(\hat{\sigma}_p)$ and $R(\hat{\sigma}_p)$ for, respectively, the weighted center and the weighted radius of σ_p, where σ_p is the subface $\sigma \setminus p$ of σ. Referring to Figure 5.4, we get:

$$R^2(\hat{\sigma}) = d^2(c(\hat{\sigma}), c(\hat{\sigma}_p)) + R^2(\hat{\sigma}_p), \qquad (5.8)$$

The set of points of $\mathbb{R}^d$ with equal weighted distances to the vertices of σ_p is an affine subspace we denote by $N(\hat{\sigma}_p)$. Writing $d(p, N(\hat{\sigma}_p))$ for the distance from p to $N(\hat{\sigma}_p)$, we have:

$$R^2(\hat{\sigma}) + w(p) = d^2(p, c(\hat{\sigma})) = d^2(p, N(\hat{\sigma}_p)) + \big(D(p,\sigma) - H(p,\hat{\sigma})\big)^2 \quad (5.9)$$

where $D(p,\sigma)$ is the altitude of p in σ and $H(p,\hat{\sigma}) = d(c(\hat{\sigma}), c(\hat{\sigma}_p))$ if p and $c(\hat{\sigma})$ are on the same side of aff(σ_p) and $H(p,\hat{\sigma}) = -d(c(\hat{\sigma}), c(\hat{\sigma}_p))$ otherwise.

Using Equations 5.8 and 5.9 together, we get:

$$w(p) = d^2(p, N(\hat{\sigma}_p)) + \big(D(p,\sigma) - H(p,\hat{\sigma})\big)^2 - R^2(\hat{\sigma})$$
$$= d^2(p, N(\hat{\sigma}_p)) + D^2(p,\sigma) - R^2(\hat{\sigma}_p) - 2D(p,\sigma)H(p,\hat{\sigma}).$$

Writing $F(p,\hat{\sigma}) = d^2(p, N(\hat{\sigma}_p)) + D^2(p,\sigma) - R^2(\hat{\sigma}_p)$, we get:

$$w(p) = F(p,\hat{\sigma}) - 2D(p,\sigma)H(p,\hat{\sigma}).$$

Hence,

$$|w(p) - F(p,\hat{\sigma})| = 2D(p,\sigma)\, d(c(\hat{\sigma}), c(\hat{\sigma}_p)). \quad (5.10)$$

Observe that $F(p,\hat{\sigma})$ depends on the locations of the vertices of σ and on the weights of the vertices of σ_p but does not depend on the weight $w(p)$ of p.

From Lemma 5.19, $D(p,\sigma) \le 2\Theta_0 \frac{\Delta(\sigma)^2}{L(\sigma)}$, and, from Equation 5.8, we get that $d(c(\hat{\sigma}), c(\hat{\sigma}_p))$ is at most $R(\hat{\sigma})$. Therefore, if $R(\hat{\sigma}) \le \varepsilon$, the weight $w(p)$ of p belongs to the interval $I(\sigma, p)$, centered at $F(p,\hat{\sigma})$, of measure

$$|I(\sigma, p)| \le 8\frac{\Delta(\sigma)^2}{L(\sigma)}\Theta_0\varepsilon. \quad (5.11)$$

In the case where σ belongs to an $(\varepsilon, \bar{\eta})$-net, we have $L(\sigma) \ge \bar{\eta}\varepsilon$ and, from Lemma 5.15, $\Delta(\sigma) \le 2\sqrt{2}\varepsilon$. The weight range $|I(\sigma, p)|$ then satisfies

$$|I(\sigma, p)| \le 64\,\Theta_0\frac{\epsilon^2}{\bar{\eta}}.$$

$\square$

5.3.4 Lovász Local Lemma

We will see in Section 5.3 how to to compute, for a given input set of points P, a weighting scheme yielding to a thick weighted Delaunay triangulation. This construction relies on the constructive proof of the Lovász local lemma due to Moser and Tardos. In this section, we recall without proof these important results.

Lovász local lemma [1] is a powerful tool to prove the existence of combinatorial objects. Let $\mathcal{A}$ be a finite collection of "bad" events in some probability space. The lemma shows that the probability that none of these events occur is positive provided that the individual events occur with a sufficiently small probability and there is limited dependence among them. Here is the lemma in a simple form that will be sufficient for our purposes.

Theorem 5.21 (Lovász local lemma)   *Let $\mathcal{A} = \{A_1, \ldots, A_N\}$ be a finite set of events in some probability space. Suppose that each event A_i is independent of all but at most Γ of the other events and that $\mathsf{Pr}[A_i] \leq \varpi$ for all $1 \leq i \leq N$. If*

$$\varpi \leq \frac{1}{e(\Gamma + 1)} \tag{5.12}$$

where e denotes the base of the natural logarithm, then the probability that none of the events in $\mathcal{A}$ occurs is strictly positive.

Assume that the events are determined by a set of independent random variables. Each event is determined by a subset of those random variables. Two events are independent if the subsets of random variables determining each of them do not overlap. In such a case, Moser and Tardos gave a constructive proof of the Lovász lemma [106, 125]. The proof leads to a simple and natural algorithm that repeatedly checks whether some event in $\mathcal{A}$ occurs. In the affirmative, the algorithm picks an arbitrary occurring event, say A, and resamples A, where we call resampling of an event A the operation that consists in choosing new random values for the variables determining A.

Moser and Tardos proved that this simple algorithm quickly terminates, providing an assignment of the random variables that avoids all of the events in $\mathcal{A}$. It is important to note that the selection mechanism for picking an occurring event in the while loop is arbitrary and does not affect the correctness of the algorithm.

Algorithm 4: Moser Tardos algorithm

Input: A finite set $\mathcal{A}$ of events determined by a finite set $\mathcal{P}$ of independent random variables

for all $P \in \mathcal{P}$ **do**

   $v_P \leftarrow$ a random evaluation of P

   while some event of $\mathcal{A}$ occurs **do**

      pick any such event $A \in \mathcal{A}$

      resample A

return $\{v_P, P \in \mathcal{P}\}$

Theorem 5.22 (Moser Tardos)   *Assume that the same conditions as in Theorem 5.21 hold. Assume, in addition, that the events are determined by a set $\mathcal{P}$ of n independent random variables. Moser Tardos randomized algorithm computes an assignment of values for the variables in $\mathcal{P}$ such that no event in $\mathcal{A}$ occurs. The algorithm resamples each event at most $\frac{1}{\Gamma}$ expected times and the expected total number of resampling steps is at most $O(n)$.*

5.3.5 Applying the Lovász Local Lemma to Remove Flakes

Let P be an $(\varepsilon, \bar{\eta})$-net of $\mathbb{R}^d$ and $\tilde{w}_0$ a constant less than $1/4$. Now we take for the weights of the points in P independent random variables and we pick the weight of each point p uniformly at random in the interval $[0, \tilde{w}_0 L^2(p)]$. An event occurs when there exists a Θ_0-flake $\sigma \subset P$ that has a weighted radius $R(\hat{\sigma})$ not greater than ε. Because we know from Lemma 5.15, that all simplices in $\mathrm{Del}(\hat{P})$ have a weighted radius $R(\hat{\sigma})$ not greater than ε, removing all events will lead to a Θ_0-thick complex. For convenience, we will often identify an event and the associated flake.

Lemma 5.23 *The probability that an event occurs is* $\varpi \leq 64 \frac{\Theta_0}{\tilde{w}_0 \bar{\eta}^3}$.

Proof Let σ be a Θ_0-flake included in P and assume that the weights of all the vertices of σ except one, say p, have already been assigned. We know from Lemma 5.20 that if the weighted radius $R(\hat{\sigma})$ is not greater than ε, the weight $w(p)$ belongs to an interval of measure less than $|I| = 64 \, \Theta_0 \frac{\varepsilon^2}{\bar{\eta}}$. It follows that the probability that an event occurs is at most

$$\frac{|I|}{\tilde{w}_0 L^2(p)} \leq 64 \frac{\Theta_0}{\tilde{w}_0 \bar{\eta}^3},$$

which implies the same bound on the probability of the event σ. $\square$

Lemma 5.24 *Each event overlaps at most* Γ *other events, where*

$$\Gamma + 1 \leq \left(\frac{13}{\bar{\eta}} \right)^{d(d+1)}.$$

Proof Let σ be a Θ_0-flake with weighted center $c(\hat{\sigma})$ and weighted radius $R(\hat{\sigma}) \leq \varepsilon$. An event that overlaps σ is a Θ_0-flake σ' with a weighted radius at most ε that shares a vertex p with σ. Let q be a vertex of σ'. We have:

$$d(c(\hat{\sigma}), q) \leq d(c(\hat{\sigma}), p) + d(p, q)$$
$$\leq \sqrt{R(\hat{\sigma})^2 + w(p)} + \Delta(\sigma')$$

Since $R(\hat{\sigma}) \leq \varepsilon$, $w(p) \leq \tilde{w}_0 L(p)^2 \leq 4\tilde{w}_0 \varepsilon^2$ by Lemma 5.1, and $\Delta(\sigma') \leq 2\sqrt{2}\varepsilon$ by Lemma 5.15, we get:

$$d(c(\hat{\sigma}), q) \leq 3\sqrt{2}\varepsilon.$$

Therefore, any vertex of an event that overlap σ lies in the ball $B(c(\hat{\sigma}), r)$ of radius $r = \bar{r}\varepsilon = 3\sqrt{2}\varepsilon$. Because P is η-separated, this ball contains at most $J(r)$ points of P, with

$$J(r) = \frac{(r + \frac{\eta}{2})^d}{(\frac{\eta}{2})^d} = \left(1 + \frac{2\bar{r}}{\bar{\eta}}\right)^d \leq \left(1 + \frac{6\sqrt{2}}{\bar{\eta}}\right)^d$$

$$\leq \left(\frac{11}{\bar{\eta}}\right)^d.$$

where the last inequality uses the fact that $\bar{\eta} \leq 2$.

Because the Θ_0-flake σ also has its vertices within the ball $B(c(\hat{\sigma}), r)$, we can bound $\Gamma + 1$ by the number of simplices with vertices within $B(c(\hat{\sigma}), r)$, i.e.,

$$\Gamma + 1 \leq \Sigma_{i=2}^{d+1} \binom{J(r)}{i} \leq (1 + J(r))^{d+1} \leq \left(1 + \left(\frac{11}{\bar{\eta}}\right)^d\right)^{d+1}.$$

Using $\bar{\eta} \leq 2$ and the fact that, for all $a \in \mathbb{R}^+$ and $b \in \mathbb{R}^+$, $a^d + b^d \leq (a+b)^d$, we get:

$$\Gamma + 1 \leq \left(\frac{13}{\bar{\eta}}\right)^{d(d+1)}.$$

□

We are now ready to apply the Lovász local lemma. We will assume that

$$\left(\frac{13}{\bar{\eta}}\right)^{d(d+1)} 64 \frac{\Theta_0}{\tilde{w}_0 \bar{\eta}^3} \leq \frac{1}{e}. \tag{5.13}$$

In view of Lemmas 5.23 and 5.24, this condition ensures that we have $\varpi \leq \frac{1}{e(\Gamma+1)}$, and therefore there exists a weight assignment on P with relative amplitude less than $\tilde{w}_0$, such that P includes no Θ_0-flakes with a weighted radius less than ε. Because any simplex in the weighted Delaunay triangulation Del($\hat{P}$) has a weighted radius less than ε (Lemma 5.15), we conclude that such an assignment yields a weighted Delaunay triangulation Del($\hat{P}$) that has no Θ_0-flakes.

Theorem 5.25 *Let P be an $(\varepsilon, \bar{\eta})$-net of $\mathbb{T}^d$ and $\tilde{w}_0 \leq \frac{1}{4}$. If Equation 5.13 is satisfied, there is a weight assignment on P with relative amplitude less than $\tilde{w}_0$ such that the weighted Delaunay triangulation Del($\hat{P}$) is Θ_0-thick.*

Observe that the thickness Θ_0 that we can guarantee is bounded by Equation 5.13 that constrains Θ_0 to be small enough with respect to $\bar{\eta}$ and $\tilde{w}_0$. Note that the bound is very small and depends as 2^{-d^2} on d. Still it does not depend on the sampling density ε.

5.3.6 Algorithm

Based on the results of the previous subsections, we will apply Moser Tardos algorithm to our context so as to obtain a weighted Delaunay triangulation that is Θ_0-thick. Algorithm 5 takes as input an $(\varepsilon, \bar{\eta})$-net P of $\mathbb{T}^d$, a constant $\tilde{w}_0 < 1/4$ and a constant Θ_0 small enough to satisfy Equation 5.13. As proved below, the algorithm outputs a weighting scheme on P whose relative amplitude is smaller than $\tilde{w}_0$ and such that the weighted Delaunay triangulation $\mathrm{Del}(\hat{P})$ is Θ_0-thick. The algorithm maintains the weighted Delaunay triangulation $\mathrm{Del}(\hat{P})$ while resampling the Θ_0-flakes that occur in $\mathrm{Del}(\hat{P})$ until they all disappear. Resampling a simplex σ consists in reassigned random weights to the vertices of σ. As already mentioned, the weights of the different vertices are picked independently and the weight $w(p)$ of vertex p is taken uniformly at random in the interval $[0, \tilde{w}_0 L^2(p)]$.

Algorithm 5: Thick weighted Delaunay triangulation

Input: P, $\tilde{w}_0$, Θ_0
Initialize all weights to 0 and compute $\mathrm{Del}(\hat{P}) = \mathrm{Del}(P)$
while there are Θ_0-flakes in $\mathrm{Del}(\hat{P})$ **do**
    choose a Θ_0-flake σ in $\mathrm{Del}(\hat{P})$
    resample σ
    update $\mathrm{Del}(\hat{P})$
Output: A weighting scheme on P and the corresponding weighted Delaunay triangulation which is granted to be Θ_0-thick.

Theorem 5.26 *If P is an $(\varepsilon, \bar{\eta})$-net of $\mathbb{T}^d$, $\tilde{w}_0$ a constant less than $1/4$ and Θ_0 a constant such that Equation 5.13 holds, Algorithm 5 outputs a weighting scheme $\hat{P}$ on P whose relative amplitude is smaller than $\tilde{w}_0$ and such that the weighted Delaunay triangulation $\mathrm{Del}(\hat{P})$ is Θ_0-thick. Its expected complexity is linear with respect to the size of P.*

Proof Algorithm 5 resamples the Θ_0-flakes that occur in the weighted Delaunay triangulation $\mathrm{Del}(\hat{P})$. Since the Θ_0-flakes in $\mathrm{Del}(\hat{P})$ have weighted radii at most ε, they are events as defined in Section 5.3.5. Therefore Algorithm 5 is a variant of Moser Tardos algorithm applied to the Θ_0-flakes with small weighted radii. The main difference is that Algorithm 5 keeps only track of Θ_0-flakes in the current $\mathrm{Del}(\hat{P})$ and not of all possible Θ_0-flakes with small weighted radii included in P. According to Theorem 5.22, Condition 5.13 ensures that Moser Tardos algorithm terminates whatever may be the order in which the events are resampled. Therefore the condition, a fortiori, guarantees the termination of Algorithm 5.

Each resampling involves the reweighting of at most $d+1$ vertices. Since P is an $(\varepsilon, \bar{\eta})$-net, and the weighting scheme has bounded relative amplitude, the weighted Delaunay complex $\mathrm{Del}(\hat{P})$ can be updated in constant time. Thus the expected complexity of Agorithm 5 is proportional to the number of resampling which is $O(|P|)$ by Theorem 5.22. □

5.4 Protection

We introduce now the notion of protection of a simplex. The notion of protection is stronger than the notion of thickness (see Lemma 5.27) and some positive protection can be obtained by perturbing the position of the points of P. This is another mean to ensure Delaunay triangulations to have positive thickness (other than weight assignment as discussed in the previous section). Protection will also be used in Section 6.2.

We say that a simplex $\sigma \subset \mathrm{Del}(P)$ is δ-*protected* if there exists a point c_σ, called a δ-*protection center* of σ such that

$$\|c_\sigma - q\| > \|c_\sigma - p\| + \delta \quad \forall p \in \sigma \text{ and } \forall q \in P \setminus \sigma. \tag{5.14}$$

We will write $\bar{\delta} = \frac{\delta}{\varepsilon}$. Note that Equation 5.14 implies the following inequality

$$\|c_\sigma - q\|^2 > \|c_\sigma - p\|^2 + \delta^2 \quad \forall p \in \sigma \text{ and } \forall q \in P \setminus \sigma. \tag{5.15}$$

Lemma 5.27 (Separation and thickness from protection) *Let P be an $(\varepsilon, \bar{\eta})$-net of a bounded domain $\Omega \subset \mathbb{R}^d$. Assume that $|P| > d+1$ and that every d-simplex in $\mathrm{Del}(P)$ is δ-protected. Then the separation ratio of P satisfies*

$$\bar{\eta} \geq \bar{\delta},$$

and the thickness of any simplex σ (of any dimension) of $\mathrm{Del}(P)$ is at least

$$\Theta(\sigma) \geq \frac{\bar{\delta}^2}{8d}.$$

Before we prove the lemma, we state and prove two easy claims that will be useful to prove the second part of the lemma.

Claim 5.28 *Let $B = B(c, R)$ and $B' = B(c', R')$ be two n-balls whose bounding spheres ∂B and $\partial B'$ intersect, and let H be the bisecting hyperplane of B and B', i.e., the hyperplane that contains the $(n-2)$-sphere $S = \partial B \cap \partial B'$. Let θ be the angle of the cone (c, S). Writing $\rho = \frac{R'}{R}$ and $\|c-c'\| = \lambda R$, we have*

$$\cos(\theta) = \frac{1 + \lambda^2 - \rho^2}{2\lambda}. \tag{5.16}$$

If $R \geq R'$, we have $\cos(\theta) \geq \frac{\lambda}{2}$.

Proof Let $q \in S$; applying the cosine rule to the triangle $[cc'q]$ gives

$$\lambda^2 R^2 + R^2 - 2\lambda R^2 \cos(\theta) = R'^2, \qquad (5.17)$$

which proves Equation 5.16. If $R \geq R'$, then $\rho \leq 1$, and $\cos(\theta) \geq \lambda/2$ immediately follows from Equation 5.16. $\square$

If $B = B(c, R)$ is a d-ball, we denote by $B^{+\delta}$ the ball $B(c, \sqrt{R^2 + \delta^2})$.

Claim 5.29 *Let* $B = B(c, R)$ *and* $B' = B(c', R')$ *be two n-balls whose bounding spheres* ∂B *and* $\partial B'$ *intersect, and let* $\tilde{\theta}$ *be the angle of the cone* $(c, \widetilde{S})$ *where* $\widetilde{S} = \partial B \cap \partial B'^{+\delta}$. *Writing* $\|c - c'\| = \lambda R$, *we have*

$$\cos(\tilde{\theta}) = \cos(\theta) - \frac{\delta^2}{2R^2\lambda}$$

Proof Let $\tilde{q} \in \widetilde{S}$, applying the cosine rule to the triangle $[cc'\tilde{q}]$ gives

$$\lambda^2 R^2 + R^2 - 2\lambda R^2 \cos(\tilde{\theta}) = R'^2 + \delta^2.$$

Subtracting Equation 5.17 from the previous equality yields $\delta^2 = 2\lambda R^2 (\cos(\theta) - \cos(\tilde{\theta}))$, which proves the lemma. $\square$

Proof of Lemma 5.27 1. Let p and q be two closest points of P. The edge $[pq]$ is an edge of Del(P). We denote by σ a d-simplex of Del(P) that contains $[pq]$ and by σ' a d-simplex of Del(P) that contains one of the two vertices of $[pq]$ but not the other. Because σ' is δ-protected, we must have $\|p - q\| \geq \delta$.

2. Since $\Theta(\tau) \geq \Theta(\sigma)$ for any simplex $\tau \subseteq \sigma$, it is sufficient to consider the case of a d-simplex σ. Because $|P| > d + 1$, there exists at least one other d-simplex σ' of Del(P) that share a facet τ with σ. Let $B(\sigma) = B(c, R)$ and $B(\sigma') = B(c', R')$ be the circumscribing balls of σ and σ', respectively. The spheres ∂B and $\partial B'^{+\delta}$ intersect in a $(d-2)$-sphere $\widetilde{S}$, which is contained in a hyperplane $\widetilde{H}$ parallel to the hyperplane $H = \text{aff}(\tau)$. For any $\tilde{q} \in \widetilde{S}$ we have

$$d(\widetilde{H}, H) = d(\tilde{q}, H) = R(\cos(\theta) - \cos(\tilde{\theta})) = \frac{\delta^2}{2\|c - c'\|},$$

where the last equality follows from Claim 5.29 and $d(\widetilde{H}, H)$ denotes the distance between the two parallel hyperplanes. See Figure 5.5 for an illustration. Because $p \in \partial B$, p belongs to $B(\sigma')^{+\delta}$ if and only if p lies in the strip bounded by H and $\widetilde{H}$, which is equivalent to

$$d(p, H) = D(p, \sigma) < \frac{\delta^2}{2\|c - c'\|}.$$

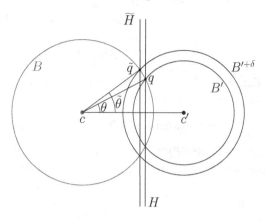

Figure 5.5 Construction used in Claims 5.28 and 5.29.

We conclude that, if σ is δ-protected, the ball

$$B(\sigma)^{+\delta} = B(c_\sigma, \sqrt{R_\sigma^2 + \delta^2}) \subseteq B(c_\sigma, R_\sigma + \delta)$$

does not contain points of $P \setminus \sigma$, which implies from the preceding inequality that

$$d(p, H) = D(p, \sigma) \geq \frac{\delta^2}{2\|c - c'\|}.$$

For any simplex σ, we have $D(p, \sigma) \leq 2R(\sigma)$ for all $p \in \sigma$, where $R(\sigma)$ denotes the radius of the circumsphere of σ. For any σ in the triangulation of an ε-net, we have $R(\sigma) \leq \varepsilon$. Thus $D(p, \sigma) \leq 2\varepsilon$, and the preceding inequality yields $\|c - c'\| \geq \frac{\delta^2}{4\varepsilon}$.

We further obtain

$$\Theta(\sigma) = \frac{\min_{p \in \sigma} D(p, \sigma)}{d\,\Delta(\sigma)} \geq \frac{\delta^2}{8d\,\varepsilon^2} = \frac{\bar{\delta}^2}{8d}.$$

$\square$

In Section 5.3.5, we have used a variant of Moser Tardos algorithm to obtain a thick *weighted* Delaunay complex. Instead of weighting the points, we can perturb their positions so that the Delaunay triangulation of the perturbed point set P' is δ-protected for some small enough $\delta > 0$. Thanks to Lemma 5.27, the Delaunay triangulation of the perturbed points will have some positive thickness (see Exercise 5.12).

5.5 Exercises

Exercise 5.1   Let Ω be a subset of $\mathbb{R}^d$ and P a finite ε-dense set of points in Ω. Show that all Delaunay simplices of P with a vertex at distance greater than 2ε from the boundary of Ω belong to $\mathrm{Del}_{|\Omega}(P)$.

Exercise 5.2 (Hypergeometric distribution)   Suppose a, b, c are positive integers, with $\max\{a, b\} \leq c$. The *hypergeometric distribution* with parameters a, b, c is the distribution of the random variable $X = |A \cap B|$, where A is a random sample of size a, from a universe C of size c, which has a subset B of size b. Prove that given $b \leq a$, the probability that the random sample A contains B, and is disjoint from another fixed set T with cardinality t, $T \cap B = \emptyset$, is at most $\left(\frac{a}{c}\right)^b \left(1 - \frac{a}{c}\right)^t$, for $a, c \gg b^2$.

Exercise 5.3 (Delaunay refinement)   Adapt Algorithm 3 to add sample points in $\mathbb{T}^d$ so that the sample P is an ε-net of $\mathbb{T}^d$.

Exercise 5.4 (k-center clustering)   Given is a set of points P and an integer k. The k-clustering problem consists in partitioning P into k clusters so as to minimize the maximum diameter of a cluster. Propose an algorithm that gives an approximation ratio of 2 for the k-clustering problem.

Exercise 5.5   Let Ω be an open subset of $\mathbb{R}^2$ and P an $(\varepsilon, \bar{\eta})$-net of Ω in general position wrt circles. Show that all triangles of $\mathrm{Del}_{|\Omega}(P)$ have all their angles greater or equal to $\arcsin(\frac{\bar{\eta}}{2})$.

Exercise 5.6 (Max-min)   Let P be a finite set of points in general position in the plane. To any triangulation T of P we attach the vector $V(T) = (\alpha_1, \ldots, \alpha_{3t})$ where the $\alpha_i \in [0, \pi]$ are the angles of the t triangles of T, sorted by increasing values. Show that $\mathrm{Del}(P)$ is, among all triangulations of P, the one that maximizes $V(T)$ for the lexicographic order. In particular, $\mathrm{Del}(P)$ maximizes the smallest angle.

Exercise 5.7   Let U and V be two vector spaces of $\mathbb{R}^d$ with $\dim U \leq \dim V$. Show that $\angle(U, V) = \angle(V^\perp, U^\perp)$ where $U^\perp$ (resp., $V^\perp$) denotes the vector space normal to U (resp., V).

Exercise 5.8   Let h and h' be two affine spaces of the same dimension embedded in $\mathbb{R}^d$, and let u be a vector of $\mathbb{R}^d$. Show that $\angle(u, h') \leq \angle(u, h) + \angle(h, h')$.

Exercise 5.9   Let τ be a j-simplex. Show that $L(\tau) \geq D(p, \tau) \geq j! \, \Theta(\tau) \Delta(\tau)$ (see Lemma 5.19 for the notations).

Exercise 5.10   Bound from below the dihedral angles of a d-simplex of $\mathbb{R}^d$ as a function of its thickness.

Exercise 5.11 (Inheritance of protection)   Let P be an $(\varepsilon, \bar{\eta})$-net of a bounded domain $\Omega \subset \mathbb{R}^d$. We say that a simplex is δ-power protected if Equation 5.15 is satisfied, i.e. there exists a point c_σ such that

$$\|c_\sigma - q\|^2 > \|c_\sigma - p\|^2 + \delta^2 \quad \forall p \in \sigma \text{ and } \forall q \in L \setminus \sigma.$$

Show that if every d-simplex in Del(P) is δ-power protected, then all simplices (of all dimensions) in Del(P) are at least δ'-power protected where $\delta' = \frac{\delta}{d}$. deduce a similar result if one replaces the power protection by the protection as defined in Section 5.4. (Hint: Use the lifting map introduced in the proofs of Theorems 4.3 and 4.6)

Exercise 5.12 (Protection via perturbation)   Let P be an $(\varepsilon, \bar{\eta})$-net P of the flat torus $\mathbb{T}^d = \mathbb{R}^d / \mathbb{Z}^d$. Propose an algorithm that perturbs the points of P so that the Delaunay triangulation of the perturbed point set P' is δ-protected for some a small enough $\delta > 0$ (and thus has some positive thickness by Lemma 5.27). If p is a point of P, the associated perturbed point is picked at random in the ball $B(p, \rho)$ for some $\rho > 0$. Use a variant of Moser Tardos algorithm.

5.6 Bibliographical Notes

The farthest point insertion algorithm (Algorithm 3) has been popularized by Gonzales in the context of clustering data sets [91] and has found numerous applications in many fields. Gonzales proved Lemma 5.9 and Feder and Greene [80] showed that no polynomial-time algorithm exists with a constant approximation ratio close to 2 unless $P = NP$. They also improved the $O(n^2)$ time complexity of Algorithm 3 to $O(n \log k)$ when the points live in Euclidean space. See also the paper by Har-Peled and Mendel [95] that contains further improvements and extensions, and, in particular, shows how to construct a hierarchical representation of a point set, called the *net-tree*, from the sequence of points provided by the farthest point insertion. The proof of the complexity of the incremental randomized construction of nets (Theorem 5.6) is due to Boissonnat, Devillers, Dutta and Glisse [26]. Their paper also contains a solution to Exercise 5.2.

The notion of thick triangulations goes back to the early work on differential topology by Cairns [32], Whitehead [130], Whitney [131], Munkres [109], and others. Thick triangulations also play a central role in the work of Cheeger et al. [55] and Fu [84] on curvature measures. Since this notion appeared in different places and contexts, various names have been used, e.g. thickness, fullness or relative thickness. Our presentation follows the work of Boissonnat, Dyer and Ghosh [14]. Lemma 5.14 is due to Whitney [131].

More recently, thick triangulations have been found important in mesh generation where numerical simulations require meshes to be thick [69]. The notion of flake simplex introduced in this chapter is an extension of the notion of sliver introduced by Cheng et al. in the context of three dimensional mesh generation [56, 69]: a sliver is a flake with an upper bound on the ratio of its cicumradius to the length of its shortest edge. Sliver removal in higher dimensions has been discussed in [99, 57].

Our weighting mechanism to remove flakes is inspired from the one used by Cheng et al. to remove slivers from three dimensional Delaunay triangulations. The weighting mechanism can be seen as a perturbation of the Euclidean metric. It is also possible to remove flakes and inconsistencies by perturbing the position of the points. This kind of perturbation may be prefered to the weighting mechanism in the context of mesh generation [99, 24, 75].

The notion of protection has been introduced by Boissonnat, Dyer and Ghosh to study the stability of Delaunay triangulations and the construction of Delaunay triangulations of manifolds [14, 13, 27]. A solution to Exercise 5.12 can be deduced from results in [13] and [15].

The Lovász local lemma, proved initially by Lovász and Erdös [1], is a celebrated result with a long history. The constructive proof of Moser and Tardos has been a break through that is still the subject of intense research [106]. Its first introduction in Computational Geometry appears in [15].

6

Delaunay Filtrations

In this chapter, we introduce two simplicial complexes that have strong ties with Delaunay complexes. Their common point is that they allow to define filtrations. Filtrations, defined in Chapter 2, are sequences of nested complexes that allow to represent a set of points at various scales. They play an important role in persistent homology, a central tool in Topological Data Analysis, as will be demonstrated in Chapter 11.

We first define the alpha-complex, or α-complex, of a finite set of points P, which is a subcomplex of the Delaunay complex. Here α is a real parameter and varying α will lead to a filtration of the Delaunay complex. The definition extends to sets of weighted points: the weighted α-complex of a set of weighted points $\hat{P}$ is a subcomplex of the weighted Delaunay triangulation of $\hat{P}$, and varying α will lead to a filtration of the weighted Delaunay complex.

The α-complex of P is a combinatorial representation of the union of the balls $B(p, \alpha)$ of radius α centered at the points of P. It is thus closely related to the Čech complex introduced in Section 2.3. In fact, the α-complex shares with the Čech complex the property of having the same homotopy type as the union of the balls. A major difference between the two complexes is related to their size: the α-complex is usually much smaller than the Čech complex and can be computed more efficiently.

Owing to their capacity of representing union of balls and their topology, α-complexes play an important role in the description of proteins and macro molecules, and in drug design. In Geometric Inference, α-complexes also play an important role and we will see in Section 8.1 that they capture the homotopy type of well sampled manifolds.

Alpha shapes are constructed from the Delaunay complex and are therefore difficult to compute in high dimensions. In Section 6.2, we will introduce another complex, the so-called *witness complex*. The witness complex is defined from two point sets: L, which is the vertex set of the complex, and

W that can be seen as an approximation of the space that contains *L*. In applications, *L* is usually a crude subset of *W* that can be extracted from *W* using, for example, the algorithms of Section 5.1. The witness complex can be defined and constructed in any discrete metric space and does not require the points to be embedded in a specific ambient metric space: we only need to know the pairwise distances between the points of *L* and *W*. This is a critical advantage in high dimensions over the Delaunay complex whose construction requires to evaluate the `in_ball` predicate whose algebraic complexity depends on the dimension *d* of the ambient space (Exercise 4.5). In the case where the points live in Euclidean space, we will see that, under appropriate conditions, witness complexes and Delaunay complexes are identical. We will also introduce a variant called the relaxed witness, which offers another filtration.

6.1 Alpha Complexes

6.1.1 Definitions

Alpha complexes. Let P be a set of points in $\mathbb{R}^d$. From Lemma 4.1, we know that the simplices in the Delaunay complex $\text{Del}(P)$ are characterized by the *empty ball property* meaning that a simplex with vertices in P belong to $\text{Del}(P)$ iff it admits an *empty* circumscribing ball, i.e., a circumscribing ball whose interior includes no point of P. We are interested here in sorting the simplices of $\text{Del}(P)$ according to the squared radius of their smallest empty circumscribing ball. For a simplex τ, we call this quantity the filtration value of τ and write it $\alpha(\tau)$.

Now, for any $\alpha \in \mathbb{R}$, we consider the subset $\mathcal{A}(P,\alpha)$ of the simplices in $\text{Del}(P)$ that have a filtration value at most α. Because a ball circumscribing a simplex circumscribes any face of this simplex, $\mathcal{A}(P,\alpha)$ is a subcomplex of $\text{Del}(P)$. It is called the α-*complex* of *P*.

Because the α-complex of *P* is a subcomplex of the Delaunay complex of *P*, it has a natural embedding if *P* is in general position wrt spheres (Theorem 4.3). The underlying space of the α-complex $\mathcal{A}(P,\alpha)$ is called the α-*shape* of *P*.

If *P* is in general position wrt spheres, the dimension of the α-complex $\mathcal{A}(P,\alpha)$ is at most the dimension *d* of the embedding space. It should be noted that the dimension of the α-complex may be strictly less that *d* and that the complex may not be pure, having some simplices which are not faces of simplices of maximal dimension.

The Delaunay filtration. The α-complex evolves when α increases, from the empty set for $\alpha < 0$, to the set of vertices of $\text{Del}(P)$ when $\alpha = 0$, and

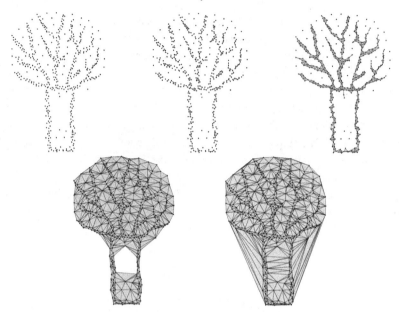

Figure 6.1 The α-complex of a set of points in $\mathbb{R}^2$ for increasing value of the parameter α.

finally to the whole Delaunay triangulation $\text{Del}(P)$ when α is large enough (see Figure 6.1). The parameter α defines an order on the simplices. This order is not total and some simplices may have the same value of the parameter. We define a total order by first sorting the simplices with a same α by increasing dimensions and then breaking ties arbitrarily. The total order we then obtain yields a filtration of the Delaunay complex.

We recall that a filtration of a simplicial complex K, as defined in Section 2.4, is a sequence of nested subcomplexes of K such that each subcomplex is obtained from the previous one by adding a simplex of K. The filtration of $\text{Del}(P)$ obtained by inserting the simplices in the order defined earlier is called a *Delaunay filtration* of P.

6.1.2 Computing Alpha Complexes and Filtrations

Let P be a set of points in $\mathbb{R}^d$ and let $\text{Del}(P)$ be the corresponding Delaunay complex. For a d-simplex τ in $\mathbb{R}^d$, there is a unique ball of $\mathbb{R}^d$ circumscribing τ. We denote by $c(\tau)$ and $r(\tau)$, respectively, the center and the radius of this ball. According to the definition, a d-simplex τ of $\text{Del}(P)$ belongs to the α-complex $\mathcal{A}(P, \alpha)$ iff $\alpha \geq r(\tau)^2$.

Things are a bit more complicated for simplices of dimension strictly less than d. Let τ be a simplex of dimension $k < d$. The centers of the d-balls circumscribing τ form a $(d - k)$-flat of $\mathbb{R}^d$ we denote by $h(\tau)$. Consider the circumscribing ball of τ that has the smallest radius. The center of this smallest circumscribing ball, $c(\tau)$, is called the center of τ and its radius, $r(\tau)$), is called the circumradius of τ. The center $c(\tau)$ is the point where $h(\tau)$ intersects the k-flat aff(τ) spanned by τ.

Given a set of points P, we say that τ is a *Gabriel* simplex if its smallest circumball contains no point of P in its interior. Plainly, a Gabriel simplex is a simplex of Del(P) but the converse is not necessarily true: a k-simplex τ of Del(P) is a Gabriel simplex iff $c(\tau)$ belongs to the face $V(\tau)$ of the Voronoi diagram Vor(P) dual to τ.

We conclude from the discussion that, if τ is a *Gabriel* simplex, its smallest enclosing ball is empty and it belongs to all α-complexes $\mathcal{A}(P, \alpha)$ for $\alpha \geq r(\tau)^2$. If τ a Delaunay simplex that is not Gabriel, the smallest empty ball that circumscribes τ circumscribes a coface of τ and therefore τ will have the same filtration value α as one of its cofaces. To prove this, consider the function $w(x)$ that associates to each point x in $h(\tau)$ its squared distance to the vertices in τ. Finding the filtration value $\alpha(\tau)$ of τ amounts to minimizing $w(x)$ under the condition that $x \in V(\tau)$. Since $w(x)$ is a convex function and $V(\tau)$ is a convex polyhedron, the minimum of $w(x)$ on $V(\tau)$ is reached at $c(\tau)$ iff $c(\tau) \in V(\tau)$ or on the boundary of $V(\tau)$ otherwise. In the first case, the simplex is a Gabriel simplex. In the last case, if we call σ the coface of higher dimension of τ whose dual Voronoi face contains $c(\tau)$ in its interior, we have $\alpha(\tau) = \alpha(\sigma)$.

For any $\tau \in$ Del(P) with dimension $k < d$, we denote by $U(\tau)$ the set of cofaces of τ in Del(P) with dimension $k + 1$. Algorithm 6 computes for each simplex τ in Del(P), the critical value $\alpha(\tau)$ at which τ enters the α-complex $\mathcal{A}(P, \alpha)$.

6.1.3 Weighted Alpha Complex

The definition of α-complexes and α-shapes extend to the weighted case. Let $\hat{P}$ be a set of weighted points and let τ be a simplex with vertex set $\hat{P}_\tau \subset \hat{P}$. Let us recall that two weighted points are said to be orthogonal when their weighted distance is zero. A weighted point is said to be orthogonal to $\hat{P}_\tau$ when it is orthogonal to all weighted points in $\hat{P}_\tau$ and it is said to be free of any weighted point in $\hat{P}$ when it has a positive or null distance to any weighted point of $\hat{P}$. From Lemma 4.5, a simplex τ with vertex set $\hat{P}_\tau \subset \hat{P}$ belongs to the weighted Delaunay triangulation Del$(\hat{P})$ iff there is a weighted

---

Algorithm 6: Computing Delaunay filtrations

Input: The set of points P in $\mathbb{R}^d$
Compute the Delaunay complex $\text{Del}(P)$
for each d-simplex $\tau \in \text{Del}(P)$ **do**
    set $\alpha(\tau) = r(\tau)^2$ (the squared circumradius of τ)
for $k = d - 1, \ldots, 0$ **do**
    for each d-simplex $\tau \in \text{Del}(P)$ **do**
        if τ is a Gabriel simplex **then**
            $\alpha(\tau) = r(\tau)^2$ (the squared smallest circumradius of τ)
        else
            $\alpha(\tau) = \min_{\sigma \in U(\tau)} \alpha(\sigma)$
Output: The critical α-value of each simplex in $\text{Del}(P)$ has been computed

---

point orthogonal to $\hat{P}_\tau$ and free of weighted points in $\hat{P}$. For any value of $\alpha \in \mathbb{R}$, we consider the subset $\mathcal{A}(\hat{P}, \alpha)$ of simplices in $\text{Del}(\hat{P})$ for which there is a weighted point with weight at most α, orthogonal to $\hat{P}_\tau$ and free of weighted points in $\hat{P}$. The simplices in $\mathcal{A}(\hat{P}, \alpha)$ form a subcomplex of $\text{Del}(\hat{P})$, which is called the *weighted α-complex* of $\hat{P}$. Under the usual general position assumption, this complex naturally embeds in $\mathbb{R}^d$ and the underlying space of $\mathcal{A}(\hat{P}, \alpha)$ is called the *weighted α-shape* of the set $\hat{P}$ for the parameter value α. Notice that α-complexes and α-shapes are special cases of respectively weighted α-complexes and weighted α-shapes, obtained when all the weights of the considered weighted points are equal.

As before, we associate to each simplex τ of $\text{Del}(\hat{P})$ a filtration value $\alpha(\tau)$ that corresponds to the first time τ enters the filtration.

Algorithm 6 extends almost verbatim to the case of weighted points, provided that we replace circumballs by orthogonal weighted points and empty balls by free weighted points. Let $\hat{P}$ be a set of weighted points in $\mathbb{R}^d$, τ a simplex of $\text{Del}(\hat{P})$ and $\hat{P}_\tau$ the subset of $\hat{P}$ associated to the vertices of τ. We now say that τ is a Gabriel simplex iff the ball with smallest radius that is orthogonal to $\hat{P}_\tau$ is free of weighted points in $\hat{P}$. Likewise, the function $w(x)$ used to prove the correctness of Algorithm 6 is now the weighted distance to the vertices of τ, i.e., $w(x) = D(x, \hat{p}) = d(x, p)^2 - w_p$, if $\hat{p} = (p, w_p)$ is the weighted point associated to the vertex p of τ.

6.1.4 Application to Union of Balls

Lemma 6.1 *Let B be a finite set of balls in $\mathbb{R}^d$. The union $U(B)$ of balls in B is homotopy equivalent to the α-complex $\mathcal{A}(B, 0)$.*

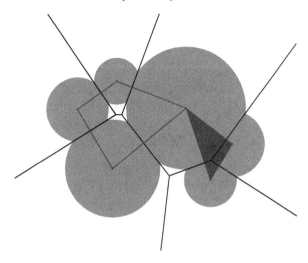

Figure 6.2 Union of balls and α-shapes.

See Figure 6.2 for an illustration of this fact.

Proof Each ball b in B may be regarded as a weighted point $(c(b), r^2(b))$ where $c(b)$ and $r^2(b)$ are respectively the center and the squared radius of b. We denote by $\mathrm{Del}(B)$, $\mathrm{Vor}(B)$ and $\mathcal{A}(B, \alpha)$, respectively, the Delaunay complex, Voronoi diagram and α-shape of the balls in B. Let $V(b)$ be the cell of b in $\mathrm{Vor}(B)$. We claim that $\{b \cap V(b), b \in B\}$ forms a finite convex cover of $U(B)$ as defined in Section 2.3. First, because b and $V(b)$ are both convex subsets of $\mathbb{R}^d$, each subset $b \cap V(b)$ is convex. We show next that $\{b \cap V(b), b \in B\}$ is a cover of $U(B)$, i.e.:

$$U(B) = \bigcup_{b \in B} b \cap V(b).$$

The inclusion $\bigcup_{b \in B} b \cap V(b) \subset U(B)$ is trivial. To show the reverse inclusion, let us consider a point p in $U(B)$. Point p belongs to at least one ball b_1 of B and let $b(p)$ be the ball in B whose Voronoi cell contains p. Because $p \in b_1$, the weighted distance $D(p, b_1)$ is negative and, because $b(p)$ minimizes the weighted distance to p, we have:

$$D(p, b(p)) \le D(p, b_1) \le 0,$$

which means that p belongs to $b(p)$ and therefore to $b(p) \cap V(b(p))$ and to $\bigcup_{b \in B} b \cap V(b)$. The claim is proved.

It follows from the claim and the Nerve theorem (Theorem 2.8) that the union $U(B)$ of balls in B is homotopy equivalent to the nerve of the cover $\bigcup_{b \in B} b \cap V(b)$. We now show that the nerve of this cover is just the α-complex

$\mathcal{A}(B, 0)$. Let $B' \subset B$ be a subset of B. The subset B' belongs to the nerve of the cover $\{b \cap V(b), b \in B\}$ iff the intersection $\bigcap_{b \in B'} b \cap V(b)$ is non empty. This in turn is equivalent to say that that there exists a point x in $\bigcap_{b \in B'} b \cap V(b)$. Such a point x is at an equal negative weighted distance $w(x)$ to the balls in B' and at a greater weighted distance to any ball of $B \setminus B'$. In other words, the weighted point $\hat{x} = (x, w(x))$ is orthogonal to any ball in B' and has a positive weighted distance to any ball in $B \setminus B'$. Therefore B' belongs to $\text{Del}(B)$ and, since $w(x) \leq 0$, to the α-complex $\mathcal{A}(B, 0)$. ☐

Let us consider the special case where all the balls in B have the same radius. Let $B(P, r)$ be the set of balls with radius r, centered at points of the set P. The union $U(B(P, r))$ of these balls is homotopy equivalent to the Čech complex $\check{\text{C}}\text{ech}(P, r)$ defined (in Section 2.5) as the nerve of the cover of $U(B(P, r))$ by balls in $B(P, r)$. Therefore, the Čech complex $\check{\text{C}}\text{ech}(P, r)$ and the α-complex $\mathcal{A}(B(P, r), 0)$ have the same homotopy type and capture both the homotopy type of the union of balls $U(B(P, r))$. However, the Čech complex $\check{\text{C}}\text{ech}(P, r)$ is often much bigger than the α-complex $\mathcal{A}(B(P, r), 0)$. In particular, the dimension of the Čech complex $\check{\text{C}}\text{ech}(P, r)$ may be larger than d, in fact it may be as large as the number of balls in $B(P, r)$. Accordingly the Čech complex $\check{\text{C}}\text{ech}(P, r)$ usually does not embed naturally in $\mathbb{R}^d$. Differently, the α-complex $\mathcal{A}(B(P, r), 0)$, being a subcomplex of $\text{Del}(B)$, embeds naturally in $\mathbb{R}^d$ under general position assumption.

6.2 Witness Complexes

In this section, we introduce the witness complex, a variant of the Delaunay complex that can be defined using only distances (and not empty spheres). Hence the witness complex can be defined in any finite metric space where the input consists of the distance matrix of the data points that stores the pairwise distances (Section 5.1.3). Not every finite metric space can be isometrically embedded in a Euclidean space but if it is the case, we provide conditions under which the witness and the Delaunay complexes are identical. A practical situation, encountered for example in the context of sensor networks, is when the points come from some Euclidean space but their actual locations are not known.

The witness complex is defined from two sets of points L and W. The first one, called the set of *landmarks*, is finite. The other one, called the set of *witnesses*, serves as an approximation of the ambient space. A typical situation is when L is a subset of W, possibly a net of W extracted using one of the algorithms of Section 5.1.3. The witness complex $\text{Wit}(L, W)$ can be seen as

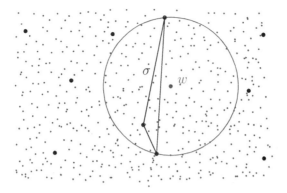

Figure 6.3 A simplex and one of its witnesses.

a weak notion of Delaunay triangulation which is easy to compute, even in high dimensions, since it only involves comparisons of distances between input points.

Definition 6.2 (Witness of a simplex)   Let σ be a simplex with vertices in $L \subset \mathbb{R}^d$, and let w be a point of $W \subseteq \mathbb{R}^d$. We say that w is a witness of σ if

$$\|w - p\| \leq \|w - q\| \quad \forall p \in \sigma \text{ and } \forall q \in L \setminus \sigma.$$

See Figure 6.3, for example.

Definition 6.3 (Witness complex)   The witness complex $\mathrm{Wit}(L, W)$ is the complex consisting of all simplexes σ such that any simplex $\tau \subseteq \sigma$ has a witness in W. In other words, $\mathrm{Wit}(L, W)$ is the maximal simplicial complex with the property that all its simplices have a witness in W.

In this section, we use the Euclidean distance to define witness complexes but the definition is general and extend to more general metric spaces and, in particular, to finite metric spaces where the only information we have about the input points is the distances between any two of them. In Euclidean space, the only predicates involved in the construction of $\mathrm{Wit}(L, W)$ are (squared) distance comparisons, i.e., polynomials of degree 2 in the coordinates of the points. This is to be compared with the predicate that decides whether a point lies inside the ball circumscribing a d-simplex, whose degree depends on d (see Exercise 4.5).

6.2.1 Identity of Witness and Delaunay Complexes

When the points W and L live in Euclidean space, the witness complex can be seen as a weak Delaunay complex. The results here make this connection more precise. We first make the following easy observation.

Lemma 6.4 *If $W' \subseteq W$, then $\mathrm{Wit}(L, W') \subseteq \mathrm{Wit}(L, W)$.*

Let Ω be a subset of $\mathbb{R}^d$. As before (see Section 5.1.2), we write $\mathrm{Del}_{|\Omega}(L)$ for the restriction of $\mathrm{Del}(L)$ to Ω, i.e., the subcomplex of $\mathrm{Del}(L)$ whose simplices have a circumcenter in Ω.

Lemma 6.5 *Let Ω be a subset of $\mathbb{R}^d$. $\mathrm{Del}_{|\Omega}(L) \subseteq \mathrm{Wit}(L, \Omega)$.*

Proof By definition, any simplex σ of $\mathrm{Del}_{|\Omega}(L)$ has an empty circumscribing ball whose center c belongs to Ω. This center is a witness of σ, and it is also a witness for all the faces of σ. $\square$

The following remarkable result provides a weak characterization of Delaunay complexes. It shows that Delaunay and witness complexes are identical when the set of witnesses cover the whole space $\mathbb{R}^d$.

Theorem 6.6 (Weak characterization) *For any convex $\Omega \subseteq \mathbb{R}^d$ and any finite point set $L \subset \Omega$, we have $\mathrm{Wit}(L, \Omega) = \mathrm{Del}_{|\Omega}(L)$.*

Proof We have already proved that $\mathrm{Del}_{|\Omega}(L) \subseteq \mathrm{Wit}(L, \Omega)$ (Lemma 6.5). We prove now the converse inclusion by an induction on the dimension k of the simplices. The claim holds for $k = 0$ because any vertex of $\mathrm{Wit}(L, \Omega)$ is a point of L and thus a vertex of $\mathrm{Del}_{|\Omega}(L)$.

Assume now that any simplex of $\mathrm{Wit}(L, \Omega)$ of dimension up to $k - 1$ is a simplex of $\mathrm{Del}_{|\Omega}(L)$ and let $\tau = [p_0, \ldots, p_k]$ be a k-simplex of $\mathrm{Wit}(L, \Omega)$ witnessed by a point w. We will say for convenience that a ball B witnesses τ if $B \cap L = \tau$. We denote by B_τ be the smallest ball centered at w that witnesses τ and by S_τ the sphere bounding B_τ.

If all the vertices of τ belong to S_τ, τ is a Delaunay simplex and we are done. Otherwise, we will show that one can find a new ball that witnesses τ such that its bounding sphere contains one more vertex of τ than S_τ. Refer to Figure 6.4. Write $\sigma = S_\tau \cap \tau$. By the induction hypothesis, σ is a simplex of $\mathrm{Del}_{|\Omega}(L)$ and therefore there exists an empty ball B_σ centered in Ω that circumscribes σ. Write c for its center. Consider the set of balls F centered on the line segment $s = [wc] \subset \Omega$ and circumscribing σ. Any ball in F is included in $B_\tau \cup B_\sigma$ and it circumscribes σ. Hence its interior contains no point of $L \setminus \tau$. Moreover, because the interior of B_σ is empty but the interior of B_τ is not, there exists a point z on s such that the ball of F centered at z, witnesses τ and contains $|\sigma| + 1$ points of τ on its boundary. Call this new ball B_τ. We can then carry on the induction and obtain a witness ball B_τ whose bounding sphere contains all the vertices of τ. Such a ball is thus a Delaunay ball and τ is a Delaunay simplex. $\square$

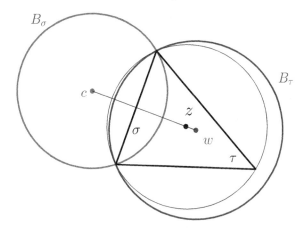

Figure 6.4 Proof of Lemma 6.6.

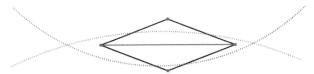

Figure 6.5 Two triangles that have a witness but not their common edge, even if $W = \mathbb{R}^d$. These two triangles are not Delaunay triangles.

It is worth noticing that, for a simplex σ to belong to the witness complex, we required all the faces of σ to have a witness. As illustrated in Figure 6.5, this is mandatory for the theorem to hold.

We deduce from Lemma 6.4 and Theorem 6.6 the following corollary

Corollary 6.7 *Let Ω be a convex subset of $\mathbb{R}^d$ and let $W \subseteq \Omega$. We have* $\mathrm{Wit}(L, W) \subseteq \mathrm{Del}_{|\Omega}(L) \subseteq \mathrm{Del}(L)$.

If the points L are in general position with respect to spheres, we know that $\mathrm{Del}(L)$ is embedded in $\mathbb{R}^d$ by Delaunay's theorem 4.3. It therefore follows from Corollary 6.7 that the same is true for $\mathrm{Wit}(L, W)$. In particular, the dimension of $\mathrm{Wit}(L, W)$ is at most d. When W is not the whole space $\mathbb{R}^d$ but a finite set of points, Theorem 6.6 no longer holds. However, the following lemma shows that both complexes are identical provided that W is dense enough and L is protected enough (refer to Section 5.4 for a definition of protection).

Lemma 6.8 (Identity from protection) *Let Ω be a convex subset of $\mathbb{R}^d$ and let W and L be two finite sets of points in Ω. If W is ε-dense in Ω and if all*

simplices (of all dimensions) of $\mathrm{Del}_{|\Omega}(L)$ are δ-protected with $\delta \geq 2\varepsilon$, then $\mathrm{Wit}(L, W)) = \mathrm{Del}_{|\Omega}(L)$.

Proof By Corollary 6.7, we have $\mathrm{Wit}(L, W) \subseteq \mathrm{Del}_{|\Omega}(L)$. We now prove the other inclusion. Let σ be a simplex in $\mathrm{Del}_{|\Omega}(L)$. By hypothesis, σ is δ-protected. Then there exists a point $c \in \Omega$ such that

$$\forall p \in \sigma, \ \forall q \in L \setminus \sigma, \quad \|c - p\| \leq \|c - q\| - \delta.$$

Because W is ε-dense in Ω, there exists a point $w \in W$ such that $\|w - c\| \leq \varepsilon$. Using the triangular inequality, we have for any $p \in \sigma$ and $q \in L \setminus \sigma$

$$\begin{aligned}
\|w - p\| &\leq \|w - c\| + (\|c - q\| - \delta) \\
&\leq \|w - q\| + 2\|w - c\| - \delta \\
&\leq \|w - q\| + 2\varepsilon - \delta
\end{aligned}$$

Hence, when $\delta \geq 2\varepsilon$, w is a witness for σ. □

This lemma requires the simplices of all dimensions to be δ-protected. In fact it is sufficient to check d-simplices only. Indeed, it can be proved that if the d-dimensional simplices are δ'-protected, for δ' slightly bigger than δ, then all simplices of all dimensions are also protected. See Exercise 5.11.

6.2.2 Computing Witness Complexes

Let L and W be two finite sets of points and $\mathrm{Wit}(L, W)$ their witness complex. We assume, for convenience, that no two points of L are at the same distance from a point in W. We describe how to compute the k-skeleton of $\mathrm{Wit}(L, W)$, denoted by $\mathrm{Wit}^k(L, W)$, for any fixed k.

Let M be a matrix of size $|W| \times k$. The lines in M are associated to the elements of W and the line $M(w)$ associated to $w \in W$ stores the list of the k landmarks that are closest to w, sorted by increasing distance from w (M can be trivially computed in time $O(|W| \times |L| \log |L|)$ and, with more clever algorithms, in time $O(|W| (\log |W| + k))$ time) (see the Bibliographical Notes in Section 6.4). We write $M(w) = (M_1(w), \ldots, M_k(w))$. Algorithm 7 below computes $\mathrm{Wit}^k(L, W)$ from M. We assume without real loss of generality that $L \subset W$.

Under this general position assumption, the number of i-simplices of $\mathrm{Wit}(L, W)$ is at most $|W|$ for any $i \leq k$. Hence, the total number of simplices of $\mathrm{Wit}^k(L, W)$ is at most $k|W| = O(|W|)$.

The total number of for loops that are executed is $|\mathrm{Wit}^k(L, W)| + |W| = O(|W|)$. Indeed, each loop either constructs a new simplex or removes a point

---

Algorithm 7: Construction of the k-skeleton of a witness complex

---

Input: W a finite point set, $L \subset W$, k, M

$\mathrm{Wit}^k(L, W) := \emptyset$

$W' := W$ {a set of active witnesses}

for $i = 0, \ldots, k - 1$ **do**

  for each $w \in W'$ **do**

    if the i-simplex $\sigma(w) = [M_1(w), \ldots, M_{i+1}(w)] \notin \mathrm{Wit}^k(L, W)$ **then**

      if all the $(i - 1)$-faces of $\sigma(w)$ are in $\mathrm{Wit}^k(L, W)$ **then**

      add $\sigma(w)$ to $\mathrm{Wit}^k(L, W)$

    else

      $W' := W' \setminus \{w\}$

Output: $\mathrm{Wit}^k(L, W)$

---

from the set of active witnesses W'. A loop has to decide if a i-simplex as well as its i facets belong to the current complex $\mathrm{Wit}^k(L, W)$. Each of these tests can be done in time $O(\log |L|)$ if one uses for example the simplex tree described in Exercise 2.1. Because $i \leq k$, the cost of a single loop is thus $O(k \log |L|)$. The overall complexity of the algorithm is therefore $O(k |W| \log |L|)$.

The algorithm is general and applies to any distance matrix M. In the case where L and W belong to $\mathbb{R}^d$, and if the points of L are in general position with respect to spheres, we know that $\mathrm{Wit}(L, W)$ is a subcomplex of $\mathrm{Del}(L)$ and thus embedded in $\mathbb{R}^d$ and of dimension at most d. Hence, the entire witness complex is computed if one takes $k = d$.

6.2.3 Relaxed Witness Complexes

As before, W and L denote two sets of points in some subset $\Omega \subset \mathbb{R}^d$. L is finite.

Definition 6.9 (Relaxed witness) Let σ be a simplex with vertices in L. We say that a point $w \in W$ is an α-witness of σ if

$$\|w - p\| \leq \|w - q\| + \alpha \quad \forall p \in \sigma \quad \text{and} \quad \forall q \in L \setminus \sigma.$$

Definition 6.10 (Relaxed witness complex) The α-relaxed witness complex $\mathrm{Wit}^\alpha(L, W)$ is the maximal simplicial complex with vertex set L whose simplices have an α-witness in W.

For $\alpha = 0$, the relaxed witness complex is the standard witness complex. The parameter α defines a filtration on the witness complex, which can be used to compute persistent homology (Chapter 11.5).

Construction

We adapt Algorithm 7. At each step j, we insert, for each witness w, the j-dimensional simplices that are α-witnessed by w. Differently from the standard witness complex, there may be more than one j-simplex that is witnessed by a given witness $w \in W$. Consequently, we do not maintain a pointer from each active witness to the last inserted simplex it witnesses. We use simple top-down insertions from the root of the simplex tree 2.7.

Given a witness w and a dimension j, we generate all the j-dimensional simplices that are α-witnessed by w. For the ease of exposition, we suppose we are given the sorted list of nearest neighbors of w in L, noted $\{z_0 \cdots z_{|L|-1}\}$, and their distance to w, noted $m_i = \mathrm{d}(w, z_i)$, with $m_0 \leq \cdots \leq m_{|L|-1}$, breaking ties arbitrarily. Note that if one wants to construct only the k-skeleton of the complex, it is sufficient to know the list of neighbors of w that are at distance at most $m_k + \alpha$ from w. We preprocess this list of neighbors for all witnesses. For $i \in \{0, \cdots, |L| - 1\}$, we define the set A_i of landmarks z such that $m_i \leq \mathrm{d}(w, z) \leq m_i + \alpha$. For $i \leq j + 1$, w α-witnesses all the j-simplices that contain $\{z_0, \cdots, z_{i-1}\}$ and a $(j + 1 - i)$-subset of A_i, provided $|A_i| \geq j + 1 - i$. We see that all j-simplices that are α-witnessed by w are obtained this way, and exactly once, when i ranges from 0 to $j + 1$.

For all $i \in \{0, \cdots, j + 1\}$, we compute A_i and generate all the simplices which contain $\{z_0, \cdots, z_{i-1}\}$ and a subset of A_i of size $(j + 1 - i)$. In order to easily update A_i when i is incremented, we maintain two pointers to the list of neighbors, one to z_i and the other to the end of A_i. We check in constant time if A_i contains more than $j + 1 - i$ vertices, and compute all the subsets of A_i of cardinality $j + 1 - i$ accordingly. See Figure 6.6.

Restricted Delaunay Complex and Relaxed Witness Complex

We consider now the case where $\Omega \subseteq \mathbb{R}^d$ is not necessarily convex and extend Lemma 6.8. Specifically, we will show that, for a large enough relaxation, $\mathrm{Del}_{|\Omega}(L)$ is contained in the relaxed witness complex.

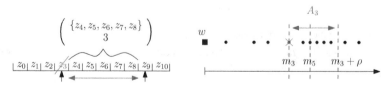

Figure 6.6 Computation of the α-witnessed simplices σ of dimension 5. If z_3 is the first neighbor of w not in σ, then σ contains in particular $\{z_0, z_1, z_2\}$ and any 3-uplet of $A_3 = \{z_4, \cdots, z_8\}$.

Lemma 6.11 *Let Ω be a subset of $\mathbb{R}^d$ (not necessarily convex). Assume that W is ε-dense in Ω and that all the simplices of $\mathrm{Del}_{|\Omega}(L)$ are δ-protected. If $\alpha \geq \max(0, 2\varepsilon - \delta)$, then $\mathrm{Del}_{|\Omega}(L) \subseteq \mathrm{Wit}^\alpha(L, W)$.*

Proof   Let σ be a d-simplex of $\mathrm{Del}_{|\Omega}(L)$ and write c_σ for its circumcenter. Since W is ε-dense in Ω, there exists a point w in W such that $\|c_\sigma - w\| \leq \varepsilon$. For any $p \in \sigma$ and $q \in L \setminus \sigma$, we then have

$$\begin{aligned}
\|w - p\| &\leq \|c_\sigma - p\| + \|c_\sigma - w\| \\
&\leq \|c_\sigma - q\| - \delta + \|c_\sigma - w\| \\
&\leq \|w - q\| + 2\|c_\sigma - w\| - \delta \\
&\leq \|w - q\| + 2\varepsilon - \delta,
\end{aligned}$$

which proves the lemma.   □

Note that if $\delta \geq 2\varepsilon$, the lemma gives $\mathrm{Del}_{|\Omega}(L) \subseteq \mathrm{Wit}(L, W)$ (as in Lemma 6.8).

6.3 Exercises

Exercise 6.1 (Full classification with respect to the α-complex)   Let $\hat{P}$ be a set of weighted points in $\mathbb{R}^d$. Each simplex τ of the Delaunay triangulation $\mathrm{Del}(\hat{P})$ can be classified with respect to the α-complex $\mathcal{A}(\hat{P}, \alpha)$ as *external* if it does not belong to $\mathcal{A}(\hat{P}, \alpha)$, *singular* if it belongs to $\mathcal{A}(\hat{P}, \alpha)$ but none of its coface in $\mathrm{Del}(\hat{P})$ does, *boundary* if it belongs to the boundary of α-complex and is not singular, which means that some of its cofaces belong to $\mathcal{A}(\hat{P}, \alpha)$ while others do not, and at last *internal* if it belongs to the interior of the α-complex, meaning that all its cofaces belong to $\mathcal{A}(\hat{P}, \alpha)$.

Modify Algorithm 6 so that it computes for any simplex τ of $\mathrm{Del}(\hat{P})$, the at most three values of the parameter α where the status of the simplex changes from external to singular and then to boundary and interior.

Exercise 6.2 (Weighted witness complex)   Show that the witness complex can be extended to weighted points and the weighted distance. Show that the identity results of Section 6.2.1 still hold when the Delaunay complex is replaced by its weighted counterpart.

Exercise 6.3   Show that, if L is a λ-sample of $\mathbb{R}^d$, the circumradius R_σ of any simplex σ in $\mathrm{Wit}(L, W)$ is at most λ. (Hint : Use Corollary 6.7).

Exercise 6.4 (Relaxed Delaunay complex) Let W and L be two finite sets of points in $\Omega \subset \mathbb{R}^d$. Let σ be a simplex with vertices in L. We say that a point $w \in W$ is an α-center of σ if

$$\|w - p\| \le \|w - q\| + \alpha \quad \forall p \in \sigma \quad \text{and} \quad \forall q \in L.$$

The α-relaxed Delaunay complex $\text{Del}^\alpha(L, W)$ is the maximal simplicial complex with vertex set L whose d-simplices have an α-center in W. Show how to construct $\text{Del}^\alpha(L, W)$. Prove that $\text{Del}(L) \subseteq \text{Del}^\alpha(L, W)$ for $\alpha \ge 2\varepsilon$ if W is an ε-sample of Ω.

6.4 Bibliographical Notes

Alpha-shapes were introduced by Edelsbrunner, Kirkpatrick and Seidel [73, 76]. Alpha-shapes are also widely used to represent union of balls [68] and to study the structure of macro molecules and various related problems like the docking of two molecules, see, e.g., [71, 100, 72].

Witness complexes and relaxed Delaunay triangulations have been introduced in the seminal work of de Silva [62] who first proved Theorem 6.6 and several of its variants including the case of weighted points (Exercise 6.2). The proof presented in Section 6.2 is due to Attali et al. [4]. The 1-skeleton of the witness complex has been introduced earlier by Martinez and Schulten [104]. They showed that $\text{Del}(L)$ and $\text{Wit}(L, \mathbb{R}^d)$ have the same 1-skeleton and they proposed a dynamic algorithm for approximating the topology of a region of space, by a graph represented as a neural network.

The identity of witness and Delaunay complexes when the number of witnesses is finite is taken from [15]. The paper describes an algorithm to obtain $\text{Del}(L)$ from $\text{Wit}(L, W)$ using the algorithmic version of the local Lovász lemma (see Exercise 5.12 and Section 5.3.4). The paper also describes an algorithm to compute the relaxed Delaunay complex in time sublinear in the number of witnesses (Exercise 6.4).

Given a set of n points $P \subset \mathbb{R}^d$, one can construct a data structure called a well-separated pair decomposition. This data structure has many applications and can be used, in particular, to compute the k-nearest neighbors of all the points in P in time $O(n \log n + kn)$ [33]. See the book of Har-Peled for a recent account on well-separated decompositions [94].

PART III

RECONSTRUCTION OF SMOOTH SUBMANIFOLDS

7

Triangulation of Submanifolds

Triangulating an object $\mathcal{M}$ entails computing a simplicial complex which is homeomorphic to $\mathcal{M}$. This is a demanding quest and, in this chapter, we will assume that $\mathcal{M}$ is a smooth and compact submanifold of $\mathbb{R}^d$ without boundary. The main goal of the chapter is to prove Theorem 7.16 that provides sufficient conditions under which a simplicial complex $\hat{\mathcal{M}}$ is a triangulation of a submanifold $\mathcal{M}$ of $\mathbb{R}^d$. These conditions require the simplices to be sufficiently small and thick and rely on the concepts of reach and of ε-net on a manifold. To prove the theorem, we will prove that the projection map that associates to a point of $\hat{\mathcal{M}}$ its closest point on $\mathcal{M}$ is a homeomorphism. The results of this chapter will be used in Chapter 8 to triangulate a submanifold $\mathcal{M}$ given only a finite point set on $\mathcal{M}$.

7.1 Reach and ε-nets on Submanifolds

7.1.1 Submanifolds

Given an open set $U \subseteq \mathbb{R}^d$ and a non-negative integer c, a map $\phi : U \to \mathbb{R}^d$ is said to be *c-differentiable*, or *of class $\mathcal{C}^c$* on U if its successive derivatives up to order c are well-defined and continuous on U. In particular, a 0-differentiable map is a continuous map. If moreover, $\phi : U \to V = \phi(U)$ is a bijection and $\phi^{-1} : V \to U$ is also c-differentiable, then ϕ is said to be a *c-differentiable diffeomorphism*.

Definition 7.1 (Submanifold) A compact subset $\mathcal{M} \subset \mathbb{R}^d$ is a c-differentiable submanifold of dimension $k \leq d$, if for any $p \in \mathcal{M}$ there exist an open set $U \subset R^d$ containing p, a c-differentiable diffeomorphism ϕ from U to an open set $V \subset \mathbb{R}^d$, and an affine k-dimensional subspace $A \subset \mathbb{R}^d$ such that

$$\phi(U \cap \mathcal{M}) = A \cap V.$$

115

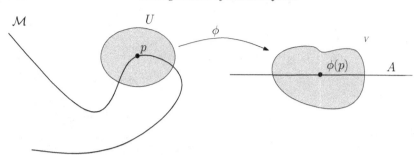

Figure 7.1 A k-dimensional submanifold M of $\mathbb{R}^d$ (here $k = 1$ and $d = 2$) is a subset of $\mathbb{R}^d$ that is locally diffeomorphic to an open set of a k-dimensional affine subspace.

Intuitively, a submanifold of dimension k is a subset of $\mathbb{R}^d$ that is locally homeomorphic to an affine space of dimension k (see Figure 7.1). A *curve* is a 1-dimensional submanifold of $\mathbb{R}^d$, and a *surface* is a 2-dimensional submanifold of $\mathbb{R}^d$. The submanifolds we will consider are differentiable and have no boundary, even if not explicitly mentioned.

The *tangent space* $T_p\mathcal{M}$ of a c-differentiable ($c > 0$) submanifold $\mathcal{M}$ at a point $p \in \mathcal{M}$ is the vector space spanned by the tangent vectors $\gamma'(0)$ where $\gamma : (-1, 1) \to M \subset \mathbb{R}^d$ belongs to the set of differentiable curves contained in M such that $\gamma(0) = p$. If $\mathcal{M}$ is of dimension k, then $T_p\mathcal{M}$ is a k-dimensional vector space. By an abuse of notation, we will also denote by $T_p\mathcal{M}$ the affine subspace spanned by $T_p\mathcal{M}$ and passing through p and we will denote by $N_p\mathcal{M}$ the $(d - k)$-dimensional affine subspace orthogonal to $T_p\mathcal{M}$ (see Figure 7.2). In the sequel, to avoid heavy notation, when there is no ambiguity, we will drop the reference to $\mathcal{M}$ and denote $T_p\mathcal{M}$ and $N_p\mathcal{M}$ by T_p and N_p, respectively.

In this chapter, we focus on submanifolds and do not consider manifolds defined in an intrinsic way, independently of any embedding in $\mathbb{R}^d$. However, the main results of the chapter and in particular the triangulation theorem (Theorem 7.16) can be extended to intrinsic smooth manifolds. See the bibliographical notes.

7.1.2 Projection Map, Medial Axis, and Reach

Let $\mathcal{M}$ be a submanifold of $\mathbb{R}^d$. The *medial axis* of $\mathcal{M}$ is defined as the closure of the set of points $x \in \mathbb{R}^d$ that have more than one closest point on $\mathcal{M}$ (see Figure 7.3). We denote it by $\text{ax}(\mathcal{M})$.

We can associate to each point of $\text{ax}(\mathcal{M})$ a ball that is centered at that point, whose interior does not intersect $\mathcal{M}$ and that is maximal for inclusion. Such a ball will be called a *medial ball*.

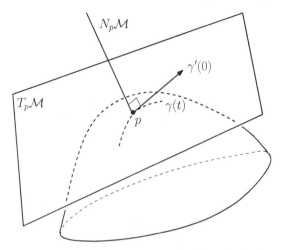

Figure 7.2 The tangent and normal spaces to a two-dimensional submanifold $\mathcal{M}$ of $\mathbb{R}^3$ at a point $p \in \mathcal{M}$.

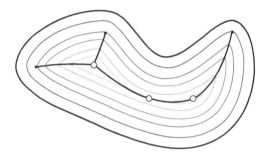

Figure 7.3 The medial axis of a closed curve. We only show the component of the medial axis that is contained in the domain bounded by the curve. Various offsets of the curve are also shown as thin curves.

We define the *projection onto* $\mathcal{M}$ as the mapping

$$\Pi : \mathbb{R}^d \setminus \text{ax}(\mathcal{M}) \to \mathcal{M}$$

that maps a point x to its (unique) closest point on $\mathcal{M}$.

The *reach* of $\mathcal{M}$, written $\text{rch}(\mathcal{M})$, is the infimum of the distance from a point of $\mathcal{M}$ to the medial axis $\text{ax}(\mathcal{M})$. As we will see, the reach encodes both local curvature considerations as well as global ones.

In this chapter, we will restrict our attention to the class of submanifolds of $\mathbb{R}^d$ with positive reach introduced by Federer [81]. This class includes all submanifolds of class C^2 and also some submanifolds whose principal curvatures may be discontinuous on subsets of measure 0. An example of such a submanifold is the *r-offset* of a solid cube, i.e., the set of points at distance at most r from the cube.

We now state some properties of submanifolds with positive reach.

Lemma 7.2 (Tubular neighborhood) *Let $\mathcal{M}$ be a manifold with positive reach* $\mathrm{rch}(\mathcal{M})$ *and let $B_{N_p}(r)$ be the intersection of the ball $B(p,r)$ with the normal space at p. If $r < \mathrm{rch}(\mathcal{M})$, then, for every point $x \in B_{N_p}(r)$, $\Pi(x) = p$.*

The proof of this lemma for C^2 submanifolds follows from rather standard arguments in differential geometry. The result for submanifolds of positive reach is due to Federer [81]. From Lemma 7.2, we easily deduce the following lemma.

Lemma 7.3 *Let $\mathcal{M}$ be a submanifold of positive reach, and let $x \in \mathcal{M}$. Any open ball that is tangent to $\mathcal{M}$ at x and whose radius is at most $\mathrm{rch}(M)$ does not intersect $\mathcal{M}$.*

Proof Let $B(c,r)$ be a ball tangent to $\mathcal{M}$ at x and assume that $r < \mathrm{rch}(\mathcal{M})$. If the intersection of $\mathcal{M}$ and the open ball $B(c,r)$ is not empty, then $\Pi(c) \neq x$, contradicting Lemma 7.2. The result for $r = \mathrm{rch}(\mathcal{M})$ now follows by taking the limit. □

Lemma 7.4 *Let B be a closed ball that intersects $\mathcal{M}$. If $B \cap \mathcal{M}$ is not a topological ball, then B contains a point of the medial axis of $\mathcal{M}$.*

Proof Write c for the center of B. The result is trivial when c belongs to the medial axis of $\mathcal{M}$. Therefore assume that $c \notin \mathrm{ax}(\mathcal{M})$.

Let y be the (unique) point of $\mathcal{M}$ closest to c. We denote by B_y the closed ball centered at c with radius $\|c - y\|$ (see Figure 7.4). Plainly, the interior of B_y does not intersect $\mathcal{M}$ and $B_y \cap \mathcal{M} = \{y\}$, otherwise c would be a point of

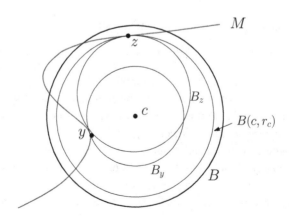

Figure 7.4 For the proof of Lemma 7.4.

the medial axis. Hence y is an isolated critical point of the distance function from c, i.e., the function $d_c : \mathbb{R}^d \to \mathbb{R}$, $d_c(x) = \|x - c\|$. d_c is minimal at y and, for a small enough radius r strictly larger than $\|y - c\|$, $B(c, r) \cap \mathcal{M}$ is a topological ball of the same dimension as $\mathcal{M}$. Because $B \cap \mathcal{M}$ is not a topological ball, it follows from a basic result in Differential Topology [105, Theorem 3.1][1] that there exists another critical point of d_c, say $z \in \mathcal{M}, z \neq y$, such that $r_c = \|c - z\| > \|c - y\|$ and the ball $B(c, r_c)$ is tangent to $\mathcal{M}$ at z. Consider the set $\mathcal{B}_z$ of closed balls that are tangent to $\mathcal{M}$ at z and are centered on the line segment $[zc]$. Note that $B(c, r_c)$ is the ball of $\mathcal{B}_z$ centered at c. Since the interior of $B(c, r_c)$ contains y and therefore intersects $\mathcal{M}$, there must exist a ball $B_z \in \mathcal{B}_z$ maximal for the inclusion whose interior does not intersect $\mathcal{M}$. The center of B_z belongs to $\mathrm{ax}(\mathcal{M})$ and also to B since $B_z \subset B(c, r_c) \subset B$. The lemma is proved. □

If $x \in \mathcal{M}$, $B(x, r)$ cannot intersect the medial axis of $\mathcal{M}$ for any $r < \mathrm{rch}(x)$. Lemma 7.4 thus implies

Corollary 7.5 *For any x of $\mathcal{M}$, and any $r < \mathrm{rch}(x)$, the intersection of $\mathcal{M}$ with the ball $B(x, r)$ centered at x of radius r is a topological ball.*

Assume that we are given a finite set of points P on $\mathcal{M}$ and let $\mathrm{Vor}(P)$ be the Voronoi diagram of P in the ambient space $\mathbb{R}^d$. The following lemma shows that the Voronoi cell of any $p \in P$ has a large extent in the normal space N_p at p.

Lemma 7.6 *Let $p \in P \subset \mathcal{M}$ and write N_p for the normal space of $\mathcal{M}$ at p. Then the ambient Voronoi cell $V(p)$ of p has a large extent in N_p. Specifically, $B(p, \mathrm{rch}(\mathcal{M})) \cap N_p \subset V(p)$, where $B(c, r)$ denotes, as usual, the open ball centered at c of radius r.*

Proof Suppose $w \in (B(p, \mathrm{rch}(\mathcal{M})) \cap N_p) \setminus V(p)$. Then the line segment $[pw]$ crosses the boundary of $V(p)$ at some point z and there exists some $u \in P \subset \mathcal{M}$, distinct from p, such that $\|z - u\| = \|z - p\|$. Because $z \in N_p$, p is the closest point to z on $\mathcal{M}$, and we have reached a contradiction with the definition of the reach. □

7.1.3 ε-nets on a Submanifold

We give a variant of the definition of ε-nets introduced in Section 5.1. This new definition is better adapted to the case of point samples on a submanifold and is sensitive to the reach of the manifold.

---

[1] Let $a = d_c(y)$ and $b = r$ and suppose that the set $d_c^{-1}(a, b)$, consisting of all $p \in \mathcal{M}$ with $a \leq d_c(p) \leq b$, contains no critical points of d_c (i.e., no point q of $\mathcal{M}$ where $B(c, \|c - q\|)$ is tangent to $\mathcal{M}$). Then $\mathcal{M}^a = \{x \in \mathcal{M}, d_c \leq a\}$ is homeomorphic to $\mathcal{M}^b = \{x \in \mathcal{M}, d_c \leq b\}$.

Definition 7.7 ($(\varepsilon, \bar{\eta})$-net)   Let $\mathcal{M}$ be a submanifold of $\mathbb{R}^d$ of positive reach. A finite point set $P \subset \mathcal{M}$ is called an $(\varepsilon, \bar{\eta})$-net of $\mathcal{M}$ if it is

1. ε-**dense:** any point x of $\mathcal{M}$ is at distance at most $\varepsilon \operatorname{rch}(\mathcal{M})$ from a point of P (the distance is the Euclidean distance in $\mathbb{R}^d$),
2. η-**separated:** for any two points p, q of P, $\|p - q\| \geq \eta \operatorname{rch}(\mathcal{M})$, where $\eta = \bar{\eta}\,\varepsilon$.

We call ε the sampling radius of P and $\bar{\eta}$ the separation ratio of P. Note that, differently from Section 5.1, ε here is a dimensionless quantity.

This definition does not allow the sampling radius to vary over the submanifold. Hence, we are confined to uniform samples, which may be quite restrictive in practice. The results of this chapter can be extended to nonuniform ε-nets but, in order to keep the exposition simple and better outline the key ideas, we will restrict our attention to *uniform ε-nets*. We leave the extension to nonuniform ε-nets as an exercise (Exercise 7.4). See also the bibliographical notes.

7.2 Projection Maps

In the rest of this chapter, $\mathcal{M}$ denotes a submanifold of $\mathbb{R}^d$ of positive reach $\operatorname{rch}(\mathcal{M})$. The tangent space at $x \in \mathcal{M}$ is denoted by T_x. The angle between two vector subspaces U and V of $\mathbb{R}^d$ is denoted by $\angle(U, V)$ (see Section 5.2.2 for a definition).

If σ is a simplex, we denote by $\Delta(\sigma)$ its diameter (i.e., the length of its longest edge) and $\Theta(\sigma)$ its thickness. We further write for convenience $\Delta(\sigma) = \delta(\sigma) \operatorname{rch}(\mathcal{M})$.

Lemma 7.8   *Let p and q be two points of $\mathcal{M}$. We have*

1. $\sin \angle(pq, T_p) \leq \frac{\|p-q\|}{2\operatorname{rch}(\mathcal{M})}$;
2. *the distance from q to T_p is at most $\frac{\|p-q\|^2}{2\operatorname{rch}(\mathcal{M})}$.*

Proof   1. Let q' be the orthogonal projection of q onto T_p and let H be the plane (pqq'). Let in addition D be the open disk of H of radius $\operatorname{rch}(\mathcal{M})$ that is tangent to $\mathcal{M}$ at p and whose center c is on the same side of $T_p \cap H$ as q (Refer to Figure 7.5). Because D is tangent to $\mathcal{M}$ and its radius is $\operatorname{rch}(\mathcal{M})$, it follows from Lemma 7.3 that $d(c, \mathcal{M}) = \|c - p\|$ and that D does not intersect $\mathcal{M}$. Hence, q does not belong to the interior of D (Lemma 7.3). Assume that the line segment $[pq]$ intersects the boundary of D in a point q'' distinct from p. We have

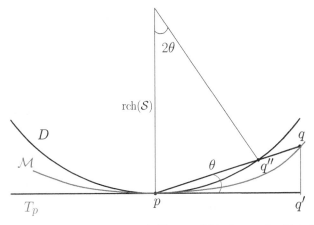

Figure 7.5 An illustration of the proof of Lemma 7.8 in the case in which $\mathcal{M}$ is a curve of $\mathbb{R}^2$. $\theta = \angle(pq, T_p)$.

$$\|p - q\| \geq \|p - q''\| = 2\,\mathrm{rch}(\mathcal{M})\,\sin\angle(pq, T_p),$$

which proves the first statement.

2. We have $\|q - q'\| = \|p - q\|\,\sin\angle(pq, T_p) \leq \frac{\|p-q\|^2}{2\,\mathrm{rch}(\mathcal{M})}$. $\qquad\square$

The previous lemma allows us to bound the Hausdorff distance between $\mathcal{M}$ and a simplex that has its vertices on $\mathcal{M}$.

Lemma 7.9 *Let σ be a simplex with its vertices on $\mathcal{M}$ and assume that $\delta(\sigma) < 1$. Then, for any point $x \in \sigma$, we have $d(x, \mathcal{M}) \leq 2\delta^2(\sigma)\,\mathrm{rch}(\mathcal{M})$.*

Proof Write x' the point of $\mathcal{M}$ closest to x and note that $\|x - x'\| = d(x, \mathcal{M}) = d(x, T_{x'})$. For any vertex p of σ, we have

$$\|p - x'\| \leq \|p - x\| + \|x - x'\| \leq 2\|p - x\| \leq 2\Delta(\sigma) = 2\delta(\sigma)\,\mathrm{rch}(\mathcal{M}).$$

Applying Lemma 7.8, we then get $d(p, T_{x'}) \leq 2\delta^2(\sigma)\,\mathrm{rch}(\mathcal{M})$. This is true for all vertices p of σ and, because the function $d(., T_{x'})$ is affine on σ, it is also true for x and we have $d(x, T_{x'}) = \|x - x'\| \leq 2\delta^2(\sigma)\,\mathrm{rch}(\mathcal{M})$. $\qquad\square$

The following lemma bounds the angle between two tangent spaces. Its proof relies on notions of differential geometry that go beyond the scope of this book. See the Bibliographic Notes (Section 7.5) for references.

Lemma 7.10 (Angle between tangent spaces) *Let $p, q \in \mathcal{M}$. Then $\sin\angle(T_p, T_q) \leq \|p - q\|/\mathrm{rch}(\mathcal{M})$.*

We now introduce the important notion of distortion of a map.

Definition 7.11 (ξ-distortion map) A map $F : U \subset \mathbb{R}^d \to \mathbb{R}^d$ is a ξ-distortion map if for all $x, y \in U$ we have

$$\left| \|F(x) - F(y)\| - \|x - y\| \right| \leq \xi \, \|x - y\|,$$

or equivalently if

$$(1 - \xi) \, \|x - y\| \leq \|F(x) - F(y)\| \leq (1 + \xi) \, \|x - y\|.$$

We will need the next lemma.

Lemma 7.12 *Let U be a subset of $\mathbb{R}^d$. A ξ-distortion map $F : U \to \mathbb{R}^d$ is an embedding (i.e., a homeomorphism onto its image) if $\xi < 1$. If it is smooth, then we have $\left| \|J u\| - 1 \right| \leq \xi$, where J denotes the Jacobian matrix of F and u is any unit vector of $\mathbb{R}^d$.*

Proof Continuity and injectivity directly follow from Definition 7.11. The continuity of the inverse follows from Exercise 7.9. This proves that F is an embedding. The second part of the lemma follows from Definition 7.11. □

We now study two maps that will play a crucial role in proving the main theorem of this chapter (Theorem 7.16). The first map has already been defined. It is the projection $\Pi : \mathbb{R}^d \setminus \mathrm{ax}(\mathcal{M}) \to \mathcal{M}$ that maps a point to its closest point on $\mathcal{M}$.

We show now that Π is Lipschitz continuous in a neighborhood of $\mathcal{M}$, and that its restriction to a simplex with vertices on $\mathcal{M}$ has a *distortion* that is bounded as a function of the diameter and of the thickness of the simplex.

Lemma 7.13 (Distortion of Π) *1. Let x and y be two points of $\mathbb{R}^d \setminus \mathrm{ax}(\mathcal{M})$. Write $x' = \Pi(x)$ and $y' = \Pi(y)$ for their (unique) projections onto $\mathcal{M}$. If $\|x - x'\| \leq \alpha \, \mathrm{rch}(\mathcal{M})$ and $\|y - y'\| \leq \alpha \, \mathrm{rch}(\mathcal{M})$ with $\alpha < 1$, then $\|x' - y'\| \leq \frac{1}{1-\alpha} \|x - y\|$.*
2. Let σ be a simplex with its vertices on $\mathcal{M}$, and assume that $\Theta(\sigma) \geq 5\delta(\sigma)$. Then the restriction of Π to σ is a ξ-distortion map where $\xi = 4\delta^2(\sigma) + \frac{16\delta^2(\sigma)}{\Theta^2(\sigma)} < 1$ and thus embeds σ in $\mathcal{M}$

Proof Refer to Figure 7.6. Let $\theta_x = \angle(y' - x', T_{x'})$ and $\theta_y = \angle(y' - x', T_{y'})$. From Lemma 7.8, both $\sin \theta_x$ and $\sin \theta_y$ are bounded by

$$\frac{\|y' - x'\|}{2 \, \mathrm{rch}(\mathcal{M})}. \tag{7.1}$$

1. Let x'' and y'' be the orthogonal projections of x and y onto the line $(x'y')$. Let H_x be the hyperplane passing through x' and orthogonal to xx', and

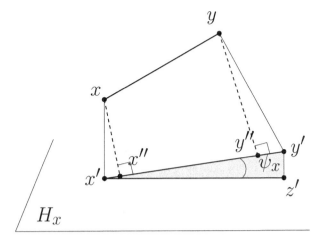

Figure 7.6 For the proof of Lemma 7.13 (1).

write $\psi_x = \angle(x' - y', H_x)$ and observe that $\psi_x = \frac{\pi}{2} - \angle(x' - y', x - x') = \angle(x' - x, x - x'')$. By definition of angles, $\psi_x \le \theta_x$ since $T_{x'} \subseteq H_x$. Using (7.1), we have

$$\|x' - x''\| = \|x - x'\| \sin \psi_x \le \|x - x'\| \sin \theta_x \le \alpha \operatorname{rch}(\mathcal{M}) \sin \theta_x \le \frac{\alpha}{2} \|y' - x'\|.$$

Likewise : $\|y' - y''\| = \le \frac{\alpha}{2} \|y' - x'\|$. So

$$\|x - y\| \ge \|x'' - y''\| \ge \|y' - x'\| - \|x' - x''\| - \|y' - y''\| \ge (1 - \alpha) \|y' - x'\|.$$

The first part of the lemma follows.

2. Refer to Figure 7.7. Let x and y be two points of σ, $x' = \Pi(x)$ and $y' = \Pi(y)$. By Lemma 7.9, we know that $\|x - x'\|$ and $\|y - y'\|$ are at most $\alpha \operatorname{rch}(\mathcal{M})$ where $\alpha = 2\delta^2(\sigma) \le 1/2$.

From the first part of the lemma, we have

$$\|x' - y'\| \le \frac{1}{1 - \alpha} \|x - y\| \le (1 + 2\alpha) \|x - y\| \le 2 \|x - y\| \qquad (7.2)$$

We now prove a lower bound on $\|x' - y'\| / \|x - y\|$.

Let, as before, H_x denote the hyperplane passing through x' and orthogonal to xx'. Let z be the projection of y onto H_x, z' the projection of y' onto H_x and write $\phi = \angle(x - y, x' - z) = \angle(x - y, H_x)$ (see Figure 7.7). We have

$$\|x' - y'\| \ge \|x' - z'\| \ge \|x' - z\| - \|z' - z\| = \|x - y\| \cos \phi - \|z' - z\| \quad (7.3)$$

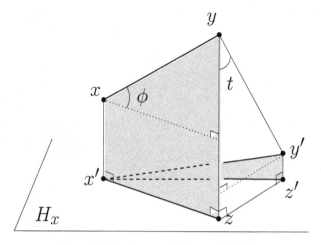

Figure 7.7 For the proof of Lemma 7.13 (2).

Let us bound $\cos \phi$ and $\|z' - z\|$. We have

$$\phi = \angle(x - y, x' - z) = \min_{v \in H_x} \angle(x - y, v)$$
$$\leq \min_{v \in T_{x'}} \angle(x - y, v)$$
$$\leq \max_{u \in \text{aff}(\sigma)} \min_{v \in T_{x'}} \angle(u, v)$$
$$= \angle(\text{aff}(\sigma), T_{x'}).$$

By the proof of Lemma 7.9, the vertices of σ are at distance at most $\alpha \, \text{rch}(\mathcal{M})$ from $T_{x'}$. We then deduce from Lemma 5.14

$$\sin \phi \leq \frac{2\alpha}{\delta(\sigma)\,\Theta(\sigma)} = \frac{4\delta(\sigma)}{\Theta(\sigma)} \quad \text{and so} \quad \cos \phi \geq 1 - \frac{16\,\delta^2(\sigma)}{\Theta^2(\sigma)} \qquad (7.4)$$

Write $\chi = \angle(T_{y'}, H_x) \leq \angle(T_{y'}, T_{x'})$. By Lemma 7.10, we have

$$\sin \chi \leq \frac{\|x' - y'\|}{\text{rch}(\mathcal{M})}.$$

Let $t = \angle(y - z, y - y') \leq \chi$. Using $\|y - y'\| \leq \alpha \, \text{rch}(\mathcal{M})$ and (7.2), we deduce

$$\|z' - z\| = \|y - y'\| \sin t \leq \alpha \|x' - y'\| \leq 2\alpha \|x - y\|. \qquad (7.5)$$

Using (7.3), (7.4) and (7.5) and $\alpha = 2\delta^2(\sigma)$, we get

$$\|x' - y'\| \geq \left(1 - 4\delta^2(\sigma) - \frac{16\delta^2(\sigma)}{\Theta^2(\sigma)}\right) \|x - y\| = (1 - \xi)\|x - y\|.$$

From (7.2) and $\alpha = 2\delta^2(\sigma)$, we also have

$$\|x' - y'\| \leq (1 + 4\delta^2(\sigma)) \|x - y\| \leq (1 + \xi) \|x - y\|.$$

We conclude that

$$(1 - \xi) \|x - y\| \leq \|x' - y'\| \leq (1 + \xi) \|x - y\|.$$

Hence, the restriction of Π to σ is a ξ-distortion map. It then follows from Lemma 7.12 that Π embeds σ in $\mathcal{M}$ if $\xi < 1$.

If $\Theta(\sigma) \geq 5\delta(\sigma)$, we have since $\Theta(\sigma) \leq 1$

$$\xi = 4\delta^2(\sigma) + \frac{16\,\delta^2(\sigma)}{\Theta^2(\sigma)} \leq \frac{20}{25} < 1.$$

$\square$

We introduce now a second map $\Pi_p : \mathbb{R}^d \to T_p$ that maps points of $\mathbb{R}^d$ to its closest point on the tangent space T_p at p. We now bound the distortion of the restriction of Π_p to a neighborhood of a p on $\mathcal{M}$ and of the restriction of Π_p to a simplex.

Lemma 7.14 (Distortion of Π_p)   *Let $p \in \mathcal{M}$, and write $B(p, r)$ for the ball of $\mathbb{R}^d$ centered at p of radius r and $B_{\mathcal{M}}(p, r)$ for $B(p, r) \cap \mathcal{M}$.*

1. *Let ρ be a positive scalar such that $\rho < \frac{1}{2}$ and let $r = \rho \operatorname{rch}(\mathcal{M})$. The restriction of Π_p to $B_{\mathcal{M}}(p, r)$ is a $4\rho^2$-distortion map.*
2. *Let σ be a simplex incident to p with its vertices on $\mathcal{M}$. If $\Theta(\sigma) > \delta(\sigma)$, then the restriction of Π_p to σ is a $\frac{\delta^2(\sigma)}{\Theta^2(\sigma)}$-distortion map which embeds σ in T_p.*

Proof   1. For all x and $y \in B_{\mathcal{M}}(p, r)$, we have from Lemmas 7.8 and 7.10

$$\sin \angle(xy, T_p) \leq \sin \angle(xy, T_x) + \sin \angle(T_x, T_p) \leq 2\rho < 1. \qquad (7.6)$$

Write $x' = \Pi_p(x)$, $y' = \Pi_p(y)$ and $\theta = \angle(xy, T_p)$. Using (7.6), we get

$$\|x - y\| - \|x' - y'\| = \|x - y\| (1 - \cos\theta)$$
$$\leq \|x - y\| (1 - \sqrt{1 - 4\rho^2})$$
$$\leq 4\rho^2 \|x - y\|.$$

Adding the fact that $\|x' - y'\| \leq \|x - y\|$, this shows that the restriction of Π_p to $B_{\mathcal{M}}(p, r)$ is a $4\rho^2$-distortion map. It then follows from Lemma 7.12 that Π_p embeds $B_{\mathcal{M}}(p, r)$ in T_p. This ends the proof of the first part of the lemma.

2. Let $x, y \in \sigma$, $x' = \Pi_p(x)$, $y' = \Pi_p(y)$, and $\phi = \angle(x - y, x' - y') \leq \angle(\mathrm{aff}(\sigma), T_p)$. By Lemma 7.8, the vertices of σ are at distance at most $h \, \mathrm{rch}(\mathcal{M})$ from T_p, where $h = \frac{\delta^2(\sigma)}{2}$. It then follows from Lemma 5.14 that

$$\sin \phi \leq \frac{2h}{\delta(\sigma)\Theta(\sigma)} = \frac{\delta(\sigma)}{\Theta(\sigma)}. \tag{7.7}$$

Using (7.7), we get

$$\|x' - y'\| = \|x - y\| \cos \phi$$

$$\geq \|x - y\| \sqrt{1 - \frac{\delta^2(\sigma)}{\Theta^2(\sigma)}}$$

$$\geq \|x - y\| \left(1 - \frac{\delta^2(\sigma)}{\Theta^2(\sigma)}\right).$$

We deduce

$$\left(1 - \frac{\delta^2(\sigma)}{\Theta^2(\sigma)}\right) \|x - y\| \leq \|x' - y'\| \leq \|x - y\| \leq \left(1 + \frac{\delta^2(\sigma)}{\Theta^2(\sigma)}\right) \|x - y\|$$

The restriction of Π_p to σ is thus a $\frac{\delta^2(\sigma)}{\Theta^2(\sigma)}$-distortion map and Lemma 7.12 ensures that Π_p embeds σ in T_p. This completes the proof of the lemma.

$\square$

7.3 Triangulation of Submanifolds

Definition 7.15 (Triangulation of a topological space)   A triangulation of a topological space X is a simplicial complex K and a homeomorphism $h : |K| \to X$.

The following theorem provides sufficient conditions for a simplicial complex $\hat{\mathcal{M}}$ to be a triangulation of a submanifold $\mathcal{M}$ embedded in $\mathbb{R}^d$. This theorem will be used in Chapter 8 to reconstruct submanifolds from finite point sets. We recall that Π denotes the projection onto $\mathcal{M}$ and Π_p the orthogonal projection onto the tangent space T_p at $p \in \mathcal{M}$.

Theorem 7.16 (Triangulation of submanifolds)   *Let $\mathcal{M}$ be a closed[2] k-submanifold of $\mathbb{R}^d$ of positive reach $\mathrm{rch}(\mathcal{M})$ and let $\hat{\mathcal{M}}$ be a combinatorial k-manifold without boundary embedded in $\mathbb{R}^d$ that satisfies the following assumptions:*

---

[2] i.e., compact and without boundary.

(a) *The vertices of $\hat{\mathcal{M}}$ belong to $\mathcal{M}$ and each connected component of $\mathcal{M}$ contains some vertices of $\mathcal{M}$,*

(b) *The diameter of any k-simplex of $\hat{\mathcal{M}}$ is less than $\Delta_0 = \delta_0 \operatorname{rch}(\mathcal{M})$ where $\delta_0 \leq 1/5$,*

(c) *The thickness of the k-simplices of $\hat{\mathcal{M}}$ is at least $\Theta_0 \geq 9\delta_0^2/\lambda_0$, where $L_0 = \lambda_0 \operatorname{rch}(\mathcal{M})$ is a lower bound on the edge lengths of the simplices,*

(d) *For any vertex $p \in \hat{\mathcal{M}}$, Π_p embeds $\operatorname{star}(p, \hat{\mathcal{M}})$.*

(e) *Let $r = \frac{7}{5}\delta_0 \operatorname{rch}(M)$. Any vertex q of $\hat{\mathcal{M}}$ that belongs to $B(p,r)$ and is mapped by Π_p onto a point $q' \in \Pi_p(\operatorname{star}(p))$ has to be a vertex of $\operatorname{star}(p)$.*

Then the following facts hold:

1. *The restriction of Π to $\hat{\mathcal{M}}$ is a homeomorphism and thus $\hat{\mathcal{M}}$ is a triangulation of $\mathcal{M}$.*

2. *The Hausdorff distance between $\hat{\mathcal{M}}$ and $\mathcal{M}$ is at most $2\delta_0^2 \operatorname{rch}(\mathcal{M})$.*

3. *If σ is a k-simplex of $\hat{\mathcal{M}}$ and p one of its vertices, we have*

$$\sin \angle (\operatorname{aff}(\sigma), T_p) \leq \frac{\delta_0}{\Theta_0}.$$

The proof is given in the following sections. A more general version of the theorem holds. Indeed, we can remove the assumption that the simplicial complex $\hat{\mathcal{M}}$ is embedded in $\mathbb{R}^d$. The fact that the complex is naturally embedded in $\mathbb{R}^d$ is a consequence of this more general version of the theorem. In the sequel, we will denote by P the set of vertices of $\hat{\mathcal{M}}$.

7.3.1 Proof of Statement 1

Write as before Π for the projection onto $\mathcal{M}$ and consider $\Pi_{|\hat{\mathcal{M}}} : \hat{\mathcal{M}} \to \mathcal{M}$, the restriction of Π to $\hat{\mathcal{M}}$. Note that $\Pi_{|\hat{\mathcal{M}}}$ is well defined because $\hat{\mathcal{M}}$ does not intersect the medial axis of $\mathcal{M}$ as $\delta_0 < 1$. We will prove that $\Pi_{|\hat{\mathcal{M}}}$ is a homeomorphism, which implies that $\hat{\mathcal{M}}$ is a triangulation of $\mathcal{M}$.

Here is an overview of the proof. We have already seen that Π embeds any simplex of $\hat{\mathcal{M}}$ into $\mathcal{M}$ (Lemma 7.13 (2)). We will extend this result and prove that $\Pi_{|\hat{\mathcal{M}}}$ is a local homeomorphism (Lemma 7.23). More specifically, we define an open cover of $\hat{\mathcal{M}}$ as follows. We attach to each vertex p of $\hat{\mathcal{M}}$ an open set V_p such that the union of the V_p, for all vertices p of $\hat{\mathcal{M}}$, covers $\hat{\mathcal{M}}$. Specifically, W_p is defined as the set of points of $\operatorname{star}(p) \subset \hat{\mathcal{M}}$ whose barycentric coordinate with respect to p is at least $\frac{1}{k+1}$, and V_p is an open set that contains W_p and is arbitrarily close to W_p. Since the barycentric coordinates in each k-simplex sum to 1, this ensures that the sets V_p cover $\hat{\mathcal{M}}$. We will show that Π embeds each V_p, which will prove that $\Pi_{|\hat{\mathcal{M}}}$ is a local homeomorphism.

We will then prove that $\Pi_{|\hat{\mathcal{M}}}$ is injective (Lemma 7.24) and surjective (Lemma 7.25). Furthermore, $\Pi_{|\hat{\mathcal{M}}}$ is continuous by Lemma 7.13(1) and its inverse is also continuous because $\hat{\mathcal{M}}$ and $\mathcal{M}$ are both k-manifolds without boundary (see Section 1.2.1). It will follow that $\Pi_{|\hat{\mathcal{M}}}$ is a homeomorphism and that $\hat{\mathcal{M}}$ and $\mathcal{M}$ are homeomorphic.

7.3.2 Whitney's Lemma

We write $\mathrm{star}'(p)$ for $\Pi_p(\mathrm{star}(p))$ and V_p' for $\Pi_p(V_p)$, With a slight abuse of notation, in the rest of the proof of Theorem 7.16, we write Π_p^{-1} for the inverse of the restriction of Π_p to $\mathrm{star}(p)$, which is well defined because Π_p embeds $\mathrm{star}(p)$ by Hypothesis (d). We further define the map $F_p : \mathrm{star}'(p) \subset T_p \to T_p$ as $F_p = \Pi_p \circ \Pi \circ \Pi_p^{-1}$. See Figure 7.8. By construction, F_p leaves the vertices of $\mathrm{star}'(p)$ fixed: if q is a vertex of $\mathrm{star}'(p)$, then $F_p(q) = q$. Our goal is to show that F_p embeds $V_p' = \Pi_p(V_p)$. To do so, we will use the following result due to Whitney[3] that we state without proof [131, App. II, Lemma 15a].

Definition 7.17 Let C be a k-simplicial complex embedded in $\mathbb{R}^k$. We say that a map $F : C \to \mathbb{R}^k$ is simplexwise positive if it is smooth and 1-1 on each k-simplex of C, and if the Jacobian of F is positive there.

Lemma 7.18 (Whitney's lemma) *Assume C is a combinatorial k-manifold with boundary embedded in $\mathbb{R}^k$. Let $F : C \to \mathbb{R}^k$ be simplexwise positive in C. Then for any connected open subset Ω of $\mathbb{R}^k \setminus F(\partial C)$, any two points of Ω not in the image of the $(k-1)$-skeleton of C are covered the same number of times. If this number is 1, then F, considered in the open subset $F^{-1}(\Omega)$ of C only, is one to one onto Ω.*

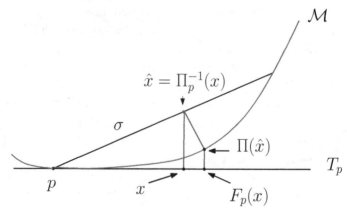

Figure 7.8 For the proof of Lemma 7.23.

---

[3] Whitney proved a more general result that does not assume that C is embedded in $\mathbb{R}^k$.

7.3.3 Satisfying the Conditions of Whitney's Lemma

We will apply Whitney's lemma to $\Omega = V_p$, $C = \text{star}'(p) = \Pi_p(\text{star}(p))$ and to $F = F_p$. This section contains the geometric arguments needed to prove that the conditions of Whitney's lemma are satisfied. After recalling that $\text{star}(p)$ is an oriented combinatorial k-manifold (Point 1), we show that F_p is simplex-wise positive (Point 2). We then exhibit a point in $F_p(V_p) \setminus F_p(\partial \text{star}(p))$ that is covered only once (Point 3) and finally prove that $F_p(V_p)$ is included in a single component of $F_p(\text{star}(p)) \setminus F_p(\partial \text{star}(p))$ (Point 4). The proofs use extensively the bounds on the distortion of the two maps Π and Π_p of Section 7.2.

1. Because $\hat{\mathcal{M}}$ is a combinatorial k-manifold and Π_p embeds $\text{star}(p)$ (Hypothesis (d)), $\text{star}'(p)$ is a combinatorial k-manifold embedded in T_p. We can then assume that it is oriented.

2. We now prove that $F_p = \Pi_p \circ \Pi \circ \Pi_p^{-1}$ is simplexwise positive.

Lemma 7.19 (Distortion of F_p on a simplex) *Under the hypotheses of Theorem 7.16, the distortion of the restriction of F_p to any simplex of $\hat{\mathcal{M}}$ is less than* $\dfrac{33\delta_0^2}{\Theta_0^2} < 1$.

Proof Rename, for convenience, Π_p^{-1} as f_1, the restriction of Π to $\text{star}(p)$ as f_2, and the restriction of Π_p to $U_p = \Pi(\text{star}(p))$ as f_3. We have $F_p = f_3 \circ f_2 \circ f_1$. Write ξ_i for the distortion of f_i, $i = 1, 2, 3$, and ξ for the distortion of F_p.

By hypothesis, the diameter of any simplex in $\text{star}(p)$ is at most δ_0 and its thickness is at least Θ_0. Moreover, U_p is contained in a ball centered at p of radius $r = \delta_0 \text{rch}(\mathcal{M})(1 + 2\delta_0) < \text{rch}(\mathcal{M})/3$ (Lemma 7.9).

Using the assumptions of Theorem 7.16 and Lemmas 7.14 and 7.13, we get

$$\xi_1 \leq \frac{\frac{\delta_0^2}{\Theta_0^2}}{1 - \frac{\delta_0^2}{\Theta_0^2}} \leq \frac{64}{63}\frac{\delta_0^2}{\Theta_0^2} \quad \text{(Exercise 7.9, Lemma 7.14(2) and } \Theta_0 \geq 8\delta_0)$$

$$\xi_2 \leq 4\delta_0^2 + \frac{16\delta_0^2}{\Theta_0^2} \leq 20\frac{\delta_0^2}{\Theta_0^2} \quad \text{(Lemma 7.13 (2) and } \Theta_0 \leq 1)$$

$$\xi_3 \leq 4\delta_0^2(1 + 2\delta_0)^2 < 8\delta_0^2 \leq 8\frac{\delta_0^2}{\Theta_0^2} \quad \left(\text{Lemma 7.14(1) and } \delta_0 \leq \frac{1}{5}\right)$$

Using Exercise 7.10 and $\Theta_0 > 9\delta_0$, we obtain

$$\xi \leq \xi_1 + \xi_2 + \xi_3 + \xi_1\xi_2 + \xi_2\xi_3 + \xi_3\xi_1 + \xi_1\xi_2\xi_3$$
$$< \frac{33\delta_0^2}{\Theta_0^2} < 1.$$

$\square$

It follows from Lemma 7.19 that F_p embeds any simplex σ of $\text{star}'(p)$ and, from Lemma 7.12, that the Jacobian of F_p does not vanish on σ.

It remains to prove that the Jacobian of F_p is positive. To do so, observe that the differential of the restriction of F_p to σ at the point $p \in \sigma$ is the identity. This follows from the observation that the differential of Π at p restricted to T_p is the identity, since p lies on the manifold.

3. We will now prove that there is a point in $F_p(V_p) \setminus F_p(\partial\text{star}(p))$ and not in the image of the $(k-1)$-skeleton that is covered once. For this purpose, we choose the image of the barycenter of a k-simplex of $\text{star}'(p)$.

Lemma 7.20 *Assume that the conditions of Theorem 7.16 hold and let b' be the barycenter of a k-simplex σ in $\text{star}'(p)$. Then the image of b', $F_p(b')$, is covered once, i.e., $F_p^{-1}(F_p(b')) = \{b'\}$.*

Proof We denote as usual by $\Delta(\sigma')$ the diameter of σ', by $L(\sigma')$ the length of the shortest edge of σ', and by $D(p, \sigma')$ the altitude of p in σ'. Let $\sigma = \Pi_p^{-1}(\sigma')$ and write ζ for the distortion of the restriction of Π_p to σ. By Lemma 7.19, we have $\zeta \leq \delta_0^2/\Theta_0^2$ and, using Conditions (b) and (c) in Theorem 7.16 and $\Theta_0 \leq 1$, we get $\zeta \leq 1/45$. We thus have $D(p, \sigma') \geq (1 - \zeta) D(p, \sigma)$. Now observe that the distance $d(b', \partial\sigma')$ from the barycenter b' to the boundary of σ' is $\min_{p \in \text{vert}(\sigma')} \frac{D(p, \sigma')}{k+1}$. A lower bound on $d(b', \partial\sigma')$ is then obtained using the definition of thickness, $k \geq 1$ and Condition (c):

$$d(b', \partial\sigma') \geq \frac{k(1-\zeta)\Theta(\sigma)\Delta(\sigma)}{k+1} \geq \frac{(1-\zeta)\Theta_0\lambda_0\,\text{rch}(\mathcal{M})}{2}$$
$$\geq \frac{9(1-\zeta)\delta_0^2\,\text{rch}(\mathcal{M})}{2}$$

Using the bound on ζ above, we obtain

$$d(b', \partial\sigma') \geq \frac{22}{5}\delta_0^2\,\text{rch}(\mathcal{M}) \tag{7.8}$$

Since the distortion of the restriction of F_p to σ' is less than 1 (Lemma 7.19), F_p embeds σ' (Lemma 7.12) and therefore no point $z' \in \sigma'$ distinct from b' can verify $F_p(z') = F_p(b')$. Let us consider now the case of a point z' of $\text{star}'(p)\setminus\sigma'$. Write $b = \Pi_p^{-1}(b')$ and $z = \Pi_p^{-1}(z')$. Using Lemma 7.9, we get

$$\|F_p(b') - b'\| = \|\Pi_p(\Pi(b) - b)\| \leq \|\Pi(b) - b\| \leq 2\delta_0^2\,\text{rch}(\mathcal{M})$$

and similarly for $\|F_p(z') - z'\|$.

Hence,

$$\|F_p(b') - F_p(z')\| \geq \|b' - z'\| - \|F_p(b') - b'\| - \|F_p(z') - z'\|$$
$$\geq d(b', \partial\sigma') - 4\delta_0^2 \operatorname{rch}(\mathcal{M})$$
$$\geq \frac{22}{5} \delta_0^2 \operatorname{rch}(\mathcal{M}) - 4\delta_0^2 \operatorname{rch}(\mathcal{M}) \qquad \text{(By Equation 7.8)}$$
$$> 0$$

It follows that $F_p(b') \neq F_p(z')$. $\qquad\square$

Because $b' \in V_p'$, the previous lemma implies that there exists a point in $F_p(V_p')$ that is covered exactly once.

4. The next lemma shows that $F_p(V_p') \cap F_p(\partial\operatorname{star}'(p)) = \emptyset$.

Lemma 7.21 *Assume that the conditions of Theorem 7.16 hold and let $x \in \sigma \subset \operatorname{star}'(p)$ and $y \in \partial(\operatorname{star}'(p))$. If the barycentric coordinate of x with respect to p is at least $\frac{1}{k+1}$, then $F_p(x) \neq F_p(y)$.*

Proof Arguing as in the proof of Lemma 7.20, we get

$$\|F_p(x) - F_p(y)\| \geq \|x - y\| - \|F_p(x) - x\| - \|F_p(y) - y\|$$
$$\geq d(x, \partial\operatorname{star}'(p)) - 4\delta_0^2 \operatorname{rch}(\mathcal{M})$$

Using Lemma 7.22, we can conclude in very much the same way as in the proof of Lemma 7.20. $\qquad\square$

Lemma 7.22 *Let σ be a k-simplex of $\operatorname{star}'(p)$ and let x be a point of σ whose barycentric coordinate associated to p in σ satisfies $\lambda_p(x) \geq \alpha$. Then $d(x, \partial\operatorname{star}'(p)) \geq \alpha k(1 - \zeta)L_0\Theta_0$, where $L_0 = \lambda_0\operatorname{rch}(\mathcal{M})$ is a lower bound on the edge lengths of the simplices and Θ_0 is a lower bound on their thickness.*

Proof Let γ_σ' be a line segment joining two points $x_{\sigma'}$ and $y_{\sigma'}$ of σ' and denote by $\lambda_p(x_{\sigma'})$ and $\lambda_p(y_{\sigma'})$ respectively their pth barycentric coordinates. Then $|\gamma_\sigma'| \geq |\lambda_p(x_{\sigma'}) - \lambda_p(y_{\sigma'})| D(p, \sigma')$, where $D(p, \sigma')$ denotes the altitude of p in σ' and we indicate the length of a curve by $|\cdot|$. As noted in the proof of Lemma 7.20, $D(p, \sigma') \geq (1 - \zeta) D(p, \sigma)$.

Let $\operatorname{star}_\alpha'(p) = \{z \in \operatorname{star}(p), \lambda_p(z) \geq \alpha\}$. Equivalently, $\operatorname{star}_\alpha'(p)$ is the image of $\operatorname{star}'(p)$ by the homothety of center p and ratio $1 - \alpha$. Consider a shortest line segment γ connecting a point of $\partial\operatorname{star}'(p)$ to a point of $\partial\operatorname{star}_\alpha'(p)$. Plainly, γ intersects $\operatorname{star}'(p)$ and $\operatorname{star}_\alpha'(p)$ only at its endpoints and the intersection of γ with any simplex σ' of $\operatorname{star}'(p)$, if non empty, is a line segment we denote by

$\gamma_{\sigma'}$. If we now note that the barycentric coordinates coincide on a face that is shared by two simplices we see that:

$$|\gamma| = \sum_{\sigma'} |\gamma'_\sigma| \geq \sum_{\sigma'} \left| \lambda_p(x'_\sigma) - \lambda_p(y'_\sigma) \right| D(p, \sigma')$$

$$\geq \sum_{\sigma'} \left| \lambda_p(x'_\sigma) - \lambda_p(y'_\sigma) \right| k\,(1 - \zeta)\,\Theta_0\,\Delta(\sigma)$$

$$\geq \sum_{\sigma'} \left| \lambda_p(x'_\sigma) - \lambda_p(y'_\sigma) \right| k\,(1 - \zeta)\,\Theta_0\,\Delta(\sigma)$$

$$\geq \alpha k\,(1 - \zeta)\,\Theta_0\,L_0$$

where x'_σ is the point where γ enters σ' and y'_σ where it leaves. $\qquad \square$

7.3.4 Local Homeomorphism

Lemma 7.23 ($\Pi_{|\hat{\mathcal{M}}}$ is a local homeomorphism) *If the conditions of Theorem 7.16 hold, then Π embeds V_p in $\mathcal{M}$ and the restriction of Π to $\hat{\mathcal{M}}$ is a local homeomorphism.*

Proof We have proved in the previous section that the conditions of Whitney's lemma are fulfilled for $F = F_p$. Hence, F_p embeds V'_p in T_p and, because $F_p = \Pi_p \circ \Pi \circ \Pi_p^{-1}$, Π must embed V_p into $\mathcal{M}$. Moreover, because the set of all V_p for all vertices of $\hat{\mathcal{M}}$ cover $\hat{\mathcal{M}}$, we have proved that the map Π restricted to $\hat{\mathcal{M}}$ is a local homeomorphism on $\mathcal{M}$. This completes the proof of Lemma 7.23. $\qquad \square$

7.3.5 The Restriction of Π to $\hat{\mathcal{M}}$ Is Injective

Lemma 7.24 (Injectivity of $\Pi_{|\hat{\mathcal{M}}}$) *Under the conditions of Theorem 7.16, Π is injective on $\hat{\mathcal{M}}$.*

Proof Let x be a point of $\Pi(\hat{\mathcal{M}})$. $\Pi_{|\hat{\mathcal{M}}}^{-1}(x)$ is nonempty and finite since Π embeds each simplex of $\hat{\mathcal{M}}$ (Lemma 7.13) and there are only finitely many simplexes in $\hat{\mathcal{M}}$. For each point $y \in \Pi^{-1}(x) \cap \hat{\mathcal{M}}$, we choose a sufficiently small open neighborhood $U(y)$ of y such that the $U(y)$ are disjoint, and each $U(y)$ is homeomorphic to a k-ball and is contained in some V_p. This is possible because the V_p, $p \in P$, constitute an open cover of $\hat{\mathcal{M}}$. Because, as already noticed, Π embeds any V_p on $\mathcal{M}$, it also embeds each $U(y)$ in $\mathcal{M}$. Hence the preimage under $\Pi_{|\hat{\mathcal{M}}}$ of any sufficiently small open neighborhood $U(x)$ of a point x of $\mathcal{M}$ is a union of disjoint open sets, each of which is contained in some $V_p \subset \hat{\mathcal{M}}$ and mapped homeomorphically onto $U(x)$ by Π. (In topological terms, $(\hat{\mathcal{M}}, \Pi)$ is a covering space of $\Pi(\hat{\mathcal{M}})$.)

We now show that the cardinality of $\Pi^{-1}_{|\hat{\mathcal{M}}}(x)$ is constant over each connected component of $\mathcal{M}$. Indeed, consider the function G that associates to a point x of $\mathcal{M}$ the cardinality of $\Pi^{-1}_{\hat{\mathcal{M}}}(x)$. From the above discussion, G is locally constant, which implies that it is constant on each connected component of $\mathcal{M}$. Hence $\Pi_{|\hat{\mathcal{M}}}$ covers all the points of a connected component of its image $\Pi(\hat{\mathcal{M}})$ the same number of times. This number is 1 as is shown next.

Assume, for a contradiction, that there exists a vertex q and a simplex σ of $\hat{\mathcal{M}}$ such that q belongs to the image $\Pi(\sigma)$ but q is not a vertex of σ. Specifically, let $x \in \sigma$ be such that $\Pi(x) = q$. In the rest of the proof, we denote by p a vertex of σ such that the associated barycentric coordinate of x satisfies $\lambda_p(x) \geq \frac{1}{k+1}$ (which must exist).

We write for convenience $x' = \Pi_p(x)$ and $q' = \Pi_p(q)$. Recall that $F_p = \Pi_p \circ \Pi \circ \Pi_p^{-1}$ and observe that $F_p(x') = F_p(q')$ for any vertex p of σ. Plainly, x' belongs to $\Pi_p(\sigma)$ but q' does not belong to $\text{star}'(p) = \Pi_p(\text{star}(p))$ by Hypothesis (e). Then, Lemma 7.21 implies that $F_p(x') \neq F_p(q')$, hence a contradiction. □

7.3.6 The Restriction of Π to $\hat{\mathcal{M}}$ Is Surjective

Lastly we prove that the restriction of Π to $\hat{\mathcal{M}}$ is surjective.

Lemma 7.25 (Surjectivity of $\Pi_{|\hat{\mathcal{M}}}$) *Under the conditions of Theorem 7.16, $\Pi_{|\hat{\mathcal{M}}}$ is surjective on $\mathcal{M}$.*

Proof Since $\hat{\mathcal{M}}$ has no boundary, the same is true for $\Pi(\hat{\mathcal{M}})$ by the invariance of domain theorem.[4] Hence any connected component of $\mathcal{M}$ that intersects $\Pi(\hat{\mathcal{M}})$ has to be totally included in $\Pi(\hat{\mathcal{M}})$. Because by Hypothesis 1 of Theorem 7.16, every connected component of $\mathcal{M}$ intersects $\Pi(\hat{\mathcal{M}})$, $\mathcal{M}$ is included in $\Pi(\hat{\mathcal{M}})$. □

7.3.7 End of Proof of Statement 1

We have shown that $\Pi_{|\hat{\mathcal{M}}}$ is a bijection from $\hat{\mathcal{M}}$ to $\mathcal{M}$. Furthermore, $\Pi_{|\hat{\mathcal{M}}}$ is continuous by Lemma 7.13(1) and its inverse is also continuous since $\hat{\mathcal{M}}$ is

---

[4] The invariance of domain theorem states that, given an open subset $U \subseteq \mathbb{R}^d$ and an injective and continuous function $f : U \to \mathbb{R}^d$ then f is a homeomorphism between U and $f(U)$. The theorem and its proof are due to L. E. J. Brouwer [110, Theorem 36.5].

compact and $\mathcal{M}$ is a metric space (see Section 1.2.1). It follows that $\Pi_{|\hat{\mathcal{M}}}$ is a homeomorphism and that $\hat{\mathcal{M}}$ and $\mathcal{M}$ are homeomorphic, which is the first statement in Theorem 7.16.

7.3.8 Proof of Statements 2 and 3, and of Theorem 7.16

To prove the second statement, let x be a point of $\mathcal{M}$ and let y be the point of $\hat{\mathcal{M}}$ such that $x = \Pi(y)$. Such a point y exists by the first statement. It then follows from Lemma 7.9 that $\|x - y\| \leq 2\delta_0^2 \operatorname{rch}(\mathcal{M})$.

The third statement of the theorem follows from Lemma 5.14 as in the proof of Lemma 7.14 (Equation (7.7)).

We have thus proved the three statements of Theorem 7.16.

7.4 Exercises

Exercise 7.1 (ε-nets on submanifolds) Let P be an ε-dense sample of a submanifold $\mathcal{M}$. Let $P' := \emptyset$ and apply the following procedure : while there exists a point p of $P \setminus P'$ whose distance to the current set P' is greater than $\varepsilon \operatorname{rch}(\mathcal{M})$, insert p in P'. Show that P' is an $(\varepsilon \operatorname{rch}(\mathcal{M}), 1)$-net of P and a $(2\varepsilon, \frac{1}{2})$-net of $\mathcal{M}$. Adapt the algorithms of Section 5.1 to the case of submanifolds.

Exercise 7.2 (Size of nets) Show that the size of an $(\varepsilon, \bar{\eta})$-net of a k-submanifold with a bounded sampling ratio $\bar{\eta}$ depends exponentially on k.

Exercise 7.3 (Computing rch($\mathcal{M}$)) Let $\mathcal{M}$ be a smooth submanifold and write $\operatorname{ax}(\mathcal{M})$ for the medial axis of $\mathcal{M}$. Show that $\operatorname{rch}(\mathcal{M})$ is the radius of a ball $B(m)$ centered at a point $m \in \operatorname{ax}(\mathcal{M})$ and tangent to $\mathcal{M}$. Show that if $B(m)$ has only one contact point, $B(m)$ is osculating $\mathcal{M}$ at the contact point. If $B(m)$ has two distinct contact points, the two contact points are the endpoints of a diameter of $B(m)$. Propose an algorithm to compute $\operatorname{rch}(\mathcal{M})$ when $\mathcal{M}$ is a hypersurface of $\mathbb{R}^d$ implicitly defined as $f(x) = 0$ where f is a differentiable function defined over $\mathbb{R}^d$ for which 0 is a regular value.

Exercise 7.4 (Non uniform nets) We define the local feature size $\operatorname{lfs}(x)$ at a point x of a submanifold $\mathcal{M}$ as the distance from x to the medial axis of $\mathcal{M}$, $\operatorname{ax}(\mathcal{M})$. We say that a finite set of points $P \subset \mathcal{M}$ is a *non uniform $(\varepsilon, \bar{\eta})$-net* if it satisfies the following two properties:

1. Any point x of $\mathcal{M}$ is at distance at most $\varepsilon \operatorname{lfs}(x)$ from a point of P.
2. For any two points p, q of P, $\|p - q\| \geq \eta \min(\operatorname{lfs}(p), \operatorname{lfs}(q))$.

Show that lfs is a 1-Lipschitz function, and, using this fact, extend the results of this chapter to sufficiently dense non uniform ε-nets.

Exercise 7.5 (Size of nonuniform nets) Provide upper and lower bounds on the size of a nonuniform $(\varepsilon, \bar{\eta})$-net of a k-submanifold as a function of k and the integral over $\mathcal{M}$ of lfs(x), the local feature size of $\mathcal{M}$ at x.

Exercise 7.6 (Geodesic distance) Let x and y be two points on $\mathcal{M}$ such that $\|x - y\| \le \alpha \operatorname{rch}(\mathcal{M})$, $\alpha < 1$. Show that the length of a shortest path on $\mathcal{M}$ joining x to y is at most $\frac{\|x-y\|}{1-\alpha}$.

Exercise 7.7 (Angle between tangent spaces) Prove Lemma 7.10 (with possibly a bigger constant) using elementary arguments.

Exercise 7.8 Let x be a point of $B_{\mathcal{M}} = B(p, r) \cap \mathcal{M}$ where $r = \rho \operatorname{rch}(\mathcal{M})$, $\rho < 1$. Show that there exists a point $y \in T_p$ such that $\Pi(y) = x$, where Π denotes the projection on $\mathcal{M}$, and $\|x - y\| \le \frac{r}{1-\rho}$.

Exercise 7.9 (Distortion) Let $F : U \subseteq R^d \to \mathbb{R}^d$ be a ξ-distortion map. Show that F^{-1} is well defined and that it is a $\frac{\xi}{1-\xi}$-distortion map.

Exercise 7.10 If F_1 is a ξ_1-distortion map and F_2 is a ξ_2-distortion map, then $F_1 \circ F_2$ is a $(\xi_1 + \xi_2 + \xi_1\xi_2)$-distortion map.

Exercise 7.11 (Ambient isotopy) Assume that the conditions of Theorem 7.16 are satisfied. Show that the restriction of Π to $\hat{\mathcal{M}}$ induces an ambient isotopy

$$\Phi^* : \mathbb{R}^d \times [0, 1] \longrightarrow \mathbb{R}^d$$

such that the map $\Phi^*(\cdot, 0)$ restricted to $\hat{\mathcal{M}}$ is the identity map on $\hat{\mathcal{M}}$ and $\Phi^*(\hat{\mathcal{M}}, 1) = \mathcal{M}$. The isotopy does not move the points by more than $O(\delta_0^2 \operatorname{rch}(\mathcal{M}))$.

Hint: Let

$$\Phi : \hat{\mathcal{M}} \times [0, 1] \longrightarrow \mathbb{R}^3, \quad (x, t) \mapsto x + t (\Pi(x) - x)$$

Note that $\Phi(\cdot, 0)$ is an identity map on $\hat{\mathcal{M}}$ and $\Phi(\cdot, 1) = \Pi_{|\hat{\mathcal{M}}}$. The map Φ is an isotopy because the maps

$$\Phi_t : \hat{\mathcal{M}} \longrightarrow \mathbb{R}^d, \quad x \mapsto \Phi(x, t)$$

are homeomorphisms between $\hat{\mathcal{M}}$ and $\Phi_t(\hat{\mathcal{M}})$.

Isotopy Φ can be extended to an ambient isotopy $\Phi^* : \mathbb{R}^d \times [0, 1] \longrightarrow \mathbb{R}^3$ such that $\Phi^*(\cdot, 0) \mid_{\hat{\mathcal{M}}} = \Phi(\cdot, 0)$ and $\Phi^*(\cdot, 1) \mid_{\hat{\mathcal{M}}} = \Phi(\cdot, 1)$

7.5 Bibliographical Notes

The medial axis was introduced as a tool in image analysis. It is by now widely used to represent and analyze shapes. For mathematical and algorithmic properties, we refer the reader to the work of Lieutier [101] and to the survey paper [3]. Lieutier proved that any bounded open subset of $\mathbb{R}^d$ is homotopy equivalent to its medial axis [101]. The notion of local feature size (Exercise 7.4) was introduced by Amenta and Bern in their seminal paper on surface reconstruction [2]. See also [22, 90]. The related notion of reach has been introduced earlier by Federer [81] who proved Lemmas 7.2, 7.8 and the first part of Lemma 7.13. Many other results on sets of positive reach can also be found in this paper. The link between the reach and the principal curvatures of a submanifold has been established by Niyogi, Smale and Weinberger [112] who also proved a weaker form of Lemma 7.10. The improved bound is due to Boissonnat, Lieutier, and Wintraecken [19].

Proving that any smooth manifold can be triangulated has been the subject of many important developments in the mathematical community by Cairns [32], Whitehead [130], Whitney [131], Munkres [109], and others. Our proof uses Lemma 7.18 which is due to Whitney. More recently, the Delaunay triangulation turned out to be a useful tool in this context leading to efficient algorithms. Variants of Theorem 7.16 have been proved by Cheng and al. [57], Boissonnat and Ghosh [18], and Dyer et al. [66]. The proof presented here is based on [16]. A proof of Exercise 7.11 can be found in [97].

8

Reconstruction of Submanifolds

Let $\mathcal{M}$ be an unknown manifold and let $P \subset \mathcal{M}$ be a known finite sample. The reconstruction problem is to recover from P alone the topological type of $\mathcal{M}$ (manifold reconstruction) or the homotopy type of $\mathcal{M}$ (homotopy reconstruction). More concretely, we look for a simplicial complex $\hat{\mathcal{M}}$, which approximates $\mathcal{M}$, and, in particular, is provably homeomorphic or homotopy equivalent to $\mathcal{M}$.

In Section 8.1, we will see that, under appropriate conditions on P, $\mathcal{M}$ has the same homotopy type as the union of balls centered on the points of P. It follows that the alpha-shape of P, for an appropriate value of α has the same homotopy type as $\mathcal{M}$. This method however has some limitations. The complex captures the homotopy type but is not in general a triangulation of $\mathcal{M}$ and computing the alpha-shape is limited to low dimensional spaces.

In the following sections, we overcome these limitations and show how to reconstruct a simplicial complex with vertex set P that is homeomorphic to $\mathcal{M}$. We have to face two main difficulties. First, even when a point set is a dense and sparse sampling on a manifold $\mathcal{M}$, the Delaunay simplexes of dimension higher than 2 are not guaranteed to be thick (see Section 5.2) and therefore not guaranteed to approximate the tangent bundle of $\mathcal{M}$ (see Lemma 5.14). This is an issue since the main theorem of Chapter 7, Theorem 7.16, that provides conditions to triangulate a submanifold, requires simplices to be thick. To be able to reconstruct manifolds of dimension greater than 2, we will need to explicitly take care of nonthick simplices using techniques similar to what has been done in Chapter 5 in the Euclidean case.

The second major difficulty comes from the so-called curse of dimensionality. We have seen (Theorems 4.4 and 5.4) that the size of the Delaunay triangulation of n points grows exponentially with the dimension d of the embedding space. As a consequence, when d is large, we cannot afford to compute the d-dimensional Delaunay triangulation Del(P) or any other subdivision of $\mathbb{R}^d$. Instead, we will introduce a subcomplex of Del(P), called the tangential Delaunay complex, whose complexity depends on the intrinsic dimension of $\mathcal{M}$ and not on the ambient dimension d. This complex is defined locally and the various local triangulations are glued together so as to constitute a manifold complex that is embedded in $\mathbb{R}^d$ and triangulates $\mathcal{M}$.

8.1 Homotopy Reconstruction Using alpha-shapes

Unions of balls play a central role in manifold reconstruction. Indeed, while Chapter 6 shows how to capture the homotopy type of a union of balls with a simplicial complex, this section shows that the homotopy type of a sampled manifold can be obtained from the homotopy type of a union of balls. More precisely, we show here that the homotopy type, hence the homology groups, of a manifold $\mathcal{M}$ with positive reach can be obtained from union of balls centered at the points of a sample of $\mathcal{M}$ provided that the sample is dense enough with respect to the reach.

Theorem 8.1 *Let $\mathcal{M}$ be a manifold with positive reach rch($\mathcal{M}$), and $P \subset \mathcal{M}$ be a point sample of $\mathcal{M}$ with sampling radius $\frac{\varepsilon}{2}$rch($\mathcal{M}$), meaning that any point x of $\mathcal{M}$ is at distance less than $\frac{\varepsilon}{2}$rch($\mathcal{M}$) from the closest sample point. If $\varepsilon < \sqrt{\frac{3}{5}}$, the union of balls with radius ε rch($\mathcal{M}$) centered on P, is homotopy equivalent to $\mathcal{M}$.*

Proof In the following, we denote by $B(p, r)$ the ball with radius r centered on p and write for short U for the union of balls with radius εrch($\mathcal{M}$) centered on points of P:

$$U = \bigcup_{p \in P} B(p, \varepsilon\text{rch}(\mathcal{M})).$$

Obviously, $\mathcal{M}$ is included in U. To prove the homotopy equivalence we prove below that U deformation retracts to $\mathcal{M}$. For all $x \in U$ and $t \in [0, 1]$, we define

$$F(x, t) = (1 - t)x + t\Pi(x),$$

where $\Pi(x)$ is the projection on $\mathcal{M}$. F is continuous from Lemma 7.13. For all $x \in U$, $F(x, 0) = x$, and $F(x, 1) = \Pi(x)$ is in $\mathcal{M}$, and for all $x \in \mathcal{M}$ and $t \in [0, 1]$, $F(x, t) = x$. Therefore F is a deformation retracts from U to $\mathcal{M}$, provided that $F(x, t)$ belongs to U for any $(x, t) \in U \times [0, 1]$, which is proved now.

Let us consider Π_U, the restriction of Π to U. The preimage $\Pi_U^{-1}(y)$ of a point $y \in \mathcal{M}$ is

$$\Pi_U^{-1}(y) = N_y \cap U \cap B(y, \text{rch}(\mathcal{M})), \tag{8.1}$$

where N_y is the normal subspace of $\mathcal{M}$ at y. The ball with radius $\mathrm{rch}(\mathcal{M})$ centered at y, $B(y, \mathrm{rch}(\mathcal{M}))$, appears in Equation 8.1 to remove orphan components of $N_y \cap U$, i.e., components that do not contain y, and may arise from the fact that $\mathcal{M}$ is curved. Therefore,

$$\Pi_U^{-1}(y) = \bigcup_{p \in P} B(p, \varepsilon\mathrm{rch}(\mathcal{M})) \cap N_y \cap B(y, \mathrm{rch}(\mathcal{M})).$$

We also consider the subset $st(y)$ defined as

$$st(y) = \bigcup_{p \in P \cap B(y, \varepsilon\mathrm{rch}(\mathcal{M}))} B(p, \varepsilon\mathrm{rch}(\mathcal{M})) \cap N_y \cap B(y, \mathrm{rch}(\mathcal{M})).$$

Obviously, $st(y) \subset \Pi_U^{-1}(y)$. Then Lemma 8.2 below proves that $st(y)$ is star shaped with respect to y and Lemma 8.3 proves that $st(y) = \Pi_U^{-1}(y)$. It follows that for any $y \in \mathcal{M}$, $\Pi_U^{-1}(y)$ is star-shaped with respect to y and that for any $(x, t) \in U \times [0, 1]$, $F(x, t)$ belongs to U. $\qquad\square$

Lemma 8.2 *The subset $st(y)$ is star shaped with respect to y.*

Proof Let z be an arbitrary point in $st(y)$. Then $z \in B(p, \varepsilon\mathrm{rch}(\mathcal{M})) \cap N_y \cap B(y, \mathrm{rch}(\mathcal{M}))$ for some $p \in P \cap B(y, \varepsilon\mathrm{rch}(\mathcal{M}))$. Because $p \in B(y, \varepsilon\mathrm{rch}(\mathcal{M}))$, $y \in B(p, \varepsilon\mathrm{rch}(\mathcal{M}))$. Because z and y are both in $B(p, \varepsilon\mathrm{rch}(\mathcal{M}))$, the segment zy is entirely contained in $B(p, \varepsilon\mathrm{rch}(\mathcal{M}))$. At the same time, zy is entirely contained in N_y and in $B(y, \mathrm{rch}(\mathcal{M}))$ and therefore in $st(y)$. $\qquad\square$

Lemma 8.3 *The subset $st(y)$ coincides with the preimage $\Pi_U^{-1}(y)$.*

Proof We are left to show that $\Pi_U^{-1}(y) \subseteq st(y)$. Let z be a point in $B(p, \varepsilon\mathrm{rch}(\mathcal{M})) \cap N_y \cap B(y, \mathrm{rch}(\mathcal{M}))$ where p is a point of P such that $p \notin B(y, \varepsilon\mathrm{rch}(\mathcal{M}))$. Lemma 8.4 shows that the distance from z to y is at most $\varepsilon^2\mathrm{rch}(\mathcal{M})$ and Lemma 8.5 shows that if P is $(\frac{\varepsilon}{2}\mathrm{rch}(\mathcal{M}))$-dense in $\mathcal{M}$ with $\varepsilon < \frac{3}{5}$, there is some point $q \in P \cap B(y, \varepsilon\mathrm{rch}(\mathcal{M}))$ such that $z \in B(q, \varepsilon\mathrm{rch}(\mathcal{M}))$ which achieves the proof. $\qquad\square$

Lemma 8.4 *Let z be a point in $B(p, \varepsilon\mathrm{rch}(\mathcal{M})) \cap N_y \cap B(y, \mathrm{rch}(\mathcal{M}))$ where p is a point of P such that $p \notin B(y, \varepsilon\mathrm{rch}(\mathcal{M}))$. The distance $d(y, z)$ from z to y is at most $\varepsilon^2\mathrm{rch}(\mathcal{M})$.*

Proof Let us consider the plane H through y, z and p. See Figure 8.1. In the plane H, we call n_y the line $H \cap N_y$, and h_y the line orthogonal to n_y that passes through y. Point z belongs to n_y and point p lies anywhere outside of the two balls with radius $\mathrm{rch}(\mathcal{M})$ tangent to h_y at y. Because the distance $d(y, z)$ is constrained by the fact that $d(p, z) \leq \varepsilon\mathrm{rch}(\mathcal{M})$, the maximum of the distance

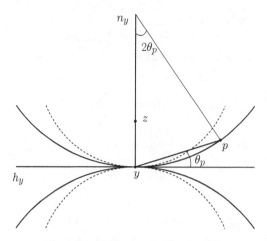

Figure 8.1 For the proof of Lemma 8.3.

$d(y, z)$ occurs in the configuration where points p and z lie on the same side of h_y, as shown in Figure 8.1. We denote by r_p the radius of the circle tangent to $\mathcal{M}$ in y and going through p, and by θ_p the angle $\angle(h_y, yp)$ between h_y and yp.

We have $r_p \geq \text{rch}(\mathcal{M})$ and $d(y, p) = 2r_p \sin \theta_p$. Furthermore, we have (see Figure 8.1):

$$
\begin{aligned}
d(y, z) &= d(y, p) \sin \theta_p + \sqrt{d(z, p)^2 - d(y, p)^2 \cos^2 \theta_p} \\
&= 2r_p \sin^2 \theta_p + \sqrt{d(z, p)^2 - r_p^2 \sin^2 2\theta_p} \\
&\leq 2r_p \sin^2 \theta_p + \sqrt{\varepsilon^2 \text{rch}(\mathcal{M})^2 - r_p^2 \sin^2 2\theta_p} \\
&\stackrel{\text{def}}{=} f(r_p, \theta_p)
\end{aligned}
\tag{8.2}
$$

We have:

$$
\begin{aligned}
\frac{df}{d\theta_p} &= 2r_p \sin 2\theta_p - \frac{2r_p^2 \sin 2\theta_p \cos 2\theta_p}{\sqrt{\varepsilon^2 \text{rch}(\mathcal{M})^2 - r_p^2 \sin^2 2\theta_p}} \\
&= 2r_p \sin 2\theta_p \left(1 - \frac{r_p \cos 2\theta_p}{\sqrt{\varepsilon^2 \text{rch}(\mathcal{M})^2 - r_p^2 \sin^2 2\theta_p}} \right).
\end{aligned}
$$

Because $\varepsilon < \sqrt{\frac{3}{5}} < 1$ and $\text{rch}(\mathcal{M}) \leq r_p$, the function f is monotonically decreasing with respect to θ_p and reaches its maximum when θ_p is minimum, i.e., when $d(y, p) = 2r_p \sin \theta_p = \varepsilon \text{rch}(\mathcal{M})$. We have then

$$f(r_p, \theta_p) = \varepsilon \mathrm{rch}(\mathcal{M}) \sin \theta_p + \sqrt{\varepsilon^2 \mathrm{rch}(\mathcal{M})^2 - \varepsilon^2 \mathrm{rch}(\mathcal{M})^2 \cos^2 \theta_p}$$

$$= 2\varepsilon \mathrm{rch}(\mathcal{M}) \sin \theta_p = \frac{\varepsilon^2 \mathrm{rch}(\mathcal{M})^2}{r_p} \leq \varepsilon^2 \mathrm{rch}(\mathcal{M}),$$

which, together with Equation 8.2, achieves the proof. □

Lemma 8.5 *Let z be a point in $B(p, \varepsilon \mathrm{rch}(\mathcal{M})) \cap N_y \cap B(y, \mathrm{rch}(\mathcal{M}))$ where p is a point of P such that $p \notin B(y, \varepsilon \mathrm{rch}(\mathcal{M}))$. If P is $(\frac{\varepsilon}{2}\mathrm{rch}(\mathcal{M}))$-dense in $\mathcal{M}$ with $\varepsilon < \sqrt{\frac{3}{5}}\mathrm{rch}(\mathcal{M})$, there is some point $q \in P \cap B(y, \varepsilon \mathrm{rch}(\mathcal{M}))$ such that $z \in B(q, \varepsilon \mathrm{rch}(\mathcal{M})) \cap N_y$.*

Proof Because P is $(\frac{\varepsilon}{2}\mathrm{rch}(\mathcal{M}))$-dense in $\mathcal{M}$, there is a point $q \in P$ at distance at most $\frac{\varepsilon}{2}\mathrm{rch}(\mathcal{M})$ from y. We prove that $z \in B(q, \varepsilon \mathrm{rch}(\mathcal{M}))$. We consider now the plane H' through y, z and q and write n'_y for the line $H' \cap N_y$, and h'_y for the line orthogonal to H' that passes through y. Figure 8.2, drawn in the plane H', shows the worst situation for the distance $d(z, q)$. Denoting now by θ_q the angle $\angle(h'_y, yq)$ between h'_y and yq, we have

$$d(z, q)^2 \leq d(y, q)^2 \cos^2 \theta_q + (d(y, q) \sin \theta_q + d(y, z))^2$$
$$\leq d(y, q)^2 + 2d(y, q)d(y, z) \sin \theta_q + d(y, z)^2.$$

Because $d(y, q) \leq \frac{\varepsilon}{2}\mathrm{rch}(\mathcal{M})$ and $d(y, z) \leq \varepsilon^2 \mathrm{rch}(\mathcal{M})$ (Lemma 8.4), we get

$$d(z, q)^2 \leq \frac{\varepsilon^2}{4}\mathrm{rch}(\mathcal{M})^2 + \varepsilon^3 \mathrm{rch}(\mathcal{M})^2 \sin \theta_q + \varepsilon^4 \mathrm{rch}(\mathcal{M})^2.$$

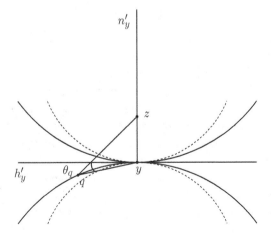

Figure 8.2 For the proof of Lemma 8.4.

We have $d(y, q) = 2r_q \sin \theta_q \leq \frac{\varepsilon}{2} \mathrm{rch}(\mathcal{M})$ where r_q is the radius of the circle tangent to $\mathcal{M}$ at y and going through q. Because point q lies outside the two balls with radii $\mathrm{rch}(\mathcal{M})$ that are tangent to T_y at y, r_q is greater than $\mathrm{rch}(\mathcal{M})$ and therefore $\sin \theta_q \leq \frac{\varepsilon}{4}$. Thus,

$$d(z, q)^2 \leq \frac{\varepsilon^2}{4} \mathrm{rch}(\mathcal{M})^2 + \frac{\varepsilon^4}{4} \mathrm{rch}(\mathcal{M})^2 + \varepsilon^4 \mathrm{rch}(\mathcal{M})^2$$
$$\leq \varepsilon^2 \mathrm{rch}(\mathcal{M})^2 \left(\frac{1}{4} + \frac{5}{4} \varepsilon^2 \right),$$

which is not greater than $\varepsilon^2 \mathrm{rch}(\mathcal{M})^2$ if $\varepsilon^2 \leq \frac{3}{5}$. $\qquad\qquad\square$

8.2 Tangential Delaunay Complex

We introduce in this section a data structure, named the tangential Delaunay complex. Let $\mathcal{M}$ be a k-submanifold of $\mathbb{R}^d$. The only knowledge we have on $\mathcal{M}$ is a finite set of points $P \in \mathcal{M}$ and the tangent spaces at each point of P. The tangential Delaunay complex $\mathrm{Del}_{T\mathcal{M}}(P)$ is a k-dimensional subcomplex of the d-dimensional Delaunay complex $\mathrm{Del}(P)$. An important property is that $\mathrm{Del}_{T\mathcal{M}}(P)$ can be constructed without computing any data structure of dimension higher than k, and in particular without computing the full Delaunay complex. We will see in Section 8.3 that $\mathrm{Del}_{T\mathcal{M}}(P)$ can be used to reconstruct a triangulation of $\mathcal{M}$.

8.2.1 Definition

Let P be a finite set of $n > k + 1$ points on $\mathcal{M}$. Let $\mathrm{Del}(P)$ be the Delaunay complex of P, i.e., the collection of all the simplices with vertices in P that admit an empty circumscribing d-dimensional ball. A ball of $\mathbb{R}^d$ is called *empty* if its interior contains no point of P. For $p \in P$, we denote by $\mathrm{Del}_p(P)$ the Delaunay complex of P restricted to the tangent space T_p, i.e., the subcomplex of $\mathrm{Del}(P)$ formed by all the simplices with vertices in P that admit an empty circumscribing ball centered on T_p. Equivalently, the simplices of $\mathrm{Del}_p(P)$ are the simplices of $\mathrm{Del}(P)$ whose Voronoi dual face intersect T_p.

In the rest of this chapter, we assume that the points of P are in general position wrt spheres so that the Delaunay complex $\mathrm{Del}(P)$ naturally embeds in $\mathbb{R}^d$ as a triangulation of P (see Section 4.3). We will further assume that P satisfies the following *transversality condition* : T_p contains no point that is equidistant from more than $k + 1$ points of P. The transversality condition

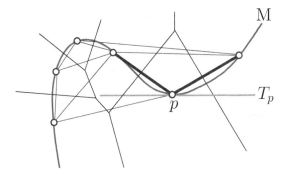

Figure 8.3 $\mathcal{M}$ is the curve in bold. The sample P is the set of circles. The line is the tangent space T_p at p. The figure shows the Voronoi diagram and the Delaunay triangulation of P with, in bold, star(p).

implies that the restricted Delaunay complex $\text{Del}_p(P)$ is a subcomplex of dimension at most k. Furthermore, if T_p intersects a $(d-k)$-face f of $\text{Vor}(P)$, the intersection consists of a single point c. The unique point c is the center of an empty ball circumscribing the k-simplex of $\text{Del}(P)$ dual to f. It is easy to see that applying an infinitesimal perturbation to P is sufficient to ensure the transversality condition.

We write star(p) for the closed star of p in $\text{Del}_p(P)$, i.e., the subcomplex of $\text{Del}_p(P)$ consisting of the simplices of $\text{Del}_p(P)$ that are incident to p together with their faces (see Figure 8.3). In the following, we will simply call star a closed star. For a k-simplex σ in star(p), we write $B_p(\sigma)$ for the ball centered on T_p that circumscribes σ, $c_p(\sigma)$ for its center and $R_p(\sigma)$ for its radius. Observe that $R_p(\sigma) \geq R(\sigma)$, where $R(\sigma)$ is the radius of the smallest ball circumscribing σ.

Definition 8.6 (Tangential Delaunay complex) We call tangential Delaunay complex, or tangential complex for short, the simplicial complex $\text{Del}_{T\mathcal{M}}(P) = \{\sigma, \sigma \in \text{star}(p), p \in P\}$.

Plainly, $\text{Del}_{T\mathcal{M}}(P)$ is a subcomplex of $\text{Del}(P)$ and is therefore a simplicial complex embedded in $\mathbb{R}^d$ if the points of P are in general position wrt spheres (see Section 4.3). The following lemma is crucial because it shows that computing the tangential complex reduces to computing n weighted Delaunay triangulations in the k-dimensional flats T_p, $p \in P$.

We define a map $\Psi_p : P \to T_p \times \mathbb{R}$ that associates to each point $p_i \in P$ a weighted point in T_p. Specifically, $\Psi_p(p_i) = (p_i', p_i'') \in T_p \times \mathbb{R}$, where p_i' is the orthogonal projection of p_i onto T_p and $p_i'' = -\|p_i - p_i'\|^2$. Observe that, under the transversality assumption, Ψ_p is 1-1.

It is known that the d-dimensional Voronoi diagram $\mathrm{Vor}(P)$ intersects T_p along the weighted k-dimensional Voronoi diagram $\mathrm{Vor}(\Psi_p(P))$ (see Exercise 4.11). Accordingly $\mathrm{Del}_p(P)$, the restriction of the d-dimensional Delaunay complex $\mathrm{Del}(P)$ to T_p, is isomorphic to the weighted Delaunay complex $\mathrm{Del}(\Psi_p(P))$. Note that the transversality condition implies the fact that the set $(\Psi_p(P))$ is in general position wrt to spheres in T_p. Therefore, the simplicial complex $\mathrm{Del}(\Psi_p(P))$ is naturally embedded in T_p. Moreover, the simplices of $\mathrm{Del}(\Psi_p(P))$ are obtained by projecting onto T_p the simplices of $\mathrm{Del}_p(P)$. Conversely, the simplices of $\mathrm{Del}_p(P)$ can be deduced from the simplices of $\mathrm{Del}(\Psi_p(P))$ by a piecewise linear map that we call the *lifting map*. Specifically, the lifting map lifts each weighted point (p', p'') associated to a vertex of $\mathrm{Del}(\Psi_p(P))$ to the unique point $p \in P$ such that $(p', p'') = \Psi_p(p)$. The lift of a simplex σ_p of $\mathrm{Del}_p(P)$ is then the geometric simplex σ whose vertices are the lifts of the vertices of σ_p. $\mathrm{Del}_p(P)$ is then the image of $\mathrm{Del}(\Psi_p(P))$ by the *lifting map*. We summarize our discussion in the following lemma:

Lemma 8.7 *If the points of P are in general position and satisfy the transversality condition, $\mathrm{Del}_p(P)$ is the lift of $\mathrm{Del}(\Psi_p(P))$, the k-dimensional weighted Delaunay triangulation of $\Psi_p(P)$ in T_p.*

We deduce from the lemma an efficient algorithm to compute $\mathrm{star}(p) = \mathrm{star}(p, \mathrm{Del}_p(P))$: project P onto T_p, compute $\mathrm{star}_{T_p}(p) = \mathrm{star}(p, \mathrm{Del}(\Psi_p(P)))$, the star of p in $\mathrm{Del}(\Psi_p(P))$, and then lift $\mathrm{star}_{T_p}(p)$ to $\mathrm{star}(p)$. Apart from the projection of the points onto T_p, this algorithm involves only operations in the k-dimensional flat T_p. If P is an $(\varepsilon, \bar{\eta})$-net of $\mathcal{M}$, we can even restrict our attention to the subset of P inside the ball of radius 2ε centered at p. The transversality condition with respect to the tangent plane T_p is therefore only required for points in that ball.

8.2.2 Inconsistent Simplices

In general, the tangential complex is *not* a combinatorial manifold (see Definition 2.17). This is due to the presence of so-called *inconsistent simplices*.

Definition 8.8 (Inconsistent simplex) A simplex $\sigma \in \mathrm{Del}_{T\mathcal{M}}(P)$ is called inconsistent if σ does not belong to the stars of *all* its vertices. Let σ be an inconsistent simplex and let p_i and p_j be two vertices of σ so that σ is in $\mathrm{star}(p_i)$ but not in $\mathrm{star}(p_j)$. We say that the pair of vertices (p_i, p_j) witnesses the inconsistent simplex σ.

Refer to Figure 8.4. Let σ be an inconsistent k-simplex witnessed by the pair of vertices (p_i, p_j). The simplex σ belongs to the star of p_i but not to the star of p_j. Equivalently, the Voronoi $(d - k)$-dimensional face $\mathrm{Vor}(\sigma)$ dual to

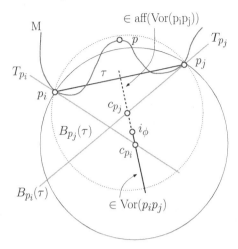

Figure 8.4 The figure shows an example of an inconsistent simplex $\sigma = [p_i, p_j]$ that belongs to star(p_i) and does not belong to star(p_j). The bisector of σ is subdivided in two line segments: the solid black line segment belongs to Vor(σ) and the dashed black line segment belongs to aff(Vor(σ)) but not to Vor(σ).

σ intersects T_{p_i} (at a point $c_{p_i}(\sigma)$) but does not intersect T_{p_j}. Observe that $c_{p_i}(\sigma)$ is the center of an empty d-dimensional ball $B_{p_i}(\sigma)$ circumscribing σ. Let $c_{p_j}(\sigma)$ denote the intersection of aff(Vor(σ)) with T_{p_j}. Differently from $B_{p_i}(\sigma)$, the d-dimensional ball $B_{p_j}(\sigma)$ centered at $c_{p_j}(\sigma)$ that circumscribes σ contains a subset $P_j(\sigma)$ of points of P in its interior. Therefore, the line segment $[c_{p_i}(\sigma)\, c_{p_j}(\sigma)]$ intersects the interior of some Voronoi cells (among which are the cells of the points of $P_j(\sigma)$). Let p_l be the point of $P \setminus \sigma$ whose Voronoi cell is hit first by the segment $[c_{p_i}(\sigma)\, c_{p_j}(\sigma)]$, when oriented from $c_{p_i}(\sigma)$ to $c_{p_j}(\sigma)$. We write σ^l for the $(k+1)$-simplex conv(σ, p_l) and $i(\sigma^l)$ for the first point of the oriented segment $[c_{p_i}(\sigma)\, c_{p_j}(\sigma)]$ that belongs to Vor(p_l). Observe that since the point $i(\sigma^l)$ belongs Vor(σ) $\cap$ Vor(p_l), σ^l is a $(k+1)$-simplex of Del(P). We say that the simplex σ^l is an *inconsistency trigger* of σ. Note that an inconsistent simplex σ may have several pairs of witnesses and several inconsistency triggers, but at most one inconsistency trigger for each pair of witnesses. Considering all pairs of witnesses of an inconsistent simplex σ, we obtain the set of inconsistency triggers of σ.

Definition 8.9 (Inconsistency trigger) An inconsistency trigger of a k-simplex σ of $\text{Del}_{T\mathcal{M}}(P)$ is a $(k+1)$-simplex of Del(P) that is the inconsistency trigger of σ for some ordered pair of vertices of σ that witnesses the inconsistency.

Because we assumed that the points satisfy the transversality condition, the tangential complex does not contain faces of dimension greater than k.

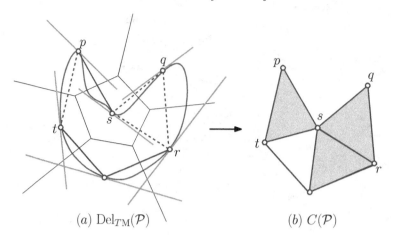

(a) $\mathrm{Del}_{TM}(\mathcal{P})$ $\qquad\qquad$ (b) $C(\mathcal{P})$

Figure 8.5 Figure (a) shows $\mathcal{M}$, the sample P, the tangent lines at the sample points, the Voronoi diagram of P and $\mathrm{Del}_{T\mathcal{M}}(P)$. The dashed lines indicate the inconsistent edges. In Figure (b), the line segments denote $\mathrm{Del}_{T\mathcal{M}}(P)$ and the grey triangles denote the inconsistency triggers.

It follows that no inconsistency trigger can belong to the tangential complex. Observe also that some of the subfaces of a inconsistency trigger may not belong to the tangential complex.

Because an inconsistency trigger σ^I is a $(k+1)$-simplex of $\mathrm{Del}(P)$, we will use the same notations for σ^I as for any other simplex, e.g., $R(\sigma^I)$ for the radius of the smallest circumscribing ball or $\Theta(\sigma^I)$ for its thickness. We write $\mathrm{Inc}(p)$ for the set of inconsistency triggers incident to p and $\mathrm{Inc}(P) = \cup_{p\in P}\mathrm{Inc}(p)$. We also define the *completed tangential complex* $\mathrm{Del}_{T\mathcal{M}}^{+I}(P) = \mathrm{Del}_{T\mathcal{M}}(P) \cup \mathrm{Inc}(P)$. See Figure 8.5.

Calculating $\mathrm{Del}_{T\mathcal{M}}^{+I}(P)$ is easy once we know $\mathrm{Del}(P)$. Indeed, it suffices to detect the inconsistent k-simplices that do not appear in the stars of all their vertices. Let σ be an inconsistent simplex witnessed by the pair (p_i, p_j). To compute the associated inconsistency trigger, we need to identify the point p_l. This can be done by computing the restriction of $\mathrm{Vor}(P)$ to the line $L_{ij} = (c_{p_i}(\sigma), c_{p_j}(\sigma))$. This in turn can be done by projecting the points of P onto L_{ij} and computing a 1-dimensional weighted Voronoi diagram (see Exercise 4.11).

8.2.3 Geometric Properties of Inconsistency Triggers

We give some simple geometric lemmas that, in particular, bound the thickness of the inconsistency triggers. We will use angles between affine spaces as defined in Section 5.2.2.

Lemma 8.10 *Let P be an ε-dense sample[1] of a submanifold $\mathcal{M}$. Let $\alpha_0 = \frac{1}{8}$ $(1 + 2\varepsilon - \sqrt{1 - 12\varepsilon + 4\varepsilon^2}) \approx \varepsilon$ and assume that $\alpha_0 < 1/4$. Then*

1. $\mathrm{Vor}(p) \cap T_p \subseteq B(p, \alpha_0 \mathrm{rch}(\mathcal{M}))$.
2. *for any k-simplex $\sigma \in \mathrm{star}(p)$, $R(\sigma) \leq R_p(\sigma) \leq \alpha_0 \mathrm{rch}(\mathcal{M})$ (recall that and $R_p(\sigma)$ is the radius of the circumscribing ball of σ centered on T_p.)*
3. *for any $\sigma \in \mathrm{Del}_{T\mathcal{M}}(P)$, $\Delta(\sigma) \leq 2\alpha_0 \mathrm{rch}(\mathcal{M})$.*

Proof We prove (i). The other statements easily follow. Let $x \in \mathrm{Vor}(p) \cap T_p$ and write $\|p - x\| = \alpha \mathrm{rch}(\mathcal{M})$. Let x' be the point of $\mathcal{M}$ closest to x and let $x'' = \Pi_p(x')$. We have $\|x - x'\| \leq \|x - p\|$ and by the triangular inequality, $\|p - x'\| \leq 2\|x - p\| = 2\alpha \mathrm{rch}(\mathcal{M})$. It then follows from Lemma 7.8 that

$$\|x' - x''\| \leq \frac{\|p - x'\|^2}{2\mathrm{rch}(\mathcal{M})} \leq 2\alpha^2 \mathrm{rch}(\mathcal{M}).$$

Now observe that $\|x' - x''\| = \|x - x'\| \cos \phi$, where $\phi = \angle(T_{x'}, T_p)$. Assuming $\alpha \leq \frac{1}{4}$, we have, by Lemma 7.10, $\cos \phi \geq 1 - 8\alpha^2$. We conclude that

$$\|x - x'\| \leq \frac{2\alpha^2 \mathrm{rch}(\mathcal{M})}{1 - 8\alpha^2}.$$

Because P is ε-dense in $\mathcal{M}$, there exists a point $q \in P$, such that $\|x' - q\| \leq \varepsilon \mathrm{rch}(\mathcal{M})$. Together with $x \in \mathrm{Vor}(p)$, this implies

$$\|x - p\| \leq \|x - q\| \leq \|x - x'\| + \|x' - q\| \leq \left(\frac{2\alpha^2}{1 - 8\alpha^2} + \varepsilon\right) \mathrm{rch}(\mathcal{M}) \quad (8.3)$$

We thus have

$$\alpha \leq \frac{2\alpha^2}{1 - 8\alpha^2} + \varepsilon \leq \frac{2\alpha^2}{1 - 2\alpha} + \varepsilon, \quad (8.4)$$

where the last inequality is obtained by taking $\alpha \leq 1/4$.

Let $\alpha_0 = \frac{1}{8}(1 + 2\varepsilon - \sqrt{1 - 12\varepsilon + 4\varepsilon^2})$ and $\alpha_1 = \frac{1}{8}(1 + 2\varepsilon + \sqrt{1 - 12\varepsilon + 4\varepsilon^2})$ and note that $\alpha_0 \approx \varepsilon$ and $\varepsilon \leq \alpha_0 < \frac{1}{4} \leq \alpha_1$. The inequality above is satisfied either when $\alpha \leq \alpha_0$ or when $\alpha \geq \alpha_1$. Hence, $\mathrm{Vor}(p)$ is contained in the union of $B(p, \alpha_0)$ and $\mathbb{R}^d \setminus B(p, \alpha_1)$. However, because $\mathrm{Vor}(p)$ is connected and contains p, $\mathrm{Vor}(p)$ must be entirely contained in $B(p, \alpha_0\mathrm{rch}(\mathcal{M}))$. $\qquad\square$

The following lemmas bound the size and shape of inconsistency triggers.

In particular, the lemmas state that if an inconsistent simplex is small, thick and has a small circumradius, its inconsistency triggers have small circumradii (Lemma 8.11) and cannot be thick (Lemma 8.12).

---

[1] See Definition 7.7.

Lemma 8.11 *Let σ be an inconsistent k-simplex and let σ^I be a $(k+1)$-simplex that triggers the inconsistency of σ. Writing $\theta = \max_{p \in \sigma} (\angle(\mathrm{aff}(\sigma), T_p))$, we have*

$$\sin \theta \leq \frac{\Delta(\sigma)}{\Theta(\sigma) \, \mathrm{rch}(\mathcal{M})} \quad \text{and} \quad R(\sigma^I) \leq \frac{R(\sigma)}{\cos \theta}.$$

Proof We assume that the vertex pair (p_i, p_j) is the witness pair of σ associated to the trigger σ^I and use the same notations as in Section 8.2.2. Therefore σ belongs to $\mathrm{Del}_{p_i}(P)$ but not to $\mathrm{Del}_{p_j}(P)$, and the vertices of σ^I lie in the closure of $B_{ij} = B_{p_j}(\sigma) \setminus B_{p_i}(\sigma)$. Observe also that c_{p_i}, c_{p_j} and $i(\sigma^I)$ lie in the $(d-k)$-flat that contains $c(\sigma)$ and is perpendicular to $\mathrm{aff}(\sigma)$. Hence the orthogonal projection of these four points onto $\mathrm{aff}(\sigma)$ is $c(\sigma)$.

We now bound $\theta = \angle(\mathrm{aff}(\sigma), T_p)$ for any $p \in \sigma$. By Lemma 7.8 (2), we have for any $p, q \in \sigma$, $d(q, T_p) \leq \frac{\Delta^2(\sigma)}{2\mathrm{rch}(\mathcal{M})}$ and by Lemma 5.14

$$\sin \theta \leq \frac{2 \frac{\Delta^2(\sigma)}{2\mathrm{rch}(\mathcal{M})}}{\Theta(\sigma) \, \Delta(\sigma)} = \frac{\Delta(\sigma)}{\Theta(\sigma) \, \mathrm{rch}(M)}.$$

Because the orthogonal projection of c_{p_i} onto $\mathrm{aff}(\sigma)$ is $c(\sigma)$, $\omega = \angle(p_i - c_{p_i}, p_i - c(\sigma)) = \min_{u \in \mathrm{aff}(\sigma)} \angle(p_i - c_{p_i}, u) \leq \theta$. We thus have

$$R_{p_i}(\sigma) = \|p_i - c_{p_i}\| = \frac{R(\sigma)}{\cos \omega} \leq \frac{R(\sigma)}{\cos \theta}.$$

and we get the same bound if p_i is replaced by p_j or by any other vertex p in this inequality. Because $i(\sigma^I) \in [c_{p_i} c_{p_j}]$, we also have $R(\sigma^I) \leq \|i(\sigma^I) - p_i\| \leq R(\sigma)/\cos \theta$. $\square$

We deduce from the lemma a bound on the thickness of inconsistency triggers. This is a crucial property to be used later to remove inconsistencies.

Lemma 8.12 *The thickness of the $(k+1)$-simplex σ^I that triggers the inconsistency of a k-simplex σ satisfies:*

$$\Theta(\sigma^I) \leq \frac{\Delta(\sigma^I)}{2(k+1)\mathrm{rch}(\mathcal{M})} \left(1 + \frac{2}{\Theta(\sigma)}\right)$$

Proof Let p_l be the vertex of σ^I that is not a vertex of σ. We bound the altitude $D(p_l, \sigma^I)$ of σ^I. Let $q \in \sigma$. We deduce

$$D(p_l, \sigma^I) = \|p_l - q\| \sin \angle(p_l - q, \mathrm{aff}(\sigma))$$
$$\leq \Delta(\sigma^I) \left(\sin \angle(p_l - q, T_q) + \sin \angle(T_q, \mathrm{aff}(\sigma))\right)$$
$$\leq \Delta(\sigma^I) \left(\frac{\Delta(\sigma^I)}{2\mathrm{rch}(\mathcal{M})} + \frac{\Delta(\sigma)}{\Theta(\sigma) \, \mathrm{rch}(\mathcal{M})}\right) \quad \text{(Lemmas 7.8 \& 8.11)}$$
$$\leq \frac{\Delta^2(\sigma^I)}{2\mathrm{rch}(\mathcal{M})} \left(1 + \frac{2}{\Theta(\sigma)}\right)$$

The bound on the thickness then follows from the definition of thickness (see Section 5.2). □

Corollary 8.13 *Let P be an ε-dense sample of $\mathcal{M}$ and let σ^I be a $(k+1)$-simplex that triggers the inconsistency of a k-simplex σ. Assume that σ is Θ_0-thick and that Θ_0 satisfies*

$$\Theta_0^{k+1} > \frac{\alpha_0}{k+1} \left(\cos \arcsin \frac{2\alpha_0}{\Theta_0^k} \right)^{-1} \left(1 + \frac{2}{\Theta_0^k} \right) \qquad (8.5)$$

where α_0 is defined in Lemma 8.10. Then σ^I is not Θ_0-thick.

Proof We need to prove that $\Theta(\sigma^I) < \Theta_0^{k+1}$. From Lemma 8.12 we have

$$\Theta(\sigma^I) \le \frac{\Delta(\sigma^I)}{2(k+1)\mathrm{rch}(\mathcal{M})} \left(1 + \frac{2}{\Theta(\sigma)} \right) \le \frac{\Delta(\sigma^I)}{2(k+1)\mathrm{rch}(\mathcal{M})} \left(1 + \frac{2}{\Theta_0^k} \right).$$

We now bound $\Delta(\sigma^I)$:

$$\Delta(\sigma^I) \le 2R(\sigma^I)$$

$$\le 2R(\sigma) \left(\cos \arcsin \frac{\Delta(\sigma)}{\Theta(\sigma)\,\mathrm{rch}(\mathcal{M})} \right)^{-1} \qquad \text{(Lemma 8.11)}$$

$$\le 2\alpha_0 \,\mathrm{rch}(\mathcal{M}) \left(\cos \arcsin \frac{2\alpha_0}{\Theta_0^k} \right)^{-1} \qquad \text{(Lemma 8.10)}$$

Hence

$$\Theta(\sigma^I) \le \frac{\alpha_0}{k+1} \left(\cos \arcsin \frac{2\alpha_0}{\Theta_0^k} \right)^{-1} \left(1 + \frac{2}{\Theta_0^k} \right).$$

It follows that if Equation 8.5 holds, $\Theta(\sigma^I) < \Theta_0^{k+1}$, which means that σ^I is not Θ_0-thick. □

Note that the condition in the corollary is satisfied when the thickness of the inconsistent simplexes satisfy $\Theta(\sigma) > \Theta_0^k = \Omega(\varepsilon^{1/(k+1)})$.

8.3 Submanifold Reconstruction

Let $\mathcal{M}$ denote a submanifold of $\mathbb{R}^d$ that is compact, closed, differentiable, and whose reach is positive. The only knowledge we have about $\mathcal{M}$ is its dimension k together with a finite point sample $P \subset \mathcal{M}$ and the tangent spaces at those points. From that knowledge, we want to construct a triangulation of $\mathcal{M}$. We assume that P is an $(\varepsilon, \bar{\eta})$-net of $\mathcal{M}$ (See Definition 7.7). The parameters ε and

$\bar{\eta}$ need not to be known but must satisfy some conditions to be made explicit in the analysis of the algorithm. In particular, we need ε to be sufficiently small.

The main idea of the proposed reconstruction algorithm is to rely on the tangential complex $\mathrm{Del}_{TM}(P)$. However, we know from the previous section that $\mathrm{Del}_{TM}(P)$ may not be a combinatorial manifold, and our first goal is to obtain a complex that is a k-combinatorial manifold. This will be achieved by assigning weights to the points of P and resorting to the weighted tangential complex $\mathrm{Del}_{TM}(\hat{P})$ which is the natural counterpart of the tangential complex when the point set P is replaced by a set $\hat{P}$ of weighted points. Properties of tangential complexes extend to weighted tangential complexes and, in particular, we will show that the occurrence of inconsistencies in $\mathrm{Del}_{TM}(\hat{P})$ is triggered by the existence of non-thick simplices of dimension at most $k + 1$ in $\mathrm{Del}(\hat{P})$. Then, since it is possible to assign weights to the points of P to get a thick weighted Delaunay complex (Section 5.3), it is a fortiori possible to get a weighted tangential complex $\mathrm{Del}_{TM}(\hat{P})$ with no inconsistency. Finally, an algorithm is derived from Moser Tardos algorithm (Section 5.2). The algorithm uses data structures of dimension at most k. Its output is a k-dimensional combinatorial manifold that we will show to be homeomorphic to $\mathcal{M}$ and close to $\mathcal{M}$.

8.3.1 Weight Assignment

We recall the definition of a *weighting scheme* introduced in Section 5.3. Given a point set $P = \{p_1, \ldots, p_n\} \subseteq \mathbb{R}^d$, a weighting scheme on P is a function w that assigns to each point $p_i \in P$ a non-negative real weight $w(p_i)$. We write $\hat{p}_i = (p_i, w(p_i))$ and $\hat{P} = \{\hat{p}_1, \ldots, \hat{p}_n\}$.

We recall the definition of the *relative amplitude* of w as $\tilde{w} = \max_{p \in P} \frac{w(p)}{L^2(p)}$ where $L(p) = \min_{q \in P \setminus \{p\}} ||p - q||$. Note that $2\varepsilon\mathrm{rch}(M) \geq L(p) \geq \bar{\eta}\varepsilon\,\mathrm{rch}(\mathcal{M})$ because P is an $(\varepsilon, \bar{\eta})$-net.

From this point onward, we assume that all weights are non-negative and that $\tilde{w} \leq \tilde{w}_0$, for some constant $\tilde{w}_0 < 1/4$. Hence, for any point $p \in P$, $w(p) \in [0, \tilde{w}_0 L^2(p)] \subset [0, 4\tilde{w}_0 \varepsilon^2 \mathrm{rch}^2(M)]$.

The condition on $\tilde{w}$ implies in particular that the weighted points in $\hat{P}$ have pairwise positive weighted distances, which ensures that any point in P appears as a vertex of the weighted Delaunay complex $\mathrm{Del}(\hat{P})$ (see Section 4.4.3).

We can extend the definition of the tangential complex to the case of a set $\hat{P}$ of weighted points. We simply need to replace in Definition 8.6 the Delaunay complex $\mathrm{Del}(P)$ by the weighted Delaunay complex $\mathrm{Del}(\hat{P})$. The role played above by Delaunay balls will be played by Delaunay weighted points, i.e., weighted points orthogonal to weighted Delaunay simplices and free of weighted points in $\hat{P}$. Lemma 8.7 remains valid provided that the mapping Ψ_p is extended to weighted points as follows. If $\hat{p}_i = (p_i, w_i) \in \mathbb{R}^d \times \mathbb{R}$ is a weighted point, we define $\Psi_p(\hat{p}_i) = (p_i, w_i - \|p_i - p_i'\|^2)$, where p_i' is the orthogonal projection of p_i on the tangent space T_p.

We now extend to the weighted case the properties of the inconsistency triggers shown in Section 8.2.

Let P be an ε-dense sample of a submanifold $\mathcal{M}$ and assume that the weighting scheme on P has a relative amplitude $\tilde{w} \leq \tilde{w}_0 < 1/4$. We denote by $\text{Del}_p(\hat{P})$ the weighted Delaunay complex restricted to T_p and by $\text{star}(\hat{p})$ the star of p in $\text{Del}_p(\hat{P})$. We further write $\text{Vor}(\hat{p})$ for the cell of p in the weighted Voronoi diagram $\text{Vor}(\hat{P})$. For any k-simplex σ in $\text{Del}_p(\hat{P})$, we denote respectively by $R(\sigma)$ and $R(\hat{\sigma})$ the circumradius and weighted radius of σ, by $R_p(\sigma)$ the radius of the ball centered on T_p that circumscribes σ and by $R_p(\hat{\sigma})$ the radius of the ball centered on T_p that is orthogonal to $\hat{\sigma}$.

Lemma 8.14 *Let*

$$\hat{\varepsilon} = \varepsilon(1 + 2\sqrt{\tilde{w}_0}),$$
$$\hat{\alpha}_0 = \frac{1}{8}(1 + 2\hat{\varepsilon} - \sqrt{1 - 12\hat{\varepsilon} + 4\hat{\varepsilon}^2}) \approx \varepsilon(1 + 2\sqrt{\tilde{w}_0}),$$
$$\hat{\alpha}_1 = \hat{\alpha}_0 + 2\varepsilon\sqrt{\tilde{w}_0} \approx \varepsilon(1 + 4\sqrt{\tilde{w}_0})$$

and assume $\hat{\alpha}_0 \leq \frac{1}{4}$. Then we have:

(i) $\text{Vor}(\hat{p}) \cap T_p \subseteq B(p, \hat{\alpha}_0 \,\text{rch}(\mathcal{M}))$,
(ii) *for any k-simplex $\sigma \in \text{star}(\hat{p})$, $R(\hat{\sigma}) \leq R_p(\hat{\sigma}) \leq \hat{\alpha}_0 \,\text{rch}(\mathcal{M})$.*
(iii) *for any $\sigma \in \text{Del}_{T\mathcal{M}}(\hat{P})$, $\Delta(\sigma) \leq 2\hat{\alpha}_1 \,\text{rch}(\mathcal{M})$.*

Proof The proof of (i) is an easy adaptation of the proof of Lemma 8.10. We define x, x' and x'' and α as in the proof of Lemma 8.10 and still get

$$\|x - x'\| \leq \frac{2\alpha^2 \,\text{rch}(\mathcal{M})}{1 - 8\alpha^2}.$$

Because P is ε-dense in $\mathcal{M}$, there exists a point $q \in P$, such that $\|x' - q\| \leq \varepsilon\,\text{rch}(\mathcal{M})$. Because x is in $\text{Vor}(\hat{p})$, this implies that

$$\|x - p\|^2 + w(p) \leq \|x - q\|^2 + w(q)$$
$$\|x - p\|^2 \leq (\|x - x'\| + \|x' - q\|)^2 + w(q),$$

which yields

$$\alpha^2 \leq \left(\frac{2\alpha^2}{1 - 8\alpha^2} + \varepsilon\right)^2 + 4\tilde{w}_0\varepsilon^2$$

Hence,

$$\alpha \le \frac{2\alpha^2}{1 - 8\alpha^2} + \varepsilon \left(1 + 2\sqrt{\tilde{w}_0} \right),$$

which is just Equation 8.4 where ε has been replaced by $\hat{\varepsilon}$ so that we can end the proof as in Lemma 8.10.

Let $c_p(\hat{\sigma})$ be the point of T_p that is orthogonal to $\hat{\sigma}$. Property (ii) follows easily because $c_p(\hat{\sigma})$ belongs to $\mathrm{Vor}(\hat{p}) \cap T_p$ and $d(c_p(\hat{\sigma}), p)^2 = R_p(\hat{\sigma})^2 + w(p)$. Hence $R_p(\hat{\sigma}) \le d(c_p(\hat{\sigma}), p) \le \hat{\alpha}_0 \, \mathrm{rch}(\mathcal{M})$.

To prove Property (iii), we bound the Euclidean distance $d(c_p(\hat{\sigma}), q)$ between $c_p(\hat{\sigma})$ and a vertex q of σ as follows:

$$
\begin{aligned}
d(c_p(\hat{\sigma}), q)^2 &= R_p(\hat{\sigma})^2 + w(q) \\
&\le \hat{\alpha}_0^2 \, \mathrm{rch}(\mathcal{M})^2 + 4\tilde{w}_0 \varepsilon^2 \mathrm{rch}(\mathcal{M})^2.
\end{aligned}
$$

Hence,

$$d(c_p(\hat{\sigma}), q) \le \left(\hat{\alpha}_0 + 2\varepsilon\sqrt{\tilde{w}_0} \right) \mathrm{rch}(\mathcal{M}) = \hat{\alpha}_1 \, \mathrm{rch}(\mathcal{M})$$

Because this bound holds for any vertex q of σ, the bound given in (iii) for the diameter $\Delta(\sigma)$ follows.   □

Lemma 8.15 *Let σ be an inconsistent k-simplex of $\mathrm{Del}_{T_\mathcal{M}}(\hat{P})$ and let σ^I be a $(k + 1)$-simplex that triggers the inconsistency of σ. If θ is defined by $\theta = \max_{p \in \sigma}(\angle(\mathrm{aff}(\sigma), T_p)$, we have*

$$\sin\theta \le \frac{\Delta(\sigma)}{\Theta(\sigma)\,\mathrm{rch}(\mathcal{M})} \quad \text{and} \quad R(\hat{\sigma}^I) \le \frac{R(\hat{\sigma})}{\cos\theta}.$$

Proof The proof is the same as the proof of Lemma 8.11   □

Lemma 8.12 applies verbatim to the weighted case and finally an easy adaptation of the proof of Corollary 8.13 yields the following weighted version.

Corollary 8.16 *Let P be an ε-dense sample of $\mathcal{M}$ and let w be a weighting scheme on P with a relative amplitude $\tilde{w} \le \tilde{w}_0 < 1/4$. Let σ be an inconsistent k-simplex and let σ^I be a $(k + 1)$-simplex that triggers the inconsistency of σ. Assume that σ is Θ_0-thick and that Θ_0 satisfies*

$$\Theta_0^{k+1} > \frac{\hat{\alpha}_1}{k+1} \left(\cos \arcsin \frac{2\hat{\alpha}_0}{\Theta_0^k} \right)^{-1} \left(1 + \frac{2}{\Theta_0^k} \right) \qquad (8.6)$$

where $\hat{\alpha}_0$ and $\hat{\alpha}_1$ are defined in Lemma 8.14. Then σ^I is not Θ_0-thick.

Proof We need to prove that $\Theta(\sigma') < \Theta_0^{k+1}$. From Lemma 8.12 we have

$$\Theta(\sigma') \leq \frac{\Delta(\sigma')}{2(k+1)\mathrm{rch}(\mathcal{M})} \left(1 + \frac{2}{\Theta(\tau)}\right) \tag{8.7}$$

We now bound $\Delta(\sigma')$. Let $c(\hat{\sigma}')$ be the weighted center of σ' and let q be any vertex of σ'. We have

$$
\begin{aligned}
d(c(\hat{\sigma}'), q)^2 &= R(\hat{\sigma}')^2 + w(q) \\
&\leq \frac{R(\hat{\sigma})^2}{\cos\theta^2} + 4\tilde{w}_0\varepsilon^2\mathrm{rch}(\mathcal{M})^2 \\
&\leq \frac{\hat{\alpha}_0^2 + 4\tilde{w}_0\varepsilon^2}{\cos\theta^2}\mathrm{rch}(\mathcal{M})^2 \leq \frac{\hat{\alpha}_1^2}{\cos\theta^2}\mathrm{rch}(\mathcal{M})^2
\end{aligned}
$$

where θ is given by Lemma 8.15 and $\hat{\alpha}_1$ is defined in Lemma 8.14. Since this is true for any vertex q of σ', $\Delta(\sigma')$ can be bound by $2\frac{\hat{\alpha}_1}{\cos\theta}\mathrm{rch}(\mathcal{M})$. Plugging this bound in Equation 8.7 yields that $\Theta(\sigma') < \Theta_0^{k+1}$ if σ is Θ_0-thick and Θ_0 satisfies Equation 8.6. $\qquad\square$

Note that Equation 8.6 in Corollary 8.16 is satisfied if $\Theta_0 = \Omega(\varepsilon^{\frac{1}{k(k+1)}})$.

8.3.2 Reconstruction Algorithm

We conclude from the previous section that if P is an $(\varepsilon, \bar{\eta})$-net of $\mathcal{M}$, the occurrence of inconsistencies in the tangential complex $\mathrm{Del}_{T\mathcal{M}}(P)$ is due to the occurrence of nonthick simplices of dimension up to $k+1$ in the Delaunay complex $\mathrm{Del}(P)$. This property still holds in the weighted case provided that the weighting scheme has a small relative amplitude. We can thus proceed in a way similar to what has been done in Section 5.3 to remove nonthick simplices from Delaunay complexes using a variant of Moser-Tardos algorithm. Here we want to find a weighting scheme on P such that the simplices of the tangential complex as well as the inconsistency triggers (all are simplices of $\mathrm{Del}(\hat{P})$) are thick. As a consequence, the tangential complex $\mathrm{Del}_{T\mathcal{M}}(\hat{P})$ won't contain any inconsistency.

The algorithm depends on two parameters $\tilde{w}_0$ and Θ_0. Here as in Section 5.3, we call resampling the operation which consists in reassigning the weights of the vertices of a simplex. The weights are taken independently. The weight of a vertex p is taken uniformly at random in $[0, \tilde{w}_0 L^2(p)]$. The algorithm maintains the weighted tangential complex $\mathrm{Del}_{T\mathcal{M}}(\hat{P})$ and *resamples* the Θ_0-flakes that may appear in $\mathrm{Del}_{T\mathcal{M}}(\hat{P})$ or in the $(k+1)$ simplices that trigger an inconsistency. Note that the algorithm does not compute the full weighted Delaunay complex $\mathrm{Del}(\hat{P})$ but only a subcomplex of dimension $k+1$.

Algorithm 8: Tangential complex with no inconsistency

Input: $P, \{T_p, p \in P\}, \tilde{w}_0, \Theta_0$

Initialize all weights to 0 and compute $\mathrm{Del}_{T\mathcal{M}}(\hat{P})$

while there are Θ_0-flakes or inconsistencies in $\mathrm{Del}_{T\mathcal{M}}(\hat{P})$ **do**

    while there is a Θ_0-flake σ in $\mathrm{Del}_{T\mathcal{M}}(\hat{P})$ **do**

        resample σ

        update $\mathrm{Del}_{T\mathcal{M}}(\hat{P})$

    if there is an inconsistent simplex σ in $\mathrm{Del}_{T\mathcal{M}}(\hat{P})$ **then**

        compute a trigger simplex σ^I associated to σ

        resample the flake $\sigma \subset \sigma^I$

        update $\mathrm{Del}_{T\mathcal{M}}(\hat{P})$

Output: A weighting scheme on P and the corresponding weighted tangential Delaunay complex $\mathrm{Del}_{T\mathcal{M}}(\hat{P})$, which is granted to be Θ_0-thick and to have no inconsistency.

Theorem 8.17 *Let $\mathcal{M}$ be a submanifold of positive reach and let P be an $(\varepsilon, \bar{\eta})$-net of $\mathcal{M}$ for a sufficiently small ε. Let in addition $\tilde{w}_0 < 1/4$ and Θ_0 be two constants satisfying Equation 8.6 and the following Equation*

$$\left[\frac{6}{\bar{\eta}} \frac{(1 + 4\sqrt{\tilde{w}_0})}{\cos \theta} \right]^{k(k+2)} \frac{32\Theta_0}{\tilde{w}_0 \bar{\eta}^3} \frac{(1 + 2\sqrt{\tilde{w}_0})(1 + 4\sqrt{\tilde{w}_0})^2}{\cos^3 \theta} \le \frac{1}{e} \qquad (8.8)$$

where

$$\theta = \arcsin \frac{2\hat{\alpha}_1}{\Theta_0^k} \approx \arcsin \frac{2\varepsilon(1 + 4\sqrt{\tilde{w}_0})}{\Theta_0^k}.$$

Then Algorithm 8 terminates and outputs a weight assignment on the points of P such that the weighted tangential complex $\mathrm{Del}_{T\mathcal{M}}(\hat{P})$ is free of inconsistencies. The expected time complexity of the algorithm is $O(|P|)$.

Proof   First note that the algorithm removed inconsistencies only when there are no Θ_0-flakes in $\mathrm{Del}_{T\mathcal{M}}(\hat{P})$. Then Equation 8.6 ensures that the trigger of an inconsistency is not Θ_0-thick (Lemma 8.16) and therefore includes a Θ_0-flake that can be resampled.

The resampled simplices are Θ_0-flakes of $\mathrm{Del}(\hat{P})$ that either belong to $\mathrm{Del}_{T\mathcal{M}}(\hat{P})$ or are included in an inconsistency trigger. Let σ be any resampled flake. From Lemmas 8.14 and 8.15, the weighted radius $R(\hat{\sigma})$ is at most

$$R(\hat{\sigma}) \le \frac{\hat{\alpha}_0}{\cos \theta} \mathrm{rch}(\mathcal{M}),$$

and, from Lemma 8.14 and the proof of Corollary 8.16, its diameter is bounded by

$$\Delta(\sigma) \le \frac{2\hat{\alpha}_1}{\cos\theta}\mathrm{rch}(\mathcal{M}).$$

Therefore Algorithm 8 is a variant of Moser-Tardos algorithm similar to the algorithm of Section 5.3.5 that removes from $\mathrm{Del}(\hat{P})$ all Θ_0-flakes with small weighted radii. Then, arguing as in Section 5.3.5, we show that Algorithm 8 terminates provided that the condition expressed in Equation 8.8 (similar to Equation 5.13) is satisfied. See Exercise 8.3 for details. The expected number of resampled simplices is $O(|P|)$. Because each resampling can be performed in constant time, the expected complexity of Algorithm 8 is also $O(|P|)$.

Assume that $\bar{\eta}$ and $\tilde{w}_0 < \frac{1}{4}$ are fixed. Then Equation 8.6 is satisfied if Θ_0 is sufficiently large with respect to ε and Algorithm 8 terminates provided that Θ_0 is sufficiently small with respect to $\bar{\eta}$ and $\tilde{w}_0$ and is sufficiently large with respect to ε. Those conditions can be satisfied if the sampling radius ε is sufficiently small. $\square$

8.3.3 Guarantees on the Reconstruction

The simplicial complex $\hat{\mathcal{M}} = \mathrm{Del}_{T\mathcal{M}}(\hat{P})$ output by the algorithm is free of inconsistencies. In addition, it is a good approximation of $\mathcal{M}$ as stated in the following theorem.

Theorem 8.18 (Guarantees) *Under the same hypotheses as in Theorem 8.17, the Delaunay tangential complex $\hat{\mathcal{M}} = \mathrm{Del}_{T\mathcal{M}}(\hat{P})$ output by the algorithm satisfies the following properties:*

1. *All the simplices in $\hat{\mathcal{M}}$ are Θ_0-thick.*
2. *$\hat{\mathcal{M}}$ is a piecewise linear k-submanifold without boundary;*
3. *$\hat{\mathcal{M}}$ is homeomorphic to $\mathcal{M}$;*
4. *The Hausdorff distance between $\hat{\mathcal{M}}$ and $\mathcal{M}$ is at most $4\varepsilon^2\mathrm{rch}(\mathcal{M})$;*
5. *If σ is a k-simplex of $\hat{\mathcal{M}}$ and p is a vertex of σ, we have*

$$\sin\angle(\mathrm{aff}(\sigma), T_p) \le \frac{2\varepsilon}{\Theta_0}.$$

Proof The first statement directly follows from the algorithm. Proving the second statement reduces to proving that the link of any vertex of $\hat{\mathcal{M}}$ is a topological $(k-1)$-sphere. We first observe that, since $\hat{\mathcal{M}}$ contains no inconsistencies, the star of any vertex p in $\hat{\mathcal{M}}$ is identical to $\mathrm{star}(\hat{p})$, the star of p in $\mathrm{Del}_p(\hat{P})$. Hence, to prove the second statement, it is enough to prove that the link of p in $\mathrm{Del}_p(\hat{P})$ is a topological $(k-1)$-sphere, which is done in the next lemma.

Lemma 8.19 *$\hat{\mathcal{M}}$ is a simplicial combinatorial manifold.*

Proof It is sufficient to prove that, for any $p \in P$, the link of p in $\hat{\mathcal{M}}$ is a topological $(k-1)$-sphere. By Lemma 8.7, $\text{star}(\hat{p})$ is isomorphic to $\text{star}_p(\hat{p})$, the star of p in $\text{Del}(\Psi_p(\hat{P}))$. Since $\text{star}_p(\hat{p})$ is a k-dimensional triangulated topological ball under the general position and transversality assumptions, the same is true for $\text{star}(\hat{p})$. To prove the lemma, it is then sufficient to show that p cannot belong to the boundary of $\text{star}_p(\hat{p})$. Consider the dual cell V of $p = \Psi_p(p)$ in the weighted Voronoi diagram $\text{Vor}(\Psi_p(\hat{P}))$. V is the intersection of the Voronoi cell of p with T_p, i.e. $V = \text{Vor}(p) \cap T_p$. By Lemma 8.10, V is bounded, which implies that p cannot belong to the boundary of $\text{star}_p(\hat{p})$. It follows that p cannot belong to the boundary of $\text{star}(\hat{p})$. □

Statements $3-5$ in Theorem 8.18 then follow from Theorem 7.16. We need to check that the five hypotheses of Theorem 7.16 are satisfied.

Hypotheses $(a)-(c)$ of the theorem are satisfied provided that ε is small enough (see Exercises 8.2 and 8.3). Hypothesis (d) is satisfied thanks to Lemma 8.7. We now prove that Hypothesis (e) holds also.

Lemma 8.20 *Hypothesis (e) of Theorem 7.16 is satisfied.*

Proof Let q be a vertex of $\hat{\mathcal{M}}$ that q belongs to $U_p = B(p,r) \cap \mathcal{M}$ where $r = \varepsilon \, \text{rch}(M)(1+2\varepsilon)$. We write $q' = \Pi_p(q)$ for the projection of q onto T_p and $\text{star}'(p) = \Pi_p(\text{star}(p))$ for the projection of $\text{star}(p)$ onto T_p. To prove that Hypothesis (e) is satisfied, it is sufficient to prove that q' is a vertex of the k-dimensional weighted Delaunay triangulation $\text{Del}(\Psi_p(P))$ (see Lemma 8.7), which is equivalent to proving the following claim.

Claim *The Voronoi cell of q intersects T_p.*

Proof of the claim To prove the claim, we will make use of Lemma 7.6 that states that $V(q)$ has a large extent in N_q and therefore intersects T_p. Denote by q'' the (unique) intersection point of N_q and T_p, and by q' the projection of q onto T_p. Because $q \in U_p$, we have $\|p-q\| < \varepsilon(1+2\varepsilon)\,\text{rch}(\mathcal{M}) = \varepsilon'\,\text{rch}(\mathcal{M})$, and it follows from Lemma 7.8 that $\|q-q'\| < \frac{\varepsilon'^2\,\text{rch}(\mathcal{M})}{2}$. Write now $\theta = \angle(T_p, T_q)$ and recall that $\theta < 2\varepsilon'$ (Lemma 7.10). It follows that

$$\|q-q''\| < \frac{\|q-q'\|}{\cos\theta} < \text{rch}(\mathcal{M})$$

by our assumption on ε. It then follows from Lemma 7.6 that $q'' \in V(q) \cap T_p$, which proves the claim. □

The claim implies that q' has a nonempty cell in the weighted Voronoi diagram $\text{Vor}(\Psi_p(P))$ embedded in T_p (see Section 8.7). Equivalently, q is a vertex of $\text{Del}_p(P)$ and q' is a vertex of $\text{Del}(\Psi_p(P))$. Since $\text{Del}(\Psi_p(P))$

is a triangulation embedded in T_p (under the transversality condition of Section 8.2.1), q' cannot belong to star$'(p)$ without being a vertex of star$'(p)$ and, accordingly, q must be a vertex of star(P). Therefore, Hypothesis 4' holds and the lemma is proved. $\qquad\square$

This ends the proof of Lemma 8.20. All hypotheses of Theorem 7.16 are satisfied. This ends the proof of Theorem 8.18. $\qquad\square$

8.4 Exercises

Exercise 8.1 Given is an $(\varepsilon, \bar{\eta})$-net P of a differentiable (unknown) submanifold $\mathcal{M} \in \mathbb{R}^d$. Propose a method to approximate the tangent space T_p of $\mathcal{M}$ at $p \in P$.

Exercise 8.2 (Distance between components) Let P be an ε-dense sample of a submanifold $\mathcal{M}$ of positive reach rch$(\mathcal{M})$. Prove that each connected component of $\mathcal{M}$ contains at least one point of P and therefore at least one vertex of Del$_{T\mathcal{M}}(P)$. (Hint: Show that the distance between any two connected components of $\mathcal{M}$ is at least 2rch$(\mathcal{M})$).

Exercise 8.3 Show that Algorithm 8 terminates if the condition expressed as Equation 8.8 is satisfied. Observe that, for given values of $\bar{\eta}$ and $\tilde{w}_0$, the condition is satisfied if Θ_0 is sufficiently small and ε is sufficiently small compared to Θ_0^k.

Sketch of the proof. Equation 8.8 is the same as Equation 5.12 of Theorem 5.21 applied to the case of Algorithm 8. We use the notations of Section 8.3.2.

Using the bounds on the weighted radius and the diameter of a resampled flake σ (Lemma 8.14), we first bound, as in Section 5.3, the measure of the weight range $I(\sigma, p)$ of a vertex p of σ:

$$
\begin{aligned}
|I(\sigma, p)| &\leq 8\Theta_0 \frac{\Delta(\sigma)^2}{L(\sigma)} R(\hat{\sigma}) \\
&\leq \frac{8\Theta_0}{\varepsilon\bar{\eta}} \frac{4\hat{\alpha}_1^2 \hat{\alpha}_0}{\cos^3 \theta} \text{rch}(\mathcal{M})^2 \\
&\leq \frac{32\Theta_0}{\bar{\eta}} \frac{(1 + 2\sqrt{\tilde{w}_0})(1 + 4\sqrt{\tilde{w}_0})^2}{\cos^3 \theta} \varepsilon^2 \text{rch}(\mathcal{M})^2.
\end{aligned}
$$

Then, the probability ϖ that such a flake occurs is at most $\frac{|I(\sigma, p)|}{\tilde{w}_0 L(p)^2}$ (Lemma 5.23), where $L(p)$ is the length of the shortest edge incident to p in Del$(\hat{P})$. Thus

$$\varpi \leq \frac{32\Theta_0}{\tilde{w}_0 \bar{\eta}^3} \frac{(1 + 2\sqrt{\tilde{w}_0})(1 + 4\sqrt{\tilde{w}_0})^2}{\cos^3 \theta}.$$

We then bound $\Gamma + 1$ where Γ is the number of events overlapping a given flake σ. Overlapping events are flakes that share at least one vertex. Because resampled flakes have their diameter bounded by $\Delta_m = \frac{2\hat{\alpha}_1 \mathrm{rch}(\mathcal{M})}{\cos \theta}$, flakes overlapping a given flake σ have their vertices within the ball $B(c(\sigma), \frac{3}{2}\Delta_m)$ where $c(\sigma)$ is the circumcenter of σ. Using then the fact that two vertices are at least $\bar{\eta}\varepsilon\mathrm{rch}(\mathcal{M})$ apart, we bound the number of vertices in this ball and then $\Gamma + 1$ using a volume argument:

$$\Gamma + 1 \leq \left(\frac{\frac{3}{2}\Delta_m}{\frac{1}{2}\bar{\eta}\varepsilon\mathrm{rch}(\mathcal{M})} \right)^{k(k+2)}$$

$$\leq \left(\frac{6\hat{\alpha}_1}{\bar{\eta}\cos\theta} \right)^{k(k+2)} \approx \left(\frac{6(1 + 4\sqrt{\tilde{w}_0})}{\bar{\eta}\cos\theta} \right)^{k(k+2)}$$

The condition for the termination of Algorithm 8 is then obtained by plugging the bounds on ϖ and $\Gamma + 1$ into Equation 5.12 of Theorem 5.21.

8.5 Bibliographical Notes

Alpha-shapes and weighted alpha-shapes are among the first tools introduced in the area of shape reconstruction where one seeks to construct an approximation of the shape of a three-dimensional object from a set of points measured on the boundary of the object. References are provided in the bibliographical notes of Chapter 6. Theorem 8.1 that states that an α-complex of a finite sample of a manifold has the same homotopy type as the manifold is due to Niyogi, Smale, and Weinberger [112].

The tangential complex has been independently defined by Freedman [82] and by Boissonnat and Flottoto [17]. Boissonnat and Ghosh later showed how to remove inconsistencies in the tangential complex by star stitching [18] and proved Theorems 8.17 and 7.16. The tangential complex can be seen as a light variant of the cocone introduced by Cheng, Dey, and Ramos [57].

The approach followed in this chapter that defines local triangulations and remove inconsistencies among the local triangulations has been pioneered by Shewchuk to maintain triangulations of moving points [122] and by Boissonnat, Wormser and Yvinec to generate anisotropic meshes [24]. The central question behind this approach is the stability of Delaunay triangulations and the existence and construction of Delaunay triangulations on manifolds [14, 13, 27].

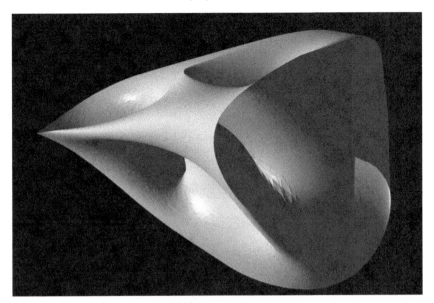

Figure 8.6 A Riemann surface embedded in $\mathbb{R}^8$ reconstructed using the tangential Delaunay complex. For visualization purposes, the surface has been projected in $\mathbb{R}^3$.

In this chapter, we have assumed that the dimension of the submanifold is known and that the tangent space can be computed at any data point. Giesen and Wagner have shown how to estimate the dimension [90]. Estimating the tangent space can be done using principal component analysis (PCA) [98].

An implementation of the tangential complex can be found in the Gudhi library [126]. Figure 8.6 shows a projection in $\mathbb{R}^3$ of the reconstruction of a Riemann surface embedded in $\mathbb{R}^8$.

PART IV

DISTANCE-BASED INFERENCE

9

Stability of Distance Functions

In the sequel, all the considered shapes and their approximations are represented by compact subsets of an Euclidean space $\mathbb{R}^d$. We use indifferently the words shape and compact set. In this chapter, we address the general problem consisting in recovering the topology of a shape from an approximation.

In general, the topological and geometric invariants of a shape cannot be directly extracted from the corresponding invariants of an approximating shape. In particular, this is always the case for a (continuous) shape K, e.g. a surface in $\mathbb{R}^3$, approximated by a finite point cloud data set K': point clouds in themselves do not carry any nontrivial topological or geometric structure. Moreover, the occurence of some features may depend on a "scale" at which the data and the shape are considered: for example, viewed with human eyes, the surface of a real world object may look very regular but at a microscopic scale it appears as a much more complicated surface with many holes and tunnels. It is thus necessary to "build" some scale-dependant geometric structure on top of such point clouds to recover informations about the shapes they approximate. For that purpose, the approach we adopt in this chapter consists in considering the distance functions to compact sets and to compare the topology of the sublevel sets (i.e., the offsets) of close compact sets. The underlying intuition is that "at some scales" (i.e., for some range values of the offsets), two close compact sets should have the same offset topology as illustrated in Figure 9.1. The goal of this chapter is to turn this intuition into a formal framework with rigorous statements. This requires to proceed in two steps. First, one needs to understand how the topology of the offsets K^r of a given compact set K evolves with the parameter r. The answer to this question is given by the theory of critical points for distance functions. Second, it is necessary to compare the topology of the offsets of two close (for the Hausdorff distance) compact sets. This leads to stability results and sampling conditions necessary to ensure correct geometric inference.

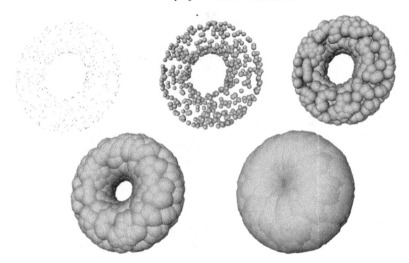

Figure 9.1 Various offsets of a point cloud data set sampled around a torus in $\mathbb{R}^3$.

The general mathematical framework introduced in this chapter allows to generalize and extend the results of Chapter 6, Section 8.1, and Chapter 8 to a wide class of nonsmooth shapes encountered in practical applications.

9.1 Distance Function and Hausdorff Distance

Given a compact subset $K \subset \mathbb{R}^d$, the *distance function* d_K to K is the non-negative function defined by

$$d_K(x) = \inf_{y \in K} d(x, y) \quad \text{for all} \quad x \in \mathbb{R}^d$$

where $d(x, y) = \|x - y\|$ is the euclidean distance between x and y in $\mathbb{R}^d$. The distance function to K is continuous and indeed 1-Lipschitz: for all $x, x' \in \mathbb{R}^d$, $|d_K(x) - d_K(x')| \leq \|x - x'\|$. Moreover, K is completely characterized by d_K since $K = d_K^{-1}(0)$.

For any non-negative real number r, the *r-offset* K^r of K is the r-sublevel set of d_K defined by

$$K^r = d_K^{-1}([0, r]) = \{x \in \mathbb{R}^d : d_K(x) \leq r\}.$$

Recall from Section 1.2.2 that if K and K' are two compact subsets of $\mathbb{R}^d$, then the Hausdorff distance $d_H(K, K')$ is the infimum of the sets of non-negative numbers $r \geq 0$ such that $K' \subset K^r$ and $K \subset K'^r$. Indeed, the Hausdorff distance can be expressed in various equivalent ways in terms of distance functions:

Proposition 9.1 *Let $K, K' \subset \mathbb{R}^d$ be two compact sets. The Hausdorff distance $d_H(K, K')$ between K and K' is defined by any of the following equivalent assertions:*

- $d_H(K, K')$ *is the smallest number r such that $K \subset K'^r$ and $K' \subset K^r$.*
- $d_H(K, K') = \max\left(\sup_{x \in K} d_{K'}(x), \sup_{x \in K'} d_K(x)\right).$
- $d_H(K, K') = \|d_K - d_{K'}\| := \sup_{x \in \mathbb{R}^d} |d_K(x) - d_{K'}(x)|.$

9.2 Critical Points of Distance Functions

Given a compact set $K \subset \mathbb{R}^d$, the distance function d_K is usually not differentiable. For example, if K is the union of the four sides of a square in the plane, d_K is not differentiable along the diagonals of K. Nevertheless, it is possible to define a generalized gradient vector field $\nabla_K : \mathbb{R}^d \to \mathbb{R}^d$ for d_K that coincides with the classical gradient at the points where d_K is differentiable.

For any point $x \in \mathbb{R}^d$ we denote by $\Gamma_K(x)$ the set of points in K closest to x:

$$\Gamma_K(x) = \{y \in K : d(x, y) = d_K(x)\} \subset \mathbb{R}^d.$$

This is a nonempty compact subset of K.

Let $B_K(x)$ be the smallest closed ball enclosing $\Gamma_K(x)$ and let $c_K(x)$ be its center and $F_K(x)$ its radius (see Figure 9.2). For $x \in \mathbb{R}^d \backslash K$, the generalized gradient $\nabla d_K(x)$ is defined by

$$\nabla d_K(x) = \frac{x - c_K(x)}{d_K(x)}$$

and for $x \in K$, $\nabla d_K(x) = 0$.

The norm of the gradient is given by

$$\|\nabla d_K(x)\|^2 = 1 - \frac{F_K^2(x)}{d_K^2(x)}. \tag{9.1}$$

Equivalently, the norm of $\nabla d_K(x)$ is the cosine of the half angle of the smallest circular cone with apex x that contains $\Gamma_K(x)$. Intuitively, the direction of $\nabla d_K(x)$ is the one along which the directional derivative of d_K is the largest or, in other words, the one in which the slope of the graph $\{(y, d_K(y)) : y \in \mathbb{R}^d\} \subset \mathbb{R}^{d+1}$ is the largest at the point $(x, d_K(x))$ (see Figure 9.3).

The map $x \in \mathbb{R}^d \to \nabla d_K(x) \in \mathbb{R}^d$ is, in general, not continuous. In other words, ∇d_K is a discontinuous vector field. Nevertheless it is possible to show [101, 117] that $x \to \|\nabla d_K(x)\|$ is a lower semicontinuous function, i.e., for any $a \in \mathbb{R}$, $\|\nabla d_K\|^{-1}((-\infty, a])$ is a closed subset of $\mathbb{R}^d$. Moreover, ∇d_K is integrable in the following sense.

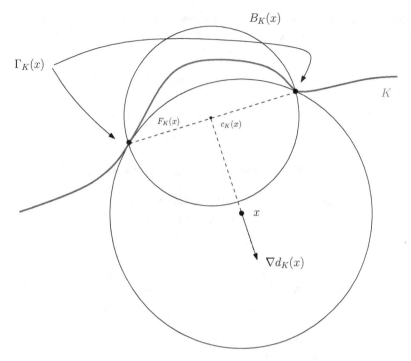

Figure 9.2 The gradient of the distance function.

Proposition 9.2 *There exists a continuous map $\mathfrak{C} : \mathbb{R}_+ \times \mathbb{R}^d \to \mathbb{R}^d$ such that for any $x \in \mathbb{R}^d$, the map $t \to \mathfrak{C}(t,x)$, called a trajectory of ∇d_K, is a solution of the differential equation*

$$\frac{dX}{dt} = \nabla d_K(X(t))$$

satisfying $X(0) = x$. Moreover this continuous trajectory can be parametrized by arc length $s \to \mathfrak{C}(t(s),x)$ and one has

$$d_K\left(\mathfrak{C}(t(l),x)\right) = d_K(x) + \int_0^l \|\nabla d_K(\mathfrak{C}(t(s),x))\|ds. \qquad (9.2)$$

This equation implies that d_K is non decreasing along the trajectories of ∇d_K. It can also be shown [101] that F_K is also nondecreasing along the trajectories of ∇d_K.

The gradient ∇d_K allows to define the notion of critical point for d_K in the same way as for differentiable functions.

Definition 9.3 (Critical point) A point x is a critical point of d_K if $\nabla d_K(x)=0$. A real $c \geq 0$ is a critical value of d_K if there exists a critical point $x \in \mathbb{R}^d$ such that $d_K(x) = c$. A regular value of d_K is a value that is not critical.

Figure 9.3 The graph of the distance to a square in the plane. Along the diagonals of the square, the direction of the gradient is given by the diagonals and its norm is the slope of the edges of the graph above the diagonals.

When there is no risk of confusion, we make the small abuse of language consisting in calling a critical (resp. regular) point of d_K a critical (resp. regular) point of K.

9.3 Topology of the Offsets

Using the notion of critical point defined in the previous section, it appears that some properties of distance functions are similar to the ones of differentiable functions. In particular, the sublevel sets of d_K are topological submanifolds of $\mathbb{R}^d$ and their topology can change only at critical points. These properties are formalized in the following two theorems.

Theorem 9.4 *Let $K \subset \mathbb{R}^d$ be a compact set and let r be a regular value of d_K. The level set $d_K^{-1}(r)$ is a $(d-1)$-dimensional topological submanifold of $\mathbb{R}^d$.*

Theorem 9.5 (Isotopy Lemma) *Let $K \subset \mathbb{R}^d$ be a compact set and let $r_1 < r_2$ be two real numbers such that $[r_1, r_2]$ does not contain any critical value of d_K. Then all the level sets $d_K^{-1}(r), r \in [r_1, r_2]$ are homeomorphic (and even isotopic) and the set $A(r_1, r_2) = \{x \in \mathbb{R}^d : r_1 \leq d_K(x) \leq r_2\}$ is homeomorphic to $d_K^{-1}(r_1) \times [r_1, r_2]$.*

An immediate consequence of these two results is that the topology of the offsets of K can only change at critical values and for any regular value r of d_K, the offset K^r is a d-dimensional topological manifold with boundary. In particular, the topology of the small offsets K^r, $r > 0$, cannot change while

r is smaller than the smallest positive critical value of d_K (if it exists). This leads to the notion of *weak feature size*.

Definition 9.6 (Weak feature size)   Let $K \subset \mathbb{R}^d$ be a compact set. The weak feature size wfs(K) of K is the infimum of the positive critical values of d_K. If d_K does not have critical values, wfs(K) $= +\infty$.

It follows from the Isotopy Lemma 9.5 that if $0 < \alpha \le \beta < \text{wfs}(K)$, then K^α and K^β are isotopic. In a more intuitive way, the knowledge of K at precision, or scale, α gives the same information for any choice of $0 < \alpha < \text{wfs}(K)$. Moreover, the following result allows to compare the topology of the offsets of two close compact sets with positive weak feature sizes.

Theorem 9.7   *Let $K, K' \subset \mathbb{R}^d$ and $\varepsilon > 0$ be such that $d_H(K, K') < \varepsilon$, wfs(K) $> 2\varepsilon$ and wfs(K') $> 2\varepsilon$. Then for any $0 < \alpha \le 2\varepsilon$, K^α and K'^α are homotopy equivalent.*

Proof   Let $\delta > 0$ be such that wfs(K) $> 2\varepsilon + \delta$ and wfs(K') $> 2\varepsilon + \delta$. It is enough to prove that $K^{\delta+2\varepsilon}$ and $K'^{\delta+\varepsilon}$ are homotopy equivalent. Because $d_H(K, K') < \varepsilon$, the following diagram, where each map is an inclusion, is commutative.

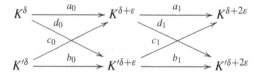

The Isotopy Lemma 9.5 implies that the inclusions a_0, a_1, b_0, and b_1 are homotopy equivalences. Let s_0, s_1, r_0 and r_1 be the homotopic inverses of a_0, a_1, b_0 and b_1, respectively.

   The following computation, where $\cong$ denotes the homotopy equivalence relation, shows that c_1 is an homotopy equivalence between $K'^{\delta+\varepsilon}$ and $K^{\delta+2\varepsilon}$ with homotopic inverse $r_1 \circ d_1 \circ s_1$:

$$c_1 \circ r_1 \circ d_1 \circ s_1 \cong c_1 \circ (r_1 \circ b_1) \circ d_0 \circ s_0 \circ s_1$$
$$\cong (c_1 \circ d_0) \circ s_0 \circ s_1$$
$$\cong a_1 \circ a_0 \circ s_0 \circ s_1 \cong id_{K^{\delta+2\varepsilon}}$$

Similarly, we get $r_1 \circ d_1 \circ s_1 \circ c_1 \cong id_{K'^{\delta+\varepsilon}}$ □

The previous theorem shows that the compact sets with positive weak feature size provide a class of compact sets with interesting topological stability properties. Moreover, it is possible to show that this class is large enough to include most of the shapes encountered in practical applications. In particular,

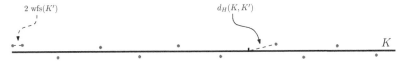

Figure 9.4 A segment K approximated by a point cloud K'. The weak feature size of K' is obviously smaller than two times the Hausdorff distance between K and K'.

smooth manifolds, polyhedra, polyhyedral sets, semi-algebraic sets and more generally the so-called subanalytic compact sets (i.e., obtained from analytic equations and inequalities) all have positive weak feature size. Nevertheless, the previous theorem suffers from a weakness that prevents it to be really useful in practice. Indeed, the assumption involving both wfs(K) and wfs(K') is hardly satisfied in practical situations. For example, if K is a continuous shape approximated by a finite point cloud K', wfs(K') is equal to half of the distance between the two closest points of K' which is usually smaller than $2d_H(K, K')$ as illustrated in Figure 9.4. As a consequence, even if the weak feature size of K is large, whatever the quality of the approximation of K by K' the assumptions of theorem 9.7 may not be satisfied. This phenomenon can also be interpreted as a lack of continuity of the map $K \to$ wfs(K) or as an instability property of the critical points of distance functions.

9.4 Stability of Critical Points

Because the topology of the offsets of a compact set can only change for critical values of d_K, it is natural to study the stability of these critical points when K is replaced by a close compact set K'. Unfortunately, it appears that the critical points are unstable, as illustrated in Figure 9.5.

To overcome this stability problem, we introduce a parametrized notion of critical point.

Definition 9.8 (μ-critical points) Let $K \subset \mathbb{R}^d$ be a compact set and let $0 \leq \mu \leq 1$. A point $x \in \mathbb{R}^d$ is μ-critical for d_K if $\|\nabla d_K(x)\| \leq \mu$.

Note that the notion of 0-critical point coincides with the notion of critical point of Definition 9.3. The family of μ-critical points satisfies the following fundamental stability property.

Theorem 9.9 (Critical point stability theorem) *Let K and K' be two compact subsets of $\mathbb{R}^d$ and $d_H(K, K') \leq \varepsilon$. For any μ-critical point x of K, there is a $(2\sqrt{\varepsilon/d_K(x)} + \mu)$-critical point of K' at distance at most $2\sqrt{\varepsilon d_K(x)}$ from x.*

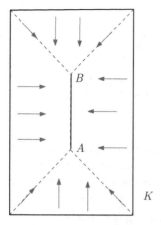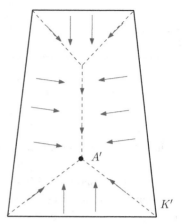

Figure 9.5 When K is a rectangle, the set of critical points of d_K is the whole segment $[AB]$. This segment collapses to a single critical point A' as one stretches the bottom side of K to obtain K'. Nevertheless, along the previously critical segment, the norm of the gradient of $d_{K'}$ remains small.

The proof of this theorem follows from two technical lemmas. The first one shows that the function d_K cannot grow too fast in a neighborhood of a μ-critical point.

Lemma 9.10 *Let $K \subset \mathbb{R}^d$ be a compact set and x one of its μ-critical points. For any $y \in \mathbb{R}^d$, we have:*

$$d_K^2(y) \le d_K^2(x) + 2\mu d_K(x)\|x - y\| + \|x - y\|^2.$$

Proof Let $\Gamma = \Gamma_K(x)$ be the set of points closest to x on K, and let S be the sphere with center x and radius $d_K(x)$. Let also $c = c_K(x)$ be the center of the minimal enclosing ball of Γ, and $\alpha = \arccos^{-1}(\mu)$ (see Figure 9.6).

For any $x' \in \Gamma$ we have

$$
\begin{aligned}
d_K^2(y) \le \|y - x'\|^2 &= ((y - x) + (x - x').(y - x) + (x - x')) \\
&= \|y - x\|^2 + \|x - x'\|^2 + 2((y - x).(x - x')) \\
&= d_K^2(x) + 2d_K(x)\|x - y\| \cos(y - x, x - x') + \|x - y\|^2
\end{aligned}
$$

To prove the lemma it is thus sufficient to prove the following claim.

Claim: there exists a point $x' \in \Gamma$ such that the angle between $(y - x)$ and $(x' - x)$ is not smaller than α.

We distinguish between two cases.

Case 1: $\mu \ne 0$

Assume that the claim is not satisfied. Then for any $x' \in \Gamma$ the angle between $(x' - x)$ and $(y - x)$ is smaller than α. Since Γ is compact, there exists $\alpha' < \alpha$

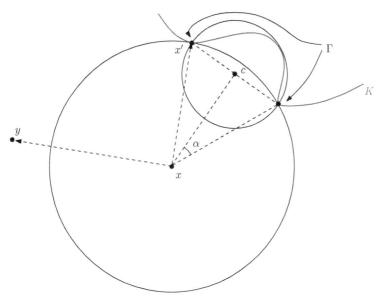

Figure 9.6 Proof of lemma 9.10

such that Γ is contained in the "circular" cone with apex x and axis the half-line directed by $y - x$ and apex angle α'. This cone intersects S along a $(d - 2)$-sphere with center c' and radius $R' = d_K(x) \sin \alpha'$. Since Γ is also contained in S, Γ is contained in the ball of center c' and radius $R' = d_K(x) \sin \alpha' < d_K(x) \sin \alpha = F_K(x)$: a contradiction.

Case 2: $\mu = 0$

$\alpha = \frac{\pi}{2}$ and Γ cannot be enclosed in any hemisphere of S. So there is at least one point $x' \in \Gamma$ such that the angle between $(y - x)$ and $(x' - x)$ is not smaller than $\frac{\pi}{2}$. □

The next lemma allows to study the behavior of the μ-critical points when K is replaced by a close approximation K'.

Lemma 9.11 *Let K and K' be two compact subsets of $\mathbb{R}^d$ and $d_H(K, K') \leq \varepsilon$. For any μ-critical point x of K and any $\rho > 0$, there is a μ'-critical point of K' at distance at most ρ from x, with:*

$$\mu' \leq \frac{\rho}{2 d_K(x)} + \frac{2\varepsilon}{\rho} + \mu$$

Proof Let us consider the trajectory $s \to C(s)$ of the vector field $\nabla d_{K'}$ parameterized by arc length and starting at x. If C reaches a critical point of K' before $s = \rho$, the lemma holds. Assume this is not the case. Letting $y = C(\rho)$, we have:

$$d_{K'}(y) - d_{K'}(x) = \int_0^\rho \|\nabla d_{K'}(C(s))\| ds$$

Therefore, there must exist a point p on the curve C between $s = 0$ and $s = \rho$ such that:

$$\|\nabla d_{K'}(p)\| \leq \frac{d_{K'}(y) - d_{K'}(x)}{\rho} \tag{9.3}$$

The curve C being parametrized by arc length, note that $\|p - x\| \leq \rho$. Now Lemma 9.10 applied to x, y, and K reads:

$$d_K(y) \leq \sqrt{d_K^2(x) + 2\mu d_K(x)\|x - y\| + \|x - y\|^2}$$

Also, because $\varepsilon = d_H(K, K')$, we have that for all $z \in \mathbb{R}^d$, $|d_K(z) - d_{K'}(z)| \leq \varepsilon$. Hence:

$$
\begin{aligned}
d_{K'}(y) - d_{K'}(x) &\leq \sqrt{d_K^2(x) + 2\mu d_K(x)\|x - y\| + \|x - y\|^2} \\
&\quad - d_K(x) + 2\varepsilon \\
&\leq d_K(x)\left[\sqrt{1 + \frac{2\mu\|x - y\|}{d_K(x)} + \frac{\|x - y\|^2}{d_K^2(x)}} - 1\right] \\
&\quad + 2\varepsilon \\
&\leq \mu\|x - y\| + \frac{\|x - y\|^2}{2d_K(x)} + 2\varepsilon,
\end{aligned}
$$

the last inequality coming from the fact that $\sqrt{1 + u} \leq 1 + \frac{u}{2}$ for $u \geq 0$. Noticing that $\|x - y\| \leq \rho$, dividing by ρ, and applying equation (9.3) shows that p satisfies the desired requirements. $\qquad\square$

Proof of Theorem 9.9 The bound of the previous lemma can be optimized by choosing $\rho = 2\sqrt{\varepsilon d_K(x)}$. It then becomes equal to $2\sqrt{\varepsilon/d_K(x)} + \mu$. The theorem follows immediately. $\qquad\square$

Remark 9.12 Note that because $d_{K'}$ is increasing along the trajectories of $\nabla d_{K'}$ (see Equation 9.2), the μ'-critical point p for $d_{K'}$ of Lemma 9.11 can be chosen such that $d_{K'}(p) \geq d_{K'}(x)$.

9.5 The Critical Function of a Compact Set

The critical point stability Theorem 9.9 plays a fundamental role to get topological stability results. It allows to introduce a general framework for inferring the topology and the geometry of a large class of (nonsmooth)

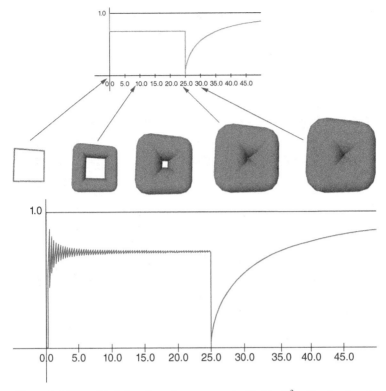

Figure 9.7 The critical function of a square embedded in $\mathbb{R}^3$ with edge length equal to 50 (top) and the critical function of a point cloud sampling this square (bottom).

compact sets. For that purpose, we first introduce a one variable real-valued function that encodes the criticality of the level sets of d_K.

Definition 9.13 The critical function of a compact set $K \subset \mathbb{R}^d$, $\chi_K :$ $(0, +\infty) \to \mathbb{R}_+$ is defined by

$$\chi_K(r) = \inf_{x \in d_K^{-1}(r)} \|\nabla d_K(x)\|$$

An example of a critical function is given in Figure 9.7. Note that from the isotopy Lemma 9.5 the zeros of the critical functions correspond to the changes in the topology of the offsets of K. As we will see later, the main interest of the critical function χ_K is to provide information about the topological stability of some offsets of the compact sets contained in a neighborhood of K. In particular, whether a compact set K is a Hausdorff approximation of a simple compact set or not can be directly read from its critical function.

Using the critical points stability Theorem 9.9, we easily get the following stability result for the critical function.

Theorem 9.14 (Critical function stability theorem) *Let K and K' be two compact subsets of $\mathbb{R}^d$ such that $d_H(K, K') \leq \varepsilon$. For all $r \geq 0$, we have:*

$$\inf\{\chi_{K'}(u) \mid u \in I(r, \varepsilon)\} \leq \chi_K(r) + 2\sqrt{\frac{\varepsilon}{r}}$$

where $I(r, \varepsilon) = [r - \varepsilon, r + 2\chi_K(r)\sqrt{\varepsilon r} + 3\varepsilon]$

This result shows that if the critical function of K' is not smaller than some value α on the interval $I(r, \varepsilon)$ then the critical function of K at the point r cannot be smaller than $\alpha - 2\sqrt{\frac{\varepsilon}{r}}$. In particular, if $\alpha > 2\sqrt{\frac{\varepsilon}{r}}$ then r cannot be a critical value of d_K. Because the topology of the offsets of K can only change at critical values, it is thus possible to locate intervals on which the topology of the offsets of K does not change. Figures 9.7 and 9.8 illustrate this property.

From an algorithmic point of view, it is not difficult to see that when K is a finite point cloud, the critical function of K can be easily computed from the Voronoi diagram of K; see Exercise 9.11.

Proof Let $r \geq 0$ and let $x \in d_K^{-1}(r)$ be such that $\|\nabla d_K(x)\| = \chi_K(r)$. The existence of such a point x comes from the fact that the infimum involved in

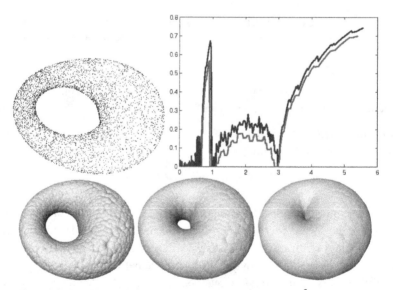

Figure 9.8 A points set (left) sampled around a torus shape in $\mathbb{R}^3$ and its critical function (the upper curve). The lowest curve represents the lower bound for the critical function of any shape K at distance less than some fixed threshold (here 0.001, the diameter of the torus being 10) from the point cloud.

the definition of χ_K is indeed a minimum. This follows from the lower semi-continuity of $\|\nabla d_K\|$ and the compactness of $d_K^{-1}(r)$. The critical point stability Theorem 9.9 implies that there exists a point p that is $\left(2\sqrt{\frac{\varepsilon}{r}} + \chi_K(r)\right)$-critical for $d_{K'}$ at distance at most $2\sqrt{\varepsilon r}$ from x. Applying Lemma 9.10 to x, p and K we get

$$d_K(p) \le \sqrt{r^2 + 4\chi_K(r)r\sqrt{\varepsilon r} + 4\varepsilon r}$$
$$\le r\sqrt{1 + 4\chi_K(r)\sqrt{\varepsilon/r} + 4\varepsilon/r}$$
$$\le r + 2\chi_K(r)\sqrt{\varepsilon r} + 2\varepsilon$$

Now, according to Remark 9.12, p can be chosen such that $d_{K'}(p) \ge d_{K'}(x)$. Using that $|d_{K'}(p) - d_K(p)| \le \varepsilon$, the theorem follows from the above inequality. $\square$

The example of Figure 9.8 illustrates the critical function Theorem 9.14. The critical function of a point cloud sampling a torus shape reveals three intervals with stable topology for K: the first one corresponds to offsets having the topology of a torus (bottom left), the second one corresponds to solid torus with a hole homeomorphic to a ball inside (bottom middle - not visible from outside) and the third one is unbounded and correspond to offsets that have the topology of a ball (bottom right).

9.6 Sampling Conditions and μ-reach

In this section we introduce the μ-reach, a stronger regularity condition than the weak feature size, that allows to give stronger reconstruction results than Theorem 9.7.

Definition 9.15 For $0 < \mu \le 1$, the μ-reach $r_\mu(K)$ of a compact set $K \subset \mathbb{R}^d$ is defined as

$$r_\mu(K) = \inf\{r > 0 : \chi_K(r) < \mu\}$$

By analogy with the wfs, the μ-reach is the infimum of the μ-critical values of d_K. When $\mu = 1$, $r_\mu(K)$ is known as the *reach* . When K is a compact smooth submanifold of $\mathbb{R}^d$, it coincides with the reach defined in Chapter 7. The function $\mu \to r_\mu(K)$ is nonincreasing and we have

$$\lim_{\mu \to 0^+} r_\mu(K) \le \text{wfs}(K)$$

Note that the above inequality can be strict (Exercise 9.10).

It follows from the critical point stability Theorem 9.9 that the positiveness of the μ-reach of a compact set K' implies some constraints on the location of the critical points of any close enough approximation K of K'. More precisely we have the following result (Exercise 9.12).

Theorem 9.16 (Critical values separation theorem) *Let K and K' be two compact subsets of $\mathbb{R}^d$, ε the Hausdorff distance between K and K', and μ a non-negative number. The distance function d_K has no critical values in the interval $(4\varepsilon/\mu^2, r_\mu(K') - 3\varepsilon)$. In addition, for any $\mu' < \mu$, χ_K is larger than μ' on the interval*

$$\left(\frac{4\varepsilon}{(\mu - \mu')^2}, r_\mu(K') - 3\sqrt{\varepsilon r_\mu(K')} \right).$$

Note that taking μ too small does not give any information on the critical values, because the lower bound then exceeds the upper bound. It is also possible to build examples showing that the bounds of the interval in the above theorem are tight.

The notion of μ-reach allows to introduce the following sampling condition.

Definition 9.17 Given two positive real numbers κ and μ, one says that a compact set $K \subset \mathbb{R}^d$ is a (κ, μ)-approximation of a compact set $K' \subset \mathbb{R}^d$ if

$$d_H(K, K') \leq \kappa r_\mu(K').$$

The notion of (κ, μ)-approximation generalizes the notion of $(\varepsilon, \bar{\eta})$-net introduced for smooth submanifolds in Chapter 7.

9.7 Offset Reconstruction

Equipped with the notion of (κ, μ)-approximation and the stability properties of critical points of distance functions proved in the previous section, we are now able to get easily offsets reconstruction results from approximations.

Theorem 9.18 (Isotopic reconstruction theorem) *Let $K' \subset \mathbb{R}^d$ be a compact set such that $r_\mu = r_\mu(K') > 0$ for some $\mu > 0$. Let K be a (κ, μ)-approximation of K' where*

$$\kappa < \min \left(\frac{\sqrt{5}}{2} - 1, \frac{\mu^2}{16 + 2\mu^2} \right).$$

Assume that r, r' are such that

$$0 < r' < \text{wfs}(K') \quad \text{and} \quad \frac{4\kappa r_\mu}{\mu^2} \leq r < r_\mu(K') - 3\kappa r_\mu.$$

Then the offset K^r and level set $d_K^{-1}(r)$ are isotopic to $K'^{r'}$ and $d_{K'}^{-1}(r')$ respectively.

The proof of the isotopy between the offsets is beyond the scope of this book. We prove here the following weaker version.

Theorem 9.19 (Homotopic reconstruction theorem) *Let $K \subset \mathbb{R}^d$ be a (κ, μ)-approximation of a compact set $K' \subset \mathbb{R}^d$. If*

$$\kappa < \frac{\mu^2}{5\mu^2 + 12}$$

then the complement of K^α is homotopy equivalent to the complement of K' and K^α is homotopy equivalent to K'^η as soon as

$$0 < \eta < \mathrm{wfs}(K') \quad \text{and} \quad \frac{4d_H(K, K')}{\mu^2} \le \alpha < r_\mu(K') - 3d_H(K, K')$$

Proof The critical values separation Theorem 9.16 applied to K and K' ensures that d_K does not have any critical value in the interval $(4\varepsilon/\mu^2, r_\mu(K') - 3\varepsilon)$ where $\varepsilon = d_H(K, K')$. It follows from the isotopy Lemma 9.5 that all the offsets of K corresponding to the values contained in this interval are isotopic. It is thus sufficient to prove the theorem for $\alpha = 4\varepsilon/\mu^2$. Since the critical functions of K and K^α are related by the relation

$$\chi_{K^\alpha}(r) = \chi_K(r + \alpha)$$

(see Exercise 9.9), we have $\mathrm{wfs}(K^\alpha) \ge r_\mu(K') - 3\varepsilon - 4\varepsilon/\mu^2$. We also have

$$d_H(K^\alpha, K') \le \varepsilon + \frac{4\varepsilon}{\mu^2}$$

According to Theorem 9.7, the theorem holds as soon as

$$d_H(K^\alpha, K') \le \frac{1}{2} \min(\mathrm{wfs}(K^\alpha), \mathrm{wfs}(K'))$$

An easy computation shows that this inequality holds when $\kappa < \frac{\mu^2}{5\mu^2+12}$. $\square$

9.8 Exercises

Exercise 9.1 Prove that d_K is 1-Lipschitz.

Exercise 9.2 Prove Proposition 9.1.

Exercise 9.3 Prove that $\sigma_K(x)$ the smallest enclosing ball containing $\Gamma_K(x)$ exists and is unique.

Exercise 9.4 Show that the map from $\mathbb{R}^d$ to the space of compact subsets of $\mathbb{R}^d$ is semi-continuous, i.e.

$$\forall x, \forall r > 0, \exists \alpha > 0, \|y - x\| \leq \alpha \Rightarrow \Gamma_K(y) \subset \{z : d(z, \Gamma_K(x)) \leq r\}$$

Exercise 9.5 Show that for any $x \in \mathbb{R}^d$, $c_K(x)$ is the point on the convex hull of $\Gamma_K(x)$ closest to x.

Exercise 9.6 Prove that for any $x \in \mathbb{R}^d$ one has the following equivalence: (x is a critical point of d_K) $\Leftrightarrow$ (x lies in the convex hull of $\Gamma_K(x)$).

Exercise 9.7 Let P be a finite set of points in $\mathbb{R}^2$ in general position. Prove that a point $x \in \mathbb{R}^2$ is a critical point of d_P if and only if it satisfies one of the following conditions:
- $x \in P$,
- x is the intersection point between a Voronoi edge and its dual Delaunay edge,
- x is a Voronoi vertex contained in its dual Delaunay triangle.

How does this result generalize for finite point clouds in higher dimensions?

Exercise 9.8 Let $K = \{p_1, \cdots p_n\} \subset \mathbb{R}^d$ be a finite point set. Prove that $\text{wfs}(K) = \frac{1}{2} \min_{i \neq j} \|p_i - p_j\|$.

Exercise 9.9 Show that for any compact set $K \subset \mathbb{R}^d$ and any $\alpha \geq 0$,

$$\chi_{K^\alpha}(r) = \chi_K(r + \alpha) \text{ for all } r \geq 0.$$

Hint: First prove the same kind of relation between d_{K^α} and d_K.

Exercise 9.10 Give an example of a compact set (e.g., a compact subset of $\mathbb{R}^2$) K such that $\lim_{\mu \to 0^+} r_\mu(K) \neq \text{wfs}(K)$.

Exercise 9.11 Let $P \subset \mathbb{R}^d$ be a finite set of points. We denote $\text{Vor}(P)$ and $\text{Del}(P)$ the Voronoi diagram and Delaunay triangulation of P. We use the notations of Section 9.2.

1. What can be said about the restriction of F_P to a Voronoi cell of $\text{Vor}(P)$?
2. For each Delaunay simplex τ, let V_τ its dual Voronoi cell and let $f_\tau : \mathbb{R}_+ \to \mathbb{R}_+$ the function defined by

$$f_\tau(r) = \sqrt{1 - \frac{F_P^2(\tau)}{r^2}} \text{ if } r \in d_P(V_\tau)$$

and $f_\tau(r) = 1$ otherwise. Show that the critical function of P is equal to the minimum, taken over all the Delaunay simplices of $\text{Del}(P)$, of the functions f_τ.
3. Deduce from the previous question an algorithm that takes $\text{Del}(P)$ as input and output the critical function of P.

Exercise 9.12 Prove the critical values separation Theorem 9.16. Hint: This is a consequence of Theorem 9.14; see also [39].

9.9 Bibliographical Notes

The distance functions framework for geometric inference has been introduced in [39] and the proof of the isotopic reconstruction Theorem 9.18 is given in [38]. It is not restricted to topological inference and shape reconstruction but has been extended to other geometric inference problems. For example, it has been used to prove stability results for normals [38] and curvatures [41] estimation of compact sets with positive μ-reach. It has also been used to prove that some smoothing operations involving offsets of shapes in Computer Aided Geometric Design are theoretically well-founded [40].

Distance functions have been widely studied and used in Riemannian geometry [54, 92] and nonsmooth analysis [58]. The notion of critical point introduced in this chapter coincides with the notion of critical point for distance function used in riemannian geometry and nonsmooth analysis where the notion of Clarke gradient [58] is closely related to the above defined gradient. The general properties of the gradient of d_K and of its trajectories given in Section 9.2, are established in [101] or, in a more general setting, in [117].

Distance functions are also particular cases of the so-called semiconcave functions. Many of the results presented in this section can be deduced from general properties of semiconcave functions [117]. This allows in particular to extend most of the results given in this section to compact subsets of Riemannian manifolds.

When K is a finite set of points, several variants of the gradient flow $\mathfrak{C}$ defined in this chapter have been previously and independently considered in the literature [70, 89, 35].

The notion of weak feature size has been introduced in [46–48]. The positiveness of the weak feature size of large classes of compact sets is discussed in [85, p. 1045] and [47], proposition 3.6. The notion of reach for compact subsets of $\mathbb{R}^d$ has been introduced by H. Federer [81] in the setting of geometric measure theory.

10

Distance to Probability Measures

As we have seen in Chapter 9, the use of distance functions provides an interesting approach for the robust estimation of the topological and geometric properties of shapes in $\mathbb{R}^d$ from approximating data. Here, approximation is meant with respect to the Hausdorff distance that requires all the data points to be located in a close neighborhood of the shape. However, in many practical applications the data come with outliers, i.e., observations (points) that are not located close to the approximated shape. For such data the Hausdorff distance is no longer relevant to formalize the notion of approximation: just adding one point p at distance R from a given data set K makes the Hausdorff distance between K and $K \cup \{p\}$ equal to R (see Figure 10.1). As a consequence, the distance-based approach of Chapter 9 fails for data corrupted by noise and outliers as illustrated in Figure 10.2. To overcome this issue, in this chapter, we adapt the distance-based framework for geometric inference to the general framework of data carrying noise and outliers.

10.1 Extending the Sampling Theory for Compact Sets

All the inference results of Chapter 9 follow from only three fundamental properties of distance functions:

- Stability of the map $K \to d_K$: for any compact subsets K, K' of $\mathbb{R}^d$ we have

$$\|d_K - d_{K'}\|_\infty = d_H(K, K')$$

  where $\|d_K - d_{K'}\|_\infty = \sup_{x \in \mathbb{R}^d} |d_K(x) - d_{K'}(x)|$.
- For any compact set $K \subset \mathbb{R}^d$, the distance function d_K is 1-Lipschitz: for any $x, x' \in \mathbb{R}^d$, $|d_K(x) - d_K(x')| \leq \|x - x'\|$.
- For any compact set $K \subset \mathbb{R}^d$, the distance function d_K^2 is 1-*semiconcave*: $x \to \|x\|^2 - d_K^2(x)$ is convex (see Exercise 10.1).

180

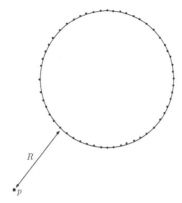

Figure 10.1 Adding just one point at distance R to a point cloud sampling a circle changes the Hausdorff distance between the shape and the sample by R.

Figure 10.2 In addition to a set of points densely sampled on the surface S of a tangle cube we consider a single "outlier" located away from S (left). When considering the offsets, the new added point creates a connected component that makes the estimation of the topology of S from the offsets of the data impossible (right): e.g., the estimated number of connected components (two) is clearly wrong.

The first property is an obvious condition to ensure that the offsets of two close compact sets are close to each other. The second and third properties are the fundamental ingredients to prove the existence and integrability of the gradient of d_K (Section 9.2) and the isotopy lemma of Section 9.3. These results still hold for general proper semiconcave functions, motivating the following definition of functions that are of particular interest for geometric inference.

Definition 10.1   A non-negative function $\phi : \mathbb{R}^d \to \mathbb{R}^+$ is a *distance-like* if

(i) ϕ is 1-Lipschitz,
(ii) ϕ^2 is 1-semiconcave, i.e., $x \to \|x\|^2 - \phi^2(x)$ is convex
(iii) ϕ is *proper*, i.e., for any compact set $K \subset \mathbb{R}$, $\phi^{-1}(K)$ is compact.

Let $\phi : \mathbb{R}^d \to \mathbb{R}$ be a *distance-like* function. The 1-semiconcavity of ϕ^2 allows to define a notion of gradient vector field $\nabla \phi(x)$ for ϕ, defined everywhere and satisfying $\|\nabla \phi(x)\| \leq 1$. Although not continuous, the vector field $\nabla \phi$ is sufficiently regular to be integrated in a continuous locally Lipschitz flow $\Phi^t : \mathbb{R}^d \to \mathbb{R}^d$, $t \geq 0$. The flow Φ^t integrates the gradient $\nabla \phi$ in the sense that for every $x \in \mathbb{R}^d$, the curve $\gamma : t \mapsto \Phi^t(x)$ is right-differentiable, and for every $t > 0$, $\frac{d\gamma}{dt}\big|_{t^-} = \nabla \phi(\gamma(t))$. Moreover, for any integral curve $\gamma : [a, b] \to \mathbb{R}^d$ parametrized by arc-length, one has:

$$\phi(\gamma(b)) = \phi(\gamma(a)) + \int_a^b \|\nabla \phi(\gamma(t))\|\, dt.$$

Definition 10.2   Let ϕ be a distance-like function. We denote by $\phi^r = \phi^{-1}([0, r])$ the r sublevel set of ϕ.

1. A point $x \in \mathbb{R}^d$ will be called α-*critical* (with $\alpha \in [0, 1]$) if the inequality $\phi^2(x+h) \leq \phi^2(x) + 2\alpha \|h\| \phi(x) + \|h\|^2$ is true for all $h \in \mathbb{R}^d$. A 0-critical point is simply called a *critical point*. It follows from the 1-semiconcavity of ϕ^2 that $\|\nabla \phi(x)\|$ is the infimum of the $\alpha \geq 0$ such that x is α-critical.
2. The *weak feature size* of ϕ at r is the maximum $r' > 0$ such that ϕ doesn't have any critical value between r and $r + r'$. We denote it by $\mathrm{wfs}_\phi(r)$. For any $0 < \alpha < 1$, the α-*reach* of ϕ is the maximum r such that $\phi^{-1}((0, r])$ does not contain any α-critical point.

Notice that the α-reach is always a lower bound for the weak-feature size, with $r = 0$.

The Isotopy Lemma 9.5 extends to distance-like functions.

Theorem 10.3 (Extended isotopy lemma)   *Let ϕ be a distance-like function and $r_1 < r_2$ be two positive numbers such that ϕ has no critical points in the subset $\phi^{-1}([r_1, r_2])$. Then all the sublevel sets $\phi^{-1}([0, r])$ are isotopic for $r \in [r_1, r_2]$.*

The proof of the following theorem, showing that the offsets of two uniformly close distance-like functions with large weak feature size have the same homotopy type, relies on Theorem 10.3 and is almost verbatim the same as the one of Theorem 9.7.

Proposition 10.4 *Let ϕ and ψ be two distance-like functions, such that $\|\phi - \psi\|_\infty \leq \varepsilon$. Suppose moreover that $\mathrm{wfs}_\phi(r) > 2\varepsilon$ and $\mathrm{wfs}_\psi(r) > 2\varepsilon$. Then, for every $0 < \eta \leq 2\varepsilon$, $\phi^{r+\eta}$ and $\psi^{r+\eta}$ have the same homotopy type.*

The Critical Point Stability Theorem 9.9 also holds for distance-like functions.

Theorem 10.5 *Let ϕ and ψ be two distance-like functions with $\|\phi - \psi\|_\infty \leq \varepsilon$. For any α-critical point x of ϕ, there exists a α'-critical point x' of ψ with $\|x - x'\| \leq 2\sqrt{\varepsilon\phi(x)}$ and $\alpha' \leq \alpha + 2\sqrt{\varepsilon/\phi(x)}$.*

Proof The proof is almost verbatim the same as the proof of Theorem 9.9
□

Corollary 10.6 *Let ϕ and ψ be two ε-close distance-like functions, and suppose that $\mathrm{reach}_\alpha(\phi) \geq R$ for some $\alpha > 0$. Then, ψ has no critical value in the interval $]4\varepsilon/\alpha^2, R - 3\varepsilon[$.*

Proof The proof is almost verbatim the same as the proof of Theorem 9.16.
□

Theorem 10.7 (Extended reconstruction theorem) *Let ϕ, ψ be two ε-close distance-like functions, with $\mathrm{reach}_\alpha(\phi) \geq R$ for some positive α. Then, for any $r \in [4\varepsilon/\alpha^2, R - 3\varepsilon]$, and for $0 < \eta < R$, the sublevel sets ψ^r and ϕ^η are homotopy equivalent, as soon as*

$$\varepsilon \leq \frac{R}{5 + 4/\alpha^2}$$

Proof By the extended isotopy Lemma 10.3, all the sublevel sets ψ^r have the same homotopy type, for r in the given range. Let us choose $r = 4\varepsilon/\alpha^2$. We have:

$$\mathrm{wfs}_\phi(r) \geq R - 4\varepsilon/\alpha^2 \text{ and } \mathrm{wfs}_\psi(r) \geq R - 3\varepsilon - 4\varepsilon/\alpha^2$$

By Proposition 10.4, the sublevel sets ϕ^r and ψ^r have the same homotopy type as soon as the uniform distance ε between ϕ and ψ is smaller than $\frac{1}{2}\mathrm{wfs}_\phi(r)$ and $\frac{1}{2}\mathrm{wfs}_\psi(r)$. This is true, provided that $2\varepsilon \leq R - \varepsilon(3 + 4/\alpha^2)$. The theorem follows.
□

Remark that in the Definition 10.2 the notion of α-reach could be made dependent on a parameter r, i.e., the (r, α)-reach of ϕ could be defined as the maximum r' such that the set $\phi^{-1}((r, r + r'])$ does not contain any α-critical value. A reconstruction theorem similar to Theorem 10.7 would still hold under the weaker condition that the (r, α)-reach of ϕ is positive.

10.2 Measures and the Wasserstein Distance W_2

To overcome the problem of outliers, a first idea is to consider geometric objects as mass distributions, i.e., measures, instead of purely geometric compact sets. Considering probability measures as the new class of studied objects leads to a much better adapted framework to cope with noise and outliers.

10.2.1 Replacing Compact Sets by Measures

The definition of measure relies on the notion of σ-algebra. All the measures considered in this book will be defined on the so-called Borel σ-algebra whose definition is given here.

Definition 10.8   A σ-algebra on a set X is a collection Σ of subsets of X such that:

  (i) $\emptyset \in \Sigma$,
 (ii) if $A \in \Sigma$, then $A^c \in \Sigma$,
(iii) if $(A_n)_{n \in \mathbb{N}}$ is a countable family of elements of σ, then $\cup_{n \in \mathbb{N}} A_n \in \Sigma$.
      The set of Borel sets of $\mathbb{R}^d$ is the smallest σ-algebra containing all the open sets of $\mathbb{R}^d$ (and thus all the closed sets).

Definition 10.9   A *Borel measure* or, for short in this book, a measure, μ on $\mathbb{R}^d$ is a map from the set of Borel subsets B of $\mathbb{R}^d$ to the set of non-negative real numbers such that whenever (B_i) is a countable family of disjoint Borel subsets of $\mathbb{R}^d$, $\mu(\cup_{i \in \mathbb{N}} B_i) = \sum_i \mu(B_i)$. A *probability measure* is a measure whose total mass $\mu(\mathbb{R}^d)$ is equal to 1.

Definition 10.10   The *support* of a measure μ is the smallest, with respect to inclusion, closed set K on which the mass of μ is concentrated, i.e., such that $\mu(\mathbb{R}^d \setminus K) = 0$.

For some compact sets such as point clouds, submanifolds of $\mathbb{R}^d$ or some more general shapes there exist natural ways to associate probability measures whose support are these compact sets as shown in the following examples.

Given a point $x \in \mathbb{R}^d$ the *Dirac measure* δ_x at x is defined as $\delta_x(B) = 1$ if $x \in B$ and $\delta_x(B) = 0$ otherwise. Given a set of n points C, the *empirical* or *uniform measure* μ_C, associated to C, is defined as $\mu_C(B) = \frac{1}{n}|B \cap C|$. It is the sum of n Dirac masses of weight $1/n$, centered at each point of C.

Given a compact k-dimensional manifold $M \subseteq \mathbb{R}^d$, let vol_M be the k-dimensional volume measure on M. As M is compact, $\mathrm{vol}_M(M)$ is finite and we define a probability measure μ_M supported on M by $\mu_M(B) = \mathrm{vol}_M(B \cap M)/$ $\mathrm{vol}_M(M)$, for any Borel set $B \subseteq \mathbb{R}^d$. For example, if M is a curve, $\mu_M(B)$ is the fraction of the total length of M that is contained in B; similarly, if M is a surface, $\mu_M(B)$ is the fraction of the total area of M that is contained in B. Notice that if M is a finite union of submanifolds $M_1, \cdots, M_k$, then we can define probability measures on M just by considering weighted sums of the measures μ_{M_i}.

10.2.2 The Wasserstein Distance W_2

There exist a whole family of Wasserstein distances W_p ($p \geq 1$) between probability measures in $\mathbb{R}^d$. Their definition relies on the notion of transport plan between measures. Although some of the results of this chapter can be stated for any distance W_p, for technical reasons that become clear in the following we only consider the W_2 distance.

A *transport plan* between two probability measures μ and ν on $\mathbb{R}^d$ is a probability measure π on $\mathbb{R}^d \times \mathbb{R}^d$ such that for every Borel sets $A, B \subseteq \mathbb{R}^d$, $\pi(A \times \mathbb{R}^d) = \mu(A)$ and $\pi(\mathbb{R}^d \times B) = \nu(B)$. Intuitively, $\pi(A \times B)$ corresponds to the amount of mass of μ contained in A that will be transported to B by the transport plan. The cost of such a transport plan π is given by

$$\mathcal{C}(\pi) = \left(\int_{\mathbb{R}^d \times \mathbb{R}^d} \|x - y\|^2 \mathrm{d}\pi(x, y) \right)^{1/2}$$

As an example, consider two probability measures with finite supports μ and ν:

$$\mu = \sum_{i=1}^{m} c_i \delta_{x_i} \quad \text{and} \quad \nu = \sum_{j=1}^{n} d_j \delta_{y_j}$$

with $\sum_{i=1}^{m} c_i = 1$ and $\sum_{j=1}^{n} d_j = 1$. A transport plan between μ and ν is then a $n \times m$ matrix $\Pi = (\pi_{i,j})$ with non-negative entries such that

$$\sum_{j=1}^{n} \pi_{i,j} = c_i \quad \text{and} \quad \sum_{i=1}^{m} \pi_{i,j} = d_j.$$

The coefficient $\pi_{i,j}$ can be seen as the amount of the mass of μ located at x_j that is transported to y_i. The cost of such a transport plan is then given by

$$\mathcal{C}(\Pi) = \left(\sum_{i=1}^{n} \sum_{j=1}^{m} \pi_{i,j} \|x_j - y_i\|^2 \right)^{1/2}.$$

Definition 10.11   The *Wasserstein distance* of order 2 between two probability measures μ and v on $\mathbb{R}^d$ is the minimum cost $\mathcal{C}(\pi)$ of a transport plan π between μ and v. It is denoted by $W_2(\mu, v)$.

Notice that $W_2(\mu, v)$ may be infinite. However, if μ and v have finite moment of order 2, i.e., $\int_{\mathbb{R}^d} \|x\|^2 d\mu(x) < +\infty$ and $\int_{\mathbb{R}^d} \|x\|^2 dv(x) < +\infty$, then $W_2(\mu, v)$ is finite and the space of probability measures with finite moment of order 2 endowed with W_2 is a metric space [128].

Even for measures with finite support, the computation of the Wasserstein distance is very expensive. However, it provides an interesting notion to quantify the resilience to outliers. To illustrate this, consider a set $C = \{x_1, x_2, \cdots, x_N\}$ of N points in $\mathbb{R}^d$ and a noisy version C' obtained by replacing the first n points in C by points y_i such that $d_C(y_i) = R > 0$ for $i = 1, \cdots, n$. If we denote by $\mu = \frac{1}{N} \sum_{p \in C} \delta_p$ and $v = \frac{1}{N} \sum_{q \in C'} \delta_q$ the empirical measures associated to C and C', respectively, then one has

$$W_2(\mu, v) \le \sqrt{\frac{n}{N}}(R + \text{diam}(C))$$

while the Hausdorff distance between C and C' is at least R. To prove this inequality, consider the transport plan Π from v to μ that moves the outliers back to their original position and leave the other points fixed. The matrix Π of this transport plan (see the aforementioned example) is defined by $\pi_{i,j} = 1/N$ if $i = j$ and 0 otherwise. Because $\|x_i - y_i\| \le R + \text{diam}(C)$ for $i = 0 \cdots n$ and $x_i = y_i$ for $i > n$, we immediately deduce that the cost of this transport plan is upper bounded by $\sqrt{n/N}(R + \text{diam}(C))$. As a consequence, replacing a small amount of points ($n \ll N$) of C by outliers results in a new measure that remains close to the original one.

From a geometric inference point of view, since, in practice, we are working with point sets sampled according to some unknown probability distribution μ, the question of the convergence of the empirical measure μ_N to μ with respect to the Wasserstein distance is of fundamental importance. This question is beyond the scope of this book but has been a subject of study in probability and statistics for a long time. For example, if μ is supported on a compact set, then μ_N converges almost surely to μ in the W_2 distance. However all the stability and inference results stated in this chapter only rely on the Wasserstein distance between the considered measures and are independent of any convergence property of empirical measures.

10.3 Distance Function to a Probability Measure

In this section, we associate to any probability measure in $\mathbb{R}^d$ a family of real valued functions that are both distance-like and robust with respect to perturbations of the probability measure.

10.3.1 Definition

The distance function to a compact set K evaluated at $x \in \mathbb{R}^d$ is defined as the smallest radius r such that the closed ball centered at x of radius r contains at least a point of K. A natural idea to adapt this definition when K is replaced by a measure μ is to consider the smallest radius r such that the ball with center x and radius r contains a given fraction m of the total mass of μ.

Definition 10.12   Let μ be a probability measure on $\mathbb{R}^d$ and $0 \leq m < 1$ a given parameter. We denote by $\delta_{\mu,m}$ the function defined by

$$\delta_{\mu,m} : x \in \mathbb{R}^d \mapsto \inf\{r > 0 \, ; \, \mu(\bar{B}(x,r)) > m\}$$

where $\bar{B}(x,r)$ denotes the closed ball with center x and radius r.

Notice that for $m = 0$, the definition coincides with the (usual) distance function to the support of the measure μ. Moreover for any $m \in [0,1)$, $\delta_{\mu,m}$ is 1-Lipschitz.

Unfortunately $\delta_{\mu,m}$ is not robust with respect to perturbations of the measure μ. Indeed, the map $\mu \rightarrow \delta_{\mu,m}$ is not continuous as shown by the following example. Let $\mu_\varepsilon = (\frac{1}{2} - \varepsilon)\delta_0 + (\frac{1}{2} + \varepsilon)\delta_1$ be the weighted sum of two Dirac measures at 0 and 1 in $\mathbb{R}$ and let $m = 1/2$. Then, for $\varepsilon \geq 0$ one has $\delta_{\mu_\varepsilon,1/2}(t) = |1 - t|$ for $t < 0$ while if $\varepsilon < 0$, one obtains $\delta_{\mu_0,1/2}(t) = |t|$ which means that $\varepsilon \mapsto \delta_{\mu_\varepsilon,1/2}$ is not continuous at $\varepsilon = 0$.

To overcome this issue we define the distance function associated to μ as a L^2 average of the pseudo-distances $\delta_{\mu,m}$ for a range $[0, m_0]$ of parameters m:

Definition 10.13 (Distance-to-measure)   Let μ be a probability measure on $\mathbb{R}^d$, and m_0 be a positive mass parameter $0 < m_0 \leq 1$. The *distance function to μ with parameter m_0* is the function $d_{\mu,m_0} : \mathbb{R}^d \rightarrow \mathbb{R}_+$ defined by :

$$d_{\mu,m_0}^2 : \mathbb{R}^n \rightarrow \mathbb{R}^+, \; x \mapsto \frac{1}{m_0} \int_0^{m_0} \delta_{\mu,m}^2(x) dm$$

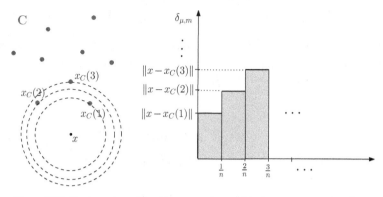

Figure 10.3 Computation of the distance to the empirical measure associated to a point set C ($x_C(k)$) denotes the kth nearest neighbor of x.

10.3.2 Distance Function to Empirical Measures

An interesting property of these defined functions is that they have a simple expression in terms of nearest neighbors. More precisely, let C be a point cloud with n points in $\mathbb{R}^d$, and μ_C be the uniform measure on it: $\mu_C = \frac{1}{n} \sum_{p \in C} \delta_p$. For $0 < m \leq 1$, the function $\delta_{\mu_C, m}$ evaluated at a given point $x \in \mathbb{R}^d$ is by definition equal to the distance between x and its kth nearest neighbor in C, where k is the smallest integer larger than mn. Hence the function $m \mapsto \delta_{\mu_C, m}(x)$ is constant and equal to the distance from x to its kth nearest neighbor in C on each interval $[\frac{k-1}{n}, \frac{k}{n})$. Integrating the square of this piecewise constant functions gives the following expression for d^2_{μ, m_0}, where $m_0 = k_0/n$:

$$d^2_{\mu, m_0}(x) = \frac{1}{m_0} \int_0^{m_0} \delta^2_{\mu, m}(x) dm = \frac{1}{m_0} \sum_{k=1}^{k_0} \frac{1}{n} \delta^2_{\mu, k/n}(x)$$

$$= \frac{1}{k_0} \sum_{p \in NN_C^{k_0}(x)} \|p - x\|^2$$

where $NN_C^{k_0}(x)$ denote the set of the first k_0 nearest neighbors of x in C. As a consequence the pointwise evaluation of $d^2_{\mu_C, k_0/n}(x)$ reduces to a k-nearest neighbor query in C.

10.3.3 Equivalent Formulation

In this paragraph, we provide another characterization of the distance function to a measure d_{μ, m_0} showing that it is in fact the distance function to a closed set, but in the non-Euclidean space of probability measures endowed with the W_2

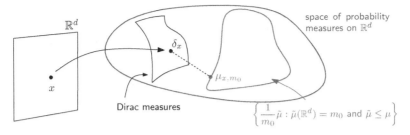

Figure 10.4 The distance function to a measure as a usual distance function in an infinite dimensional space.

metric (see Figure 10.4). This equivalent formulation will be used to deduce that $\mu \to d_{\mu,m_0}$ is Lipschitz and $x \to d^2_{\mu,m_0}(x)$ is semiconcave.

Definition 10.14 A measure ν is a *submeasure* of another measure μ if for every Borel subset B of $\mathbb{R}^d$, $\nu(B) \leq \mu(B)$. The set of all submeasures of a given measure is denoted by $\text{Sub}(\mu)$, while the set of submeasures of μ with a prescribed total mass $m_0 > 0$ is denoted by $\text{Sub}_{m_0}(\mu)$.

Proposition 10.15 *For any probability measure μ on $\mathbb{R}^d$, the distance function to μ evaluated at x is defined as:*

$$d_{\mu,m_0}(x) = \min \left\{ m_0^{-1/2} W_2(m_0 \delta_x, \nu) ; \nu \in \text{Sub}_{m_0}(\mu) \right\} \qquad (10.1)$$

Moreover, for any measure μ_{x,m_0} that realizes the above minimum one has:

$$d_{\mu,m_0}(x) = \left(\frac{1}{m_0} \int_{\mathbb{R}^d} \|x - h\|^2 \, d\mu_{x,m_0}(h) \right)^{1/2}$$

Said otherwise, the distance d_{μ,m_0} evaluated at a point $x \in \mathbb{R}^d$ is the minimal Wasserstein distance between the Dirac mass $m_0 \delta_x$ and the set of submeasures of μ with total mass m_0.

The set $\mathcal{R}_{\mu,m_0}(x)$ of submeasures minimizing the above expression corresponds to the nearest neighbors of the Dirac measure $m_0 \delta_x$ on the set of submeasures $\text{Sub}_{m_0}(\mu)$. It is not empty but it might not be reduced to a single element. Indeed, it coincides with the set of submeasures μ_{x,m_0} of total mass m_0 whose support is contained in the closed ball $\bar{B}(x, \delta_{\mu,m_0}(x))$, and whose restriction to the *open* ball $B(x, \delta_{\mu,m_0}(x))$ coincides with μ.

10.3.4 Stability of the Distance Function to a Measure

The characterization of d_{μ,m_0} given in Proposition 10.15 provides a rather easy way to prove the stability of $\mu \mapsto d_{\mu,m_0}$.

Theorem 10.16 (Distance function stability) *If μ and μ' are two probability measures on $\mathbb{R}^d$ and $m_0 > 0$, then $\left\| d_{\mu,m_0} - d_{\mu',m_0} \right\|_\infty \le \frac{1}{\sqrt{m_0}} W_2(\mu, \mu')$.*

The proof of theorem 10.16 follows from the following proposition.

Proposition 10.17 *Let μ and μ' be two probability measures on $\mathbb{R}^d$. Then,*

$$d_H(\mathrm{Sub}_{m_0}(\mu), \mathrm{Sub}_{m_0}(\mu')) \le W_2(\mu, \mu')$$

where $d_H(.,.)$ is the Hausdorff distance in the space of probability measures endowed with the W_2 metric.

Proof (sketch of) Let ε be the Wasserstein distance of order 2 between μ and μ', and π be a corresponding optimal transport plan, i.e., a transport plan between μ and μ' such that $\int_{\mathbb{R}^d \times \mathbb{R}^d} \|x - y\|^2 \, d\pi(x, y) = \varepsilon^2$. Given a submeasure ν of μ, one can find a submeasure π' of π that transports ν to a submeasure ν' of μ' (notice that this later claim is not completely obvious and its formal proof is beyond the scope of this book. It can be proven using the Radon-Nykodim theorem). Then,

$$W_2(\nu, \nu')^2 \le \int_{\mathbb{R}^d \times \mathbb{R}^d} \|x - y\|^2 \, d\pi'(x, y) \le \varepsilon^2$$

This shows that $\mathrm{dist}(\nu, \mathrm{Sub}_{m_0}(\mu')) \le \varepsilon$ for every submeasure $\nu \in \mathrm{Sub}_{m_0}(\mu)$. The same holds by exchanging the roles of μ and μ', thus proving the bound on the Hausdorff distance. $\qquad\square$

Proof **[of Theorem 10.16]** The following sequence of equalities and inequalities, that follows from Propositions 10.15 and 10.17, proves the theorem:.

$$d_{\mu,m_0}(x) = \frac{1}{\sqrt{m_0}} \mathrm{dist}_{W_2}(m_0\delta_x, \mathrm{Sub}_{m_0}(\mu))$$

$$\le \frac{1}{\sqrt{m_0}}(d_H(\mathrm{Sub}_{m_0}(\mu), \mathrm{Sub}_{m_0}(\mu')) + \mathrm{dist}_{W_2}(m_0\delta_x, \mathrm{Sub}_{m_0}(\mu')))$$

$$\le \frac{1}{\sqrt{m_0}} W_2(\mu, \mu') + d_{\mu',m_0}(x) \qquad\qquad\square$$

10.3.5 The Distance to a Measure is a Distance-like Function

The subdifferential of a function $f : \Omega \subseteq \mathbb{R}^d \to \mathbb{R}$ at a point x, is the set of vectors v of $\mathbb{R}^d$, denoted by $\partial_x f$, such that for all small enough vector h, $f(x + h) \ge f(x) + h.v$. This gives a characterization of convexity: a function $f : \mathbb{R}^d \to \mathbb{R}$ is convex if and only if its subdifferential $\partial_x f$ is non-empty for every point x. If this is the case, then f admits a derivative at a point x if and only if the subdifferential $\partial_x f$ is a singleton, in which case the gradient $\nabla_x f$ coincides with its unique element [58].

Proposition 10.18 *The function* $v_{\mu,m_0} : x \in \mathbb{R}^d \mapsto \|x\|^2 - d^2_{\mu,m_0}$ *is convex, and its subdifferential at a point* $x \in \mathbb{R}^d$ *is given by*

$$\partial_x v_{\mu,m_0} = \left\{ 2x - \frac{2}{m_0} \int_{h \in \mathbb{R}^d} (x - h) \, d\mu_{x,m_0}(h) \, ; \, \mu_{x,m_0} \in \mathcal{R}_{\mu,m_0}(x) \right\}$$

Proof For any two points x and y of $\mathbb{R}^d$, let μ_{x,m_0} and μ_{y,m_0} be in $\mathcal{R}_{\mu,m_0}(x)$ and $\mathcal{R}_{\mu,m_0}(y)$, respectively. Thanks to Proposition 10.15, we have the following sequence of equalities and inequalities:

$$\begin{aligned}
d^2_{\mu,m_0}(y) &= \frac{1}{m_0} \int_{h \in \mathbb{R}^d} \|y - h\|^2 \, d\mu_{y,m_0}(h) \\
&\leq \frac{1}{m_0} \int_{h \in \mathbb{R}^d} \|y - h\|^2 \, d\mu_{x,m_0}(h) \\
&\leq \frac{1}{m_0} \int_{h \in \mathbb{R}^d} \|x - h\|^2 + 2(x - h).(y - x) + \|y - x\|^2 \, d\mu_{x,m_0}(h) \\
&\leq d^2_{\mu,m_0}(x) + \|y - x\|^2 + v.(y - x)
\end{aligned}$$

where v is the vector defined by

$$v = \frac{2}{m_0} \int_{h \in \mathbb{R}^d} (x - h) \, d\mu_{x,m_0}(h).$$

The inequality can be rewritten as:

$$\left(\|y\|^2 - d^2_{\mu,m_0}(y) \right) - \left(\|x\|^2 - d^2_{\mu,m_0}(x) \right) \geq (2x - v).(y - x)$$

which shows that the vector $(2x - v)$ belongs to the subdifferential of v_{μ,m_0} at x. By the characterization of convex functions by that we recalled earlier, one deduces that v_{μ,m_0} is convex.

The proof of the reverse inclusion is slightly more technical and beyond the scope of the book. □

Corollary 10.19 *The function* d^2_{μ,m_0} *is* 1-*semiconcave. Moreover,*

(i) d^2_{μ,m_0} *is differentiable almost everywhere in* $\mathbb{R}^d$, *with gradient defined by*

$$\nabla_x d^2_{\mu,m_0} = \frac{2}{m_0} \int_{h \in \mathbb{R}^d} [x - h] \, d\mu_{x,m_0}(h)$$

where μ_{x,m_0} *is the only measure in* $\mathcal{R}_{\mu,m_0}(x)$.

(ii) *the function* $x \in \mathbb{R}^d \mapsto d_{\mu,m_0}(x)$ *is* 1-*Lipschitz.*

Proof   (i) It follows from the fact that a convex function is differentiable at almost every point, at which its gradient is the only element of the subdifferential at that point.

(ii) The gradient of d_{μ,m_0} can be written as:

$$\nabla_x d_{\mu,m_0} = \frac{\nabla_x d^2_{\mu,m_0}}{2 d_{\mu,m_0}} = \frac{1}{\sqrt{m_0}} \frac{\int_{h \in \mathbb{R}^d} [x - h] \, d\mu_{x,m_0}(h)}{\left(\int_{h \in \mathbb{R}^d} \|x - h\|^2 \, d\mu_{x,m_0}(h) \right)^{1/2}}$$

Using the Cauchy-Schwartz inequality we find $\left\| \nabla_x d_{\mu,m_0} \right\| \leq 1$, which proves the statement.   □

10.4 Applications to Geometric Inference

Reconstruction from point clouds in presence of outliers was the main motivation for introducing the distance function to a measure. In this section, we show how the extended reconstruction Theorem 10.7 can be applied to distance to measure functions. It is also possible to adapt most of the topological and geometric inference results of Chapter 9 in a similar way.

10.4.1 Distance to a Measure vs. Distance to Its Support

In this section, we compare the distance functions d_{μ,m_0} to a measure μ and the distance function d_S to its support S, and study the convergence properties of d_{μ,m_0} to d_S as the mass parameter m_0 converges to zero. Remark that the function δ_{μ,m_0} (and hence the distance d_{μ,m_0}) is always larger than the distance function d_S, i.e., for any $x \in \mathbb{R}^d$, $d_S(x) \leq d_{\mu,m_0}(x)$. As a consequence, to obtain a convergence result of d_{μ,m_0} to d_S as m_0 goes to zero, we just need to upper bound $d_{\mu,m_0} - d_S$ by a function converging to 0 as m_0 goes to 0. It turns out that the convergence speed of d_{μ,m_0} to d_S depends on the way the mass of μ contained within any ball $B(p, r)$ centered at a point p of the support increases with r. Let us define:

(i) We say that a nondecreasing positive function $f : \mathbb{R}^+ \to \mathbb{R}^+$ is a *uniform lower bound on the growth of μ* if for every point p in the support of μ and every $\varepsilon > 0$, $\mu(B(p, \varepsilon)) \geq f(\varepsilon)$;

(ii) The measure μ has *dimension at most k* if there is a constant $C(\mu)$ such that $f(\varepsilon) = C(\mu)\varepsilon^k$ is a uniform lower bound on the growth of μ, for ε small enough.

Lemma 10.20   *Let μ be a probability measure and f be a uniform lower bound on the growth of μ. Then $\left\| d_{\mu,m_0} - d_S \right\|_\infty < \varepsilon$ as soon as $m_0 < f(\varepsilon)$.*

Proof Let ε and m_0 be such that $m_0 < f(\varepsilon)$ and let x be a point in $\mathbb{R}^d$, p a projection of x on S, i.e., a point p such that $\|x - p\| = d_S(x)$. By assumption, $\mu(B(x, d_S(x) + \varepsilon)) \geq \mu(B(p, \varepsilon)) \geq m_0$. Hence, $\delta_{\mu,m_0}(x) \leq d_S(x) + \varepsilon$. The function $m \mapsto \delta_{\mu,m}(x)$ being non-decreasing, we get: $m_0 d_S^2(x) \leq \int_0^{m_0} \delta_{\mu,m}^2(x) dm \leq m_0(d_S(x) + \varepsilon)^2$. Taking the square root of this expression proves the lemma. $\qquad\square$

Corollary 10.21 *(i) If the support S of μ is compact, then d_S is the uniform limit of* d_{μ,m_0} *as m_0 converges to 0:*

$$\|d_{\mu,m_0} - d_S\|_\infty = \sup_{x \in \mathbb{R}^d} |d_{\mu,m_0}(x) - d_S(x)| \xrightarrow{m_0 \to 0} 0$$

(ii) If the measure μ has dimension at most $k > 0$, then

$$\left\|\mathrm{d}_{\mu,m_0} - \mathrm{d}_S\right\|_\infty \leq C(\mu)^{-1/k} m_0^{1/k}$$

Proof (i) If S is compact, there exists a sequence $x_1, x_2, \cdots$ of points in S such that for any $\varepsilon > 0$, $S \subseteq \cup_{i=1}^n B(x_i, \varepsilon/2)$ for some $n = n(\varepsilon)$. By definition of the support of a measure, $\eta(\varepsilon) = \min_{i=1\cdots n} \mu(B(x_i, \varepsilon/2))$ is positive. Now, for any point $x \in S$, there is a x_i such that $\|x - x_i\| \leq \varepsilon/2$. Hence, $B(x_i, \varepsilon/2) \subseteq B(x, \varepsilon)$, which means that $\mu(B(x, \varepsilon)) \geq \eta(\varepsilon)$. (ii) Follows straightforwardly from the lemma. $\qquad\square$

For example, the uniform probability measure on a k-dimensional compact submanifold S has dimension at most k. The following proposition gives a more precise convergence speed estimate based on curvature.

Proposition 10.22 *Let S be a smooth k-dimensional submanifold of $\mathbb{R}^d$ whose curvature radii are lower bounded by R, and μ the uniform probability measure on S, then*

$$\left\|\mathrm{d}_S - \mathrm{d}_{\mu,m_0}\right\|_\infty \leq C(S)^{-1/k} m_0^{1/k}$$

for m_0 small enough and $C(S) = (2/\pi)^k \beta_k / \mathrm{vol}^k(S)$ where β_k is the volume of the unit ball in $\mathbb{R}^k$.

Notice in particular that the convergence speed of d_{μ,m_0} to d_S depends only on the *intrinsic* dimension k of the submanifold S, and not on the ambient dimension d. The proof of this result is beyond the scope of this book and relies on the so-called Günther-Bishop theorem (cf [88, Section 3.101]).

10.4.2 Shape Reconstruction from Noisy Data

The previous results lead to shape reconstruction theorems that work for noisy data with outliers. To fit in our framework we consider shapes that are defined as supports of probability measures. Let μ be a probability measure of dimension at most $k > 0$ with compact support $K \subset \mathbb{R}^d$ and let $d_K : \mathbb{R}^d \to \mathbb{R}_+$ be the (Euclidean) distance function to K. If μ' is another probability measure (e.g., the empirical measure given by a point cloud sampled according to μ), one has

$$\left\| d_K - d_{\mu',m_0} \right\|_\infty \le \left\| d_K - d_{\mu,m_0} \right\|_\infty + \left\| d_{\mu,m_0} - d_{\mu',m_0} \right\|_\infty \qquad (10.2)$$

$$\le C(\mu)^{-1/k} m_0^{1/k} + \frac{1}{\sqrt{m_0}} W_2(\mu, \mu') \qquad (10.3)$$

This inequality insuring the closeness of d_{μ',m_0} to the distance function d_K for the sup-norm follows immediately from the stability Theorem 10.16 and Corollary 10.21. As expected, the choice of m_0 is a trade-off: small m_0 lead to better approximation of the distance function to the support, while large values of m_0 make the distance functions to measures more stable. Eq. (10.3) leads to the following corollary of Theorem 10.7:

Corollary 10.23 *Let μ be a measure and K its support. Suppose that μ has dimension at most k and that $\mathrm{reach}_\alpha(d_K) \ge R$ for some $R > 0$. Let μ' be another measure, and ε be an upper bound on the uniform distance between d_K and d_{μ',m_0}. Then, for any $r \in [4\varepsilon/\alpha^2, R - 3\varepsilon]$, the r-sublevel sets of d_{μ,m_0} and the offsets K^η, for $0 < \eta < R$ are homotopy equivalent as soon as:*

$$W_2(\mu, \mu') \le \frac{R\sqrt{m_0}}{5 + 4/\alpha^2} - C(\mu)^{-1/k} m_0^{1/k+1/2}$$

Figure 10.5 On the left, a point cloud sampled on a mechanical part to which 10% of outliers (uniformly sampled in a box enclosing the model) have been added. On the right, the reconstruction of an isosurface of the distance function d_{μ_C,m_0} to the uniform probability measure on this point cloud.

Figure 10.5 illustrates Theorem 10.7 on a sampled mechanical part with 10% of outliers. In this case μ' is the normalized sum of the Dirac measures centered on the data points and the (unknown) measure μ is the uniform measure on the mechanical part.

10.5 Exercises

Exercise 10.1 Let $K \subset \mathbb{R}^d$ be a compact set. Show that the map $x \rightarrow \|x\|^2 - d_K^2(x)$ is convex.

Hint: Recall that the supremum of any family of convex functions is convex and show that $x \rightarrow \|x\|^2 - d_K^2(x)$ is the supremum of a set of affine functions.

Exercise 10.2 Let $\mu_1, \cdots, \mu_k$ be measures on $\mathbb{R}^d$ and let $\lambda_1, \cdots, \lambda_k \in \mathbb{R}$. Show that if all the λ_i are non-negative then $\mu = \sum_{i=1}^{k} \lambda_i \mu_i$ is a measure. Show that the set of probability measures on $\mathbb{R}^d$ is convex.

Exercise 10.3 Let μ and ν be two probability measures with finite supports:

$$\mu = \sum_{j=1}^{m} c_j \delta_{x_j} \text{ and } \nu = \sum_{i=1}^{n} d_i \delta_{y_i}$$

where $x_1, \cdots, x_m$ and $y_1, \cdots, y_n$ are points in $\mathbb{R}^d$ and $\sum_{j=1}^{m} c_j = \sum_{i=1}^{n} d_i = 1$. Show that any transport plan between μ and ν can be represented as a $n \times m$ matrix $\Pi = (\pi_{i,j})$ with non-negative entries such that

$$\sum_{i=1}^{n} \pi_{i,j} = c_j \text{ and } \sum_{j=1}^{m} \pi_{i,j} = d_i.$$

Exercise 10.4 Let μ be a probability measure on $\mathbb{R}^d$ and let $m \in [0, 1)$. Show that $\delta_{\mu,m}$ is 1-Lipschitz:

$$\forall x, y \in \mathbb{R}^d, |\delta_{\mu,m}(x) - \delta_{\mu,m}(y)| \leq \|x - y\|.$$

Exercise 10.5 Let μ be a probability measure on $\mathbb{R}^d$ and let $0 < m_0 < 1$ and $x \in \mathbb{R}^d$. Recall that we denote by $\mathcal{R}_{\mu,m_0}(x)$ the set of submeasures minimizing the right hand term of Equation (10.1). Give an example of a probability measure μ such that $\mathcal{R}_{\mu,m_0}(x)$ contains only one element and an example such that $\mathcal{R}_{\mu,m_0}(x)$ contains an infinite number of elements.

Hint: For $\mathcal{R}_{\mu,m_0}(x)$ to contain more than one submeasure, the measure $\mu(S(x, \delta_{\mu,m_0}))$ of the sphere of center x and radius δ_{μ,m_0} must be positive.

10.6 Bibliographical Notes

Most of the chapter comes from [42] that introduces and studies stability properties of distance functions to a probability measure. Approximation and computation of the distance to measure function and its connections with power distances has been studied in [93]. Extensions of the distance-to-measure framework to general metric spaces has been considered in [29]. Statistical aspects of distance-to-measure functions in relation with density estimation and deconvolution have been considered in [9, 31, 45, 49].

Wasserstein distances are closely related to the theory of optimal transportation (see, e.g., [128]). The distance W_1 is also known as the earth-mover distance, and has been used in various domains such as, e.g., vision [116] or image retrieval [120].

General results about semiconcave functions can be found in [117, 34].

The convergence properties of empirical measure with respect to the Wasserstein metric have been widely studied and quantitative results can be found in [28].

The complete proofs of Propositions 10.15, 10.18, and 10.4 are given in [42].

The Günther-Bishop Theorem is stated in [88, Section 3.101] and the proof of Proposition 10.22 can be found in [42].

11

Homology Inference

Although the distance-based approach introduced in the two previous chapters provides a powerful mathematical framework for shape reconstruction, it is not always possible, nor desirable, to fully reconstruct the approximated shapes from data. This chapter focuses on weaker topological invariants, homology, Betti numbers and persistent homology, that turn out to be easier to infer and that are widely used in applied topology and topological data analysis. The introduction of homology is restricted to the minimum that is necessary to understand the basic ideas of homology inference and persistent homology and its usage in topological data analysis.

11.1 Simplicial Homology and Betti Numbers

In this section we introduce the basic notions of simplicial homology that are necessary to define and study topological persistence. To avoid minor technical discussions about the orientation of simplices, we restrict to the homology with coefficients in the finite field $\mathbb{Z}/2\mathbb{Z} = \{0, 1\}$. In the sequel of this chapter, K denotes a finite d-dimensional simplicial complex.

11.1.1 The Space of k-chains

For any non-negative integer k, the space of k-chains is the vector space of all the formal sums (with coefficient in $\mathbb{Z}/2\mathbb{Z}$) of k-dimensional simplices of K. More precisely, if $\{\sigma_1, \cdots, \sigma_p\}$ is the set of k-simplices of K any k-chain c can be uniquely written

$$c = \sum_{i=1}^{p} \varepsilon_i \sigma_i \text{ with } \varepsilon_i \in \mathbb{Z}/2\mathbb{Z}$$

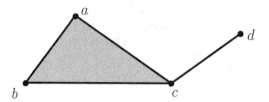

Figure 11.1 A very simple simplicial complex made of 4 vertices, 4 edges and 1 triangle.

If $c' = \sum_{i=1}^{p} \varepsilon'_i \sigma_i$ is another k-chain, the sum of two k-chains and the product of a chain by a scalar are defined by

$$c + c' = \sum_{i=1}^{p} (\varepsilon_i + \varepsilon'_i)\sigma_i \text{ and } \lambda.c = \sum_{i=1}^{p} (\lambda \varepsilon_i)\sigma_i$$

where the sums $\varepsilon_i + \varepsilon'_i$ and the products $\lambda \varepsilon_i$ are modulo 2.

Definition 11.1 The space of k-chains is the set $C_k(K)$ of the simplicial k-chains of K with the two operations defined earlier. This is a $\mathbb{Z}/2\mathbb{Z}$-vector space whose zero element is the empty chain $0 = \sum_{i=1}^{p} 0.\sigma_i$.

Notice that the set of k-simplices of K is a basis of $C_k(K)$. For example, for the simplicial complex K of Figure 11.1, $C_1(K)$ is the $\mathbb{Z}/2\mathbb{Z}$-vector space generated by the edges $e_1 = [a, b]$, $e_2 = [b, c]$, $e_3 = [c, a]$, $e_4 = [c, d]$, i.e.,

$$C_1(K) = \{0, e_1, e_2, e_3, e_4, e_1 + e_2, e_1 + e_3, e_1 + e_4, e_2 + e_3, e_2 + e_4, e_3$$
$$+ e_4, e_1 + e_2 + e_3, \cdots\}$$

Summing $e_1 + e_2$ with $e_2 + e_3 + e_4$ gives $e_1 + e_3 + e_4$.

Chains with coefficient in $\mathbb{Z}/2\mathbb{Z}$ have an obvious geometric interpretation: since any k-chain can be uniquely written as $c = \sigma_{i_1} + \sigma_{i_2} + \cdots + \sigma_{i_m}$ where the σ_{i_j} are k-simplices, c can be considered as the union of the simplices σ_{i_j}. The sum of two k-chains is equal to their symetric difference.

11.1.2 The Boundary Operator and Homology Groups

Definition 11.2 (Boundary of a simplex) The boundary $\partial(\sigma)$ of a k-simplex σ is the sum of its $(k-1)$-faces. This is a $(k-1)$-chain.

If $\sigma = [v_0, \cdots, v_k]$ is a k-simplex, then

$$\partial(\sigma) = \sum_{i=0}^{k} [v_0 \cdots \hat{v}_i \cdots v_k]$$

where $[v_0 \cdots \hat{v}_i \cdots v_k]$ is the $(k-1)$-simplex spanned by the sets of all the vertices of σ except v_i.

Remark 11.3 Notice that in the general case where the coefficient of the chains are taken in another field than $\mathbb{Z}/2\mathbb{Z}$ it is important to take into account the ordering of the vertices in σ and the boundary of σ has to be defined as $\partial(\sigma) = \sum_{i=0}^{k}(-1)^i[v_0 \cdots \hat{v}_i \cdots v_k]$ - see [110].

The boundary operator, defined on the simplices of K, extends linearly to $C_k(K)$.

Definition 11.4 The boundary operator is the linear map defined by

$$
\begin{aligned}
\partial_k : \quad C_k(K) \quad &\rightarrow \quad C_{k-1}(K) \\
c \quad &\rightarrow \quad \partial c = \sum_{\sigma \in c} \partial(\sigma)
\end{aligned}
$$

To avoid heavy notations, when there is no risk of confusion, the index k is usually ommited and the boundary operator is denoted by ∂.

Proposition 11.5 *The boundary of the boundary of a chain is always zero:*

$$\partial\partial := \partial \circ \partial = 0.$$

Proof Because the boundary operator is linear, it is sufficient to check the property for a simplex. Let $\sigma = [v_0 \cdots v_k]$ be a k-simplex.

$$
\begin{aligned}
\partial\partial\sigma &= \partial\left(\sum_{i=0}^{k}[v_0 \cdots \hat{v}_i \cdots v_k]\right) \\
&= \sum_{i=0}^{k} \partial[v_0 \cdots \hat{v}_i \cdots v_k] \\
&= \sum_{j<i}[v_0 \cdots \hat{v}_j \cdots \hat{v}_i \cdots v_k] + \sum_{j>i}[v_0 \cdots \hat{v}_i \cdots \hat{v}_j \cdots v_k] \\
&= 0
\end{aligned}
$$

$\square$

The boundary operator defines a sequence of linear maps between the spaces of chains.

Definition 11.6 (Chain complex) The chain complex associated to a complex K of dimension d is the following sequence of linear operators

$$\{0\} \rightarrow C_d(K) \xrightarrow{\partial} C_{d-1}(K) \xrightarrow{\partial} \cdots \xrightarrow{\partial} C_{k+1}(K) \xrightarrow{\partial} C_k(K) \xrightarrow{\partial} \cdots \xrightarrow{\partial} C_0(K) \xrightarrow{\partial} \{0\}$$

For $k \in \{0, \cdots, d\}$, the set $Z_k(K)$ of k-*cycles* of K is the kernel of $\partial : C_k \rightarrow C_{k-1}$:

$$Z_k(K) := \ker(\partial : C_k \rightarrow C_{k-1}) = \{c \in C_k : \partial c = 0\}$$

The image $B_k(K)$ of $\partial : C_{k+1} \rightarrow C_k$ is the set of k-chains bounding a $(k+1)$-chain:

$$B_k(K) := \text{im}(\partial : C_{k+1} \rightarrow C_k) = \{c \in C_k : \exists\, c' \in C_{k+1}, c = \partial c'\}$$

B_k and Z_k are subspaces of C_k and according to Proposition 11.5, one has

$$B_k(K) \subset Z_k(K) \subset C_k(K).$$

Examples of chains, cycles, and boundaries are given in Figure 11.2.

Definition 11.7 (Homology groups)   The kth homology group of K is the quotient vector space

$$H_k(K) = Z_k/B_k$$

$H_k(K)$ is a vector space and its elements are the homology classes of K. The dimension $\beta_k(K)$ of $H_k(K)$ is the kth Betti number of K (see Figure 11.3).

The homology class of a cycle $c \in Z_k(K)$ is the set $c + B_k(K) = \{c + b : b \in B_k(K)\}$. Two cycles c, c' that are in the same homology class are said to be *homologous*.

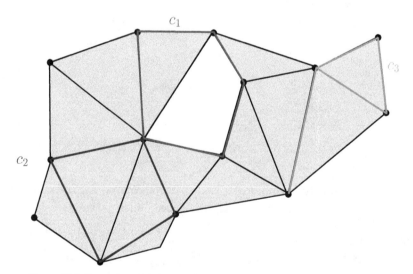

Figure 11.2 Examples of chains, cycles, and boundaries: c_1 is a cycle that is not a boundary, c_2 is a boundary, and c_3 is a chain that is not a cycle.

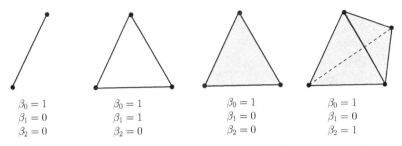

$\beta_0 = 1$ $\beta_0 = 1$ $\beta_0 = 1$ $\beta_0 = 1$
$\beta_1 = 0$ $\beta_1 = 1$ $\beta_1 = 0$ $\beta_1 = 0$
$\beta_2 = 0$ $\beta_2 = 0$ $\beta_2 = 0$ $\beta_2 = 1$

Figure 11.3 Examples of Betti numbers for simple simplicial complexes: from left to right, an edge, the boundary of a triangle, a triangle and the boundary of a tetrahedron.

11.2 An Algorithm to Compute Betti Numbers

Let K be a finite simplicial complex of dimension d and

$$\emptyset = K^0 \subset K^1 \subset \cdots \subset K^m = K$$

a filtration of K such that for any $i = 0, \cdots m - 1$,

$$K^{i+1} = K^i \cup \sigma^{i+1} \quad \text{where} \quad \sigma^{i+1} \text{ is a simplex.}$$

By considering the evolution of the Betti numbers of the filtration as we add the simplices σ^i we get the following algorithm.

Algorithm 9: Betti numbers computation

Input: A filtration of a d-dimensional simplicial complex K containing m simplices.
$\beta_0 \leftarrow 0; \ \beta_1 \leftarrow 0; \cdots ; \beta_d \leftarrow 0$
for $i = 1$ to m **do**
    $k = \dim \sigma^i - 1$
    if σ^i is contained in a $(k+1)$-cycle in K^i **then**
        $\beta_{k+1} \leftarrow \beta_{k+1} + 1$
    else
        $\beta_k \leftarrow \beta_k - 1$
Output: The Betti numbers $\beta_0, \beta_1, \cdots, \beta_d$ of K.

To prove the correctness of the algorithm, one has to understand how the topology of the filtration evolves each time we add a simplex. Let assume that the Betti numbers of K^{i-1} have been computed and add the simplex σ^i of dimension $k + 1$ to get K^i. Remark that according to the definition of filtration, σ^i cannot be part of the boundary of any $(k + 2)$-simplex of K^i.

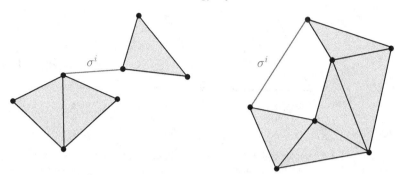

Figure 11.4 Examples of insertion of a 1-simplex σ^i to a subcomplex K^{i-1}. When σ^i is not contained in a 1-cycle (left), its insertion results in the connection of two connected components of K^{i-1}. When σ^i is contained in a 1-cycle (right), its insertion create a new 1-cycle that is not homologous to any previously existing in K^{i-1}.

As a consequence if σ^i is contained in a $(k+1)$-cycle in K^i, this cycle is not the boundary of a $(k+2)$-chain in K^i. Let consider the two alternatives of the algorithm that are illustrated in Figure 11.4:

Case 1: assume that σ^i is contained in a $(k+1)$-cycle c in K^i. Then c cannot be homologous to any $(k+1)$-cycle in K^{i-1}. Indeed, otherwise there would exist a cycle c' in K^{i-1} such that $c + c'$ is the boundary of a $(k+2)$-chain d. But since σ^i cannot be contained in c', it has to be contained in $c + c' = \partial d$ contradicting the aforementioned remark. So, c creates a new homology class which is linearly independent of the classes created by the cycles in K^{i-1}. As a consequence, $\beta_{k+1}(K^i) \geq \beta_{k+1}(K^{i-1}) + 1$. To conclude this first case, it is sufficient to remark that adding the $(k+1)$-simplex σ^i to K^{i-1} cannot increase the dimension of the kth homology group by more than one: if c and c' are two $(k+1)$-cycles containing σ^i, then $c+c'$ is a $(k+1)$-cycle in K^{i-1} implying that c' is contained in the linear subspace spanned by $Z_{k+1}(K^{i-1})$ and c. It follows that $\dim Z_{k+1}(K^i) \leq \dim Z_{k+1}(K^{i-1}) + 1$ and since $B_{k+1}(K^{i-1}) \subset B_{k+1}(K^i)$, $\beta_{k+1}(K^i) \leq \beta_{k+1}(K^{i-1}) + 1$.

Case 2: assume that σ^i is not contained in any $(k+1)$-cycle in K^i. Then the k-cycle $\partial\sigma^i$ is not a boundary in K^{i-1}. Indeed, otherwise there would exist a chain c in K^{i-1} such that $\partial c = \partial\sigma^i$ or equivalently $\partial(c+\sigma^i) = 0$. Thus $c+\sigma^i$ is a $(k+1)$-cycle in K^i containing σ^i: a contradiction. As a consequence, because the k-cycle $\partial\sigma^i$ which is not a boundary in K^{i-1} becomes a boundary in K^i, one has $\beta_k(K^i) \leq \beta_k(K^{i-1}) - 1$. One proves as in Case 1 that this inequality is indeed an equality.

The aforementioned discussion suggests to distinguish between the two types of simplices in the filtration of K that will play an important role in the definition of topological persistence.

Definition 11.8 Let K be a d-dimensional simplicial complex and let

$$\emptyset = K^0 \subset K^1 \subset \cdots \subset K^m = K$$

be a filtration of K. A simplex σ^i is called positive if it is contained in a $(k+1)$-cycle in K^i (which is necessarily not a boundary in K^i according to the remark at the beginning of the proof of the correctness of the algorithm) and negative otherwise.

With the aforementioned definition, the kth Betti number of K is equal to the difference between the number of positive k-simplices (which are creating k-cycles) and the number of negative $(k + 1)$-simplices (which are "killing" k-cycles).

As an example, if one considers the simplicial complex K of Figure 11.1 with the filtration defined by the simplices ordering $\emptyset$, a, b, c, ab, bc, d, ac, cd, abc, then the positive simplices are a, b, c, d, and ac. The Betti numbers of K are $\beta_0 = 1$, $\beta_1 = 0$ and $\beta_2 = 0$.

It is important to notice that the above algorithm needs to be able to decide whether a simplex is positive or negative. This is not, a priori, an obvious question but an answer will be given in Section 11.5. It is also important to notice that the algorithm not only computes the Betti numbers of K but also the Betti numbers of all the subcomplexes K^i of the filtration.

11.3 Singular Homology and Topological Invariance

The homology groups and Betti numbers are topological invariants: if K and K' are two simplicial complexes with homeomorphic geometric realizations then their homology groups are isomorphic and their Betti numbers are equal. This result is still true if the geometric realizations of K and K' are just homotopy equivalent. The proof of this invariance property is a classical, but not obvious, result in algebraic topology. It is beyond the scope of this book (see [110, 96] for details).

Singular homology is another notion of homology that allows to consider general spaces that are not necessarily homeomorphic to simplicial complexes. The definition of singular homology is similar to the one of simplicial homology except that it relies on the notion of singular simplex. Let Δ_k be the standard k-dimensional simplex in $\mathbb{R}^{k+1}$, i.e., the geometric simplex spanned by the vertices x_i, $i = 1, \cdots k + 1$, whose all coordinates are 0 except the ith one which is equal to 1. Given a topological space X, a *singular k-simplex* σ is a continuous map $\sigma : \Delta_k \to X$. As in the case of simplicial homology, the space of singular k-chains is the vector space of formal linear combinations of singular k-simplices. The boundary $\partial\sigma$ of a singular k-simplex is the sum of the restriction of σ to each of the $(k - 1)$-faces of Δ_k. Proposition 11.5 still holds for the (singular) boundary operator and the kth singular homology group of X is defined similarly as the quotient of the space of cycles by the space of boundaries.

A remarkable fact is that simplicial and singular homology are related in the following way: if X is a topological space homeomorphic to the support of a simplicial complex K, then the singular homology groups of X are isomorphic to the simplicial homology groups of K. For example, if X is a surface and if K and K' are two triangulations of X, then the homology groups $H_k(K)$ and $H_k(K')$ are isomorphic. Thus they have the same Betti numbers that are, indeed, the ones of X. As a consequence, in the sequel of the chapter, we will consider indifferently simplicial or singular homology.

Another important property of singular (and thus simplicial) homology is that continuous maps between topological spaces canonically induce homomorphisms between their homology groups. Indeed, if $f : X \to Y$ is a continuous map between two topological spaces and if $\sigma : \Delta_k \to X$ is a singular simplex in X, then $f \circ \sigma : \Delta_k \to Y$ is a singular simplex in Y. So, f induces a linear map between the spaces of chains on X and Y that preserves cycles and boundaries. As a consequence, f also induces a homomorphism $f_\star : H_k(X) \to H_k(Y)$. Moreover if f is an homeomorphism, $f_\star$ is an isomorphism and $(f_\star)^{-1} = (f^{-1})_\star$. Similarly, if f is an homotopy equivalence with homotopic inverse $g : Y \to X$, then $f_\star$ is an isomorphism with inverse $g_\star$. As a consequence, two spaces that are homotopy equivalent have the same Betti numbers. Notice that, when X is not homotopy equivalent to a finite simplicial complex, its Betti numbers might not be finite.

11.4 Betti Numbers Inference

Singular homology allows to consider Betti numbers of compact sets in $\mathbb{R}^d$ and of their offsets. Using its connexion to simplicial homology and the distance functions framework of Chapter 9, we derive explicit methods to infer the Betti numbers of compact subsets with positive weak feature size.

Let $K \subset \mathbb{R}^d$ be a compact set with $\mathrm{wfs}(K) > 0$ and let $P \in \mathbb{R}^d$ be a finite set of points such that $d_H(K, P) < \varepsilon$ for some given $\varepsilon > 0$. Recall that, from the isotopy Lemma 9.5, all the *r*-offsets K^r of K, for $0 < r < \text{wfs}(K)$, are homeomorphic and thus have isomorphic homology groups. The goal of this section is to provide an effective method to compute the Betti numbers $\beta_k(K^r)$, $0 < r < \text{wfs}(K)$, from P.

Theorem 11.9 *Let $K \subset \mathbb{R}^d$ be a compact set with $\text{wfs}(K) > 0$ and let $P \in \mathbb{R}^d$ be a finite set of points such that $d_H(K,P) < \varepsilon$ for some given $\varepsilon > 0$. Assume that $\text{wfs}(K) > 4\varepsilon$. For $\alpha > 0$ such that $4\varepsilon + \alpha < \text{wfs}(K)$, let $i : P^{\alpha+\varepsilon} \hookrightarrow P^{\alpha+3\varepsilon}$ be the canonical inclusion. Then for any non-negative integer k and any $0 < r < \text{wfs}(K)$,*

$$H_k(K^r) \cong \text{im}\left(i_* : H_k(P^{\alpha+\varepsilon}) \to H_k(P^{\alpha+3\varepsilon})\right)$$

where im *denotes the image of the homomorphism and $\cong$ means that the two groups are isomorphic.*

Proof Because $d_H(K,P) < \varepsilon$, we have the following sequence of inclusion maps

$$K^\alpha \subseteq P^{\alpha+\varepsilon} \subseteq K^{\alpha+2\varepsilon} \subseteq P^{\alpha+3\varepsilon} \subseteq K^{\alpha+4\varepsilon}$$

that induces the following sequence of homomorphisms (the one induced by the canonical inclusion maps) at the homology level

$$H_k(K^\alpha) \to H_k(P^{\alpha+\varepsilon}) \to H_k(K^{\alpha+2\varepsilon}) \to H_k(P^{\alpha+3\varepsilon}) \to H_k(K^{\alpha+4\varepsilon}).$$

Because $\text{wfs}(K) > \alpha + 4\varepsilon$, it follows from the isotopy Lemma 9.5 that the homomorphisms $H_k(K^\alpha) \to H_k(K^{\alpha+2\varepsilon})$ and $H_k(K^{\alpha+2\varepsilon}) \to H_k(K^{\alpha+4\varepsilon})$ induced by the inclusion maps are indeed isomorphisms. Notice that the aforementioned sequence implies that the rank of these isomorphisms is finite (see Exercise 11.5). It immediately follows that the rank of $H_k(P^{\alpha+\varepsilon}) \to H_k(P^{\alpha+3\varepsilon})$ is equal to the rank of these isomorphisms, which is equal to $\beta_k(K^\alpha)$.   □

Theorem 11.9 shows that the Betti numbers of the offsets of K can be deduced from the offsets of P. However, the direct computation of the homology groups of a union of balls, which is a continuous object and not a finite simplicial complex, is not obvious. To overcome this issue, recall that the Nerve Theorem 2.8 implies that for any $r \geq 0$, P^r is homotopy equivalent to Čech(P, r). As a consequence $H_k(P^r)$ and $H_k(\text{Čech}(P, r))$ are isomorphic. Moreover, one can show that the isomorphisms can be chosen to commute with the ones induced by inclusions maps [50], making the following diagram commutative

$$
\begin{array}{ccc}
H_k(P^r) & \to & H_k(P^{r'}) \\
\uparrow & & \uparrow \\
H_k(\check{C}ech(P,r)) & \to & H_k(\check{C}ech(P,r'))
\end{array}
\qquad (11.1)
$$

We immediately obtain the following result.

Proposition 11.10 *Assume that* $\mathrm{wfs}(K) > 4\varepsilon$. *For* $\alpha > 0$ *such that* $4\varepsilon + \alpha <$ $\mathrm{wfs}(K)$, *let* $i : \check{C}ech(P, \alpha + \varepsilon) \hookrightarrow \check{C}ech(P, \alpha + 3\varepsilon)$ *be the canonical inclusion. Then for any non-negative integer* k *and any* $0 < r < \mathrm{wfs}(K)$,

$$
H_k(K^r) \cong im(i_\star : H_k(\check{C}ech(P, \alpha + \varepsilon)) \to H_k(\check{C}ech(P, \alpha + 3\varepsilon))).
$$

Thanks to the previous proposition, inferring the Betti numbers of K^r now boils down to homology computation on finite Čech complexes. However, as already noticed in Section 2.5, computing Čech complexes require to determine if finite sets of balls intersect, which quickly becomes prohibitive as d and the cardinality of P increase. Using the interleaving property between Čech and Vietoris-Rips filtrations established in Lemma 2.13, we obtain the following theorem.

Theorem 11.11 *Assume that* $\mathrm{wfs}(K) > 9\varepsilon$. *For any* $2\varepsilon \le \alpha \le \frac{1}{4}(\mathrm{wfs}(K) - \varepsilon)$ *and any* $0 < r < \mathrm{wfs}(K)$ *we have*

$$
\beta_k(K^r) = \mathrm{rk}(H_k(\mathrm{Rips}(P, \alpha) \to H_k(\mathrm{Rips}(P, 4\alpha))
$$

where $\mathrm{rk}(H_k(\mathrm{Rips}(P, \alpha) \to H_k(\mathrm{Rips}(P, 4\alpha))$ *denotes the rank of the homomorphism induced by the inclusion* $\mathrm{Rips}(P, \alpha) \subseteq \mathrm{Rips}(P, 4\alpha)$.

This last result raises two questions. The first one is about how to compute the rank of the homomorphisms induced by the inclusion maps between the homology groups of the subcomplexes of the *Vietoris − Rips* complex. This question will be answered in next Section when the persistence algorithm will be presented. The second, and more tricky, question is about the effective choice of α when K and $\mathrm{wfs}(K)$ are not known. This is an ill-posed problem because $\mathrm{wfs}(K)$ does not depend continuously of K; see Section 9.3. However, it is possible for the user to try to guess a good choice of α using the following algorithm.

When applied to a point cloud sampled around a compact subset of $\mathbb{R}^d$ with positive weak feature size, the algorithm provides the diagrams of rank numbers $\beta_{k,4\alpha}^{16\alpha}$ that are constant on some intervals of values α as illustrated in Figure 11.5. Identifying these intervals allows the user to determine the scales at which the topological features of K^r can be infered. Notice that intervals on which the persistent Betti numbers are constant can appear at different scales, reflecting multiscale topological features of the offsets of K; see Figure 11.6.

Algorithm 10: Betti numbers inference

Input: $P \subset \mathbb{R}^d$ a finite set.

Let $L := \emptyset$, $\alpha := +\infty$;

while $L \subsetneq P$ **do**

  Let $p := \mathrm{argmax}_{w \in P} \min_{v \in L} \|w - v\|$; // *pick arbitrary p if* $L = \emptyset$

  $L \leftarrow L \cup \{p\}$;

  $\alpha \leftarrow \max_{w \in P} \min_{v \in L} \|w - v\|$;

  Update $\mathrm{Rips}(L, 4\alpha)$ and $\mathrm{Rips}(L, 16\alpha)$;

  Compute $\beta_{k,4\alpha}^{16\alpha} = \mathrm{rk}(i_\star : H_k(\mathrm{Rips}(L, 4\alpha)) \to H_k(\mathrm{Rips}(L, 16\alpha)))$;

Output: diagram showing the evolution of persistent Betti numbers, i.e. the ranks of $i_\star$ versus α.

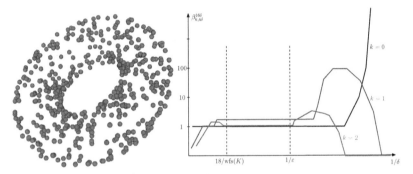

Figure 11.5 An example of persistent Betti numbers curves obtained from a point cloud sampled on a torus. They are plotted as functions of $1/\alpha$. These numbers are constant on an interval containing $[18/\mathrm{wfs}(K), 1/\varepsilon]$ and correspond to the three first Betti numbers of the torus: $\beta_0 = 1$, $\beta_1 = 2$ and $\beta_2 = 1$.

The previous algorithm comes with the following theoretical guarantees justifying the existence of intervals of constant persistent Betti numbers [50].

Theorem 11.12 *Let* $K \subset \mathbb{R}^d$ *be a compact set with* $\mathrm{wfs}(K) > 0$ *and let* $P \in \mathbb{R}^d$ *be a finite set of points such that* $d_H(K, P) < \varepsilon$ *for some given* $\varepsilon > 0$. *Assume that* $\mathrm{wfs}(K) > 18\varepsilon$. *Then at each iteration of the algorithm such that* $\varepsilon < \alpha < \frac{1}{18}\mathrm{wfs}(K)$,

$$\beta_k(K^r) = \beta_{k,4\alpha}^{16\alpha}$$

for any $r \in (0, \mathrm{wfs}(K))$ *and any non-negative integer* k.

The example of Figure 11.6 where P is sampled around a smooth two-dimensional torus in $\mathbb{R}^{1000}$ illustrates this property: it would not have been possible to do the computation if the complexity was exponential in $d = 1000$.

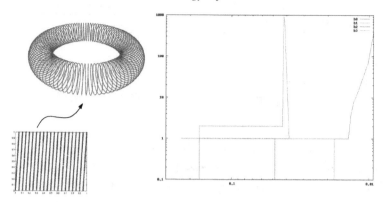

Figure 11.6 The persistent Betti numbers curves obtained from a point cloud sampled on a closed curve spiraling on a torus which was itself non linearly embedded into $\mathbb{R}^{1000}$. They are plotted as functions of $1/\delta$. We distinguish two intervals on which the computed ranks are constant. The right-most one (corresponding to the smaller range of δ) exhibits the Betti numbers of a circle $(1, 1, 0)$, while left most one (intuitively corresponding to a larger scale) exhibits the Betti numbers of the torus $(1, 2, 0)$.

11.5 Persistent Homology

The algorithm of Section 11.2 to compute the Betti numbers of a filtered simplicial complex also provides the Betti numbers of all the subcomplexes of the filtration. Intuitively, the goal of persistent homology is to keep track of all this information and to pair the creation and destruction time of homology classes appearing during the process.

11.5.1 A Simple Example

Before formally indroducing persistent homology, we first consider a very simple example. Let $f : [0, 1] \to \mathbb{R}$ be the function whose graph is represented in Figure 11.7. We are interested in studying the evolution of the topology of the sublevel sets $f^{-1}((-\infty, t])$ as t increases. The topology of the sublevel sets changes when t crosses the critical values a, b, c, d, and e. Passing through the critical value a creates a connected component and for $a \leq t < b$, $f^{-1}((-\infty, t])$ is a connected set (an interval). When t passes through the critical value b a second connected component appears and for $b \leq t < c$, $f^{-1}((-\infty, t])$ has two connected components. When t reaches the value c, the two connected components are merged: the most recently created component, when t passed through b, is merged into the older one. One then pairs the two values b and c corresponding to the "birth" and "death" of the component.

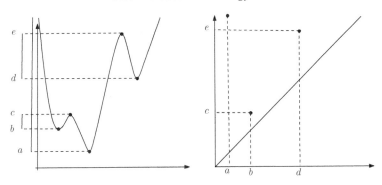

Figure 11.7 The persistence diagram of a real valued function.

In the persistent homology framework, this pairing is either represented by the interval on the left of the graph of f in Figure 11.7 or by the point with coordinates (b, c) in the plane on the right of Figure 11.7. The length $c-b$ of the interval (b, c) represents the lifespan of the component created at b. Intuitively, the larger the interval is, the more relevant the corresponding component is. Now, continuing to increase t, a new connected component is created when one reaches d, which is merged at $t = e$ giving rise to a new persistence interval (d, e). Notice that a is not paired to any (finite) value since the first created component is never merged into another one. As a consequence it is paired with $+\infty$ and represented by the interval $(a, +\infty)$. At the end, the pairs are either represented as a set of intervals (called a *barcode*) or as a diagram in the plane (called the *persistence diagram*; see Figure 11.7 on the right). For technical reasons that will become clear later in this chapter the diagonal $\{y = x\}$ is added to the diagram.

When one considers functions f defined over higher dimensional spaces, passing through critical values may not only change the connectedness of the sublevel sets but also other topological features: creation/destruction of cycles, voids, etc. All these events corresponds to a change in the corresponding homology groups (H_0 for connected components, H_1 for cycles, H_2 for voids,...). In the sequel of this section we show that we can define pairs and persistence diagrams for each dimension.

Now, if we replace the function f by a function g on the Figure 11.8 which is close to f, we observe that the number of pairs of g is much larger than the one of f. However most of these pairs correspond to intervals with short length (points close to the diagonal) while the pairs corresponding to long interval are close to the ones of f. In other words, the topological features having a large persistence with respect to the size of the perturbation are preserved while

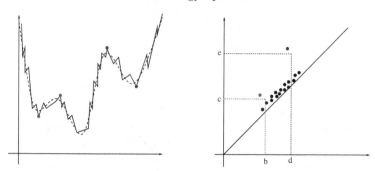

Figure 11.8 An approximation g of f and its persistence diagram.

the topological features created by the perturbation have a small persistence. We will see that this is a general phenomenon: two close functions have close persistence diagrams. The stability properties of persistence diagrams are of fundamental importance to formalize and quantify the notion of topological noise and to handle noisy data.

11.5.2 Persistent Homology of a Filtration

We first define the notion of persistence for a filtration of a simplicial complex. Its goal is to study the evolution of the homology of the subcomplexes of the filtration.

Let K be a d-dimensional simplicial complex and let

$$\emptyset = K^0 \subset K^1 \subset \cdots \subset K^m = K$$

be a filtration of K such that, for any $i = 0, \cdots, m - 1$, $K^{i+1} = K^i \cup \sigma^{i+1}$ where σ^{i+1} is a simplex.

For any $0 \le n \le m$, we denote by C_k^n the set of k-chains (with coefficients in $\mathbb{Z}/2\mathbb{Z}$) of K^n. Notice that the restriction of the boundary operator to C_k^n has its image contained in C_{k-1}^{n-1}. We denote by Z_k^n and B_k^n the sets of k-cycles and k-boundaries of K^n, respectively. The kth homology group of K^n is thus

$$H_k^n = Z_k^n / B_k^n$$

With these notations, we have the following inclusions

$$Z_k^0 \subset Z_k^1 \subset \cdots \subset Z_k^n \cdots \subset Z_k^m = Z_k(K)$$

$$B_k^0 \subset B_k^1 \subset \cdots \subset B_k^n \cdots \subset B_k^m = B_k(K)$$

Definition 11.13 (Persistent Betti numbers) For $p \in \{0, \cdots, m\}$ et $l \in \{0, \cdots, m - p\}$, the kth persistent Betti number of K^l is the dimension of the vector space $H_k^{l,p} = Z_k^l / \left(B_k^{l+p} \cap Z_k^l \right)$.

The kth persistent Betti number of K^l represents the number of independent homology classes of k-cycles in K^l that are not boundaries in K^{l+p}. Intuitively, a k-cycle in K^l generating a nonzero element in $H_k^{l,p}$ is a cycle that has appeared in the filtration before the step $l + 1$ and that is still not a boundary at step $l + p$. We have seen in Section 11.2 that a homology class is created when a positive simplex is added in the filtration and that a homology class is destroyed when a negative simplex is added. Persistent homology provides a natural way to pair positive and negative simplices such that whenever a positive simplex is added to the filtration it creates a homology class and a corresponding cycle that becomes a boundary when the negative simplex to which it is paired is added.

Cycle Associated to a Positive Simplex

Lemma 11.14 *Let $\sigma = \sigma^i$ be a positive k-simplex in the filtration of K. There exists a unique k-cycle c that is not a boundary in K^i, that contains σ and that does not contain any other positive k-simplex.*

Proof The lemma is proven by induction on the order of the positive k-simplices in the filtration. Assume that for any positive k-simplex added to the filtration before σ there exists a k-cycle, that is not a boundary and that contains σ but no other positive k-simplex. Because σ is positive, there exists a k-cycle d that is not a boundary in K^i and that contains σ. Let $\sigma_{i_j}, j = 1, \cdots, p$ be the positive k-simplices different from σ contained in d and let c_j be the cycles that are not boundaries containing them and not containing any other positive simplices. Then

$$c = d + c_1 + \cdots + c_p$$

is a k-cycle in which σ is the only positive simplex. Because $\sigma = \sigma^i$ is the last simplex added in K^i there does not exist any $(k + 1)$-simplex in K^i containing σ in its boundary. As a consequence, c cannot be a boundary cycle.

The uniqueness of c is proven in a similar way. $\qquad\qquad\square$

Persistent Homology Basis and Persistent Pairs

The k-cycles associated to the positive k-simplices in Lemma 11.14 allow to maintain a basis of the k-dimensional homology groups of the subcomplexes of the filtration. At the beginning, the basis of $H_k(K^0)$ is empty. Bases of the $H_k(K^i)$ are built inductively in the following way. Assume that the basis of

H_k^{i-1} has been built and that the ith simplex σ^i is positive and of dimension k. We add to the basis of H_k^{i-1} the homology class of the cycle c^i associated to σ^i to obtain a basis of H_k^i. Indeed, because c^i is the sum of σ^i and negative simplices, it is not homologous to any linear combination of cycles defining the basis of H_k^{i-1}. Because $\dim H_k^i = \dim H_k^{i-1} + 1$ we thus obtain a basis of H_k^i.

Now assume that the basis of H_k^{j-1} is built and the jth simplex σ^j is negative and of dimension $k+1$. Let $c^{i_1}, \cdots, c^{i_p}$ be the cycles associated to the positive simplices $\sigma^{i_1}, \cdots \sigma^{i_p}$ whose homology classes form a basis of H_k^{j-1}. The boundary $d = \partial \sigma^j$ of σ^j is a k-cycle in K^{j-1}, which is not a boundary in K^{j-1} but is a boundary in K^j (see the proof of the algorithm to compute Betti numbers in the previous section). So it can be written in a unique way as

$$d = \partial \sigma^j = \sum_{k=1}^{p} \varepsilon_k c^{i_k} + b$$

where $\varepsilon_k \in \{0, 1\}$ and b is a boundary. We then denote $l(j) = \max\{i_k : \varepsilon_k = 1\}$ and we remove the homology class of $c^{l(j)}$ from the basis of H_k^{j-1}.

Claim: We obtain a basis of H_k^j.

Because $\dim H_k^{j-1} = \dim H_k^j + 1$ we just need to prove that $c^{l(j)}$ is, up to a boundary, a linear combination of the cycles c^{i_k} in Z_k^j, $i_k \neq l(j)$, which is equivalent to the aforementioned decomposition of d.

Definition 11.15 (Persistent pairs) The pairs of simplices $(\sigma^{l(j)}, \sigma^j)$ are called the persistence pairs of the filtration of K.

Intuitively, the homology class created by $\sigma^{l(j)}$ in $K^{l(j)}$ is destroyed by σ^j in K^j. The persistence of this pair is $j - l(j) - 1$. From the aforementioned discussion, we deduce a first algorithm to compute the persistent pairs of a filtration of a simplicial complex K of dimension d with m simplices.

Algorithm 11: Persistent pairs computation

Input: A filtration of a d-dimensional simplicial complex K containing m simplices.
$L_0 = L_1 = \cdots = L_{d-1} = \emptyset$
for $j = 0$ to m **do**
  $k = \dim \sigma^j - 1$
  if σ^j is negative **then**
    $l(j) =$ the largest index of the positive k-simplices associated to $\partial \sigma^j$;

    $L_k \leftarrow L_k \cup \{(\sigma^{l(j)}, \sigma^j)\}$;
Output: Return the persistent pairs in each dimension $L_0, L_1, \cdots, L_{d-1}$;

Notice that, as for the algorithm to compute the Betti numbers, the main issue with this algorithm is to determine $l(j)$. We overcome it by considering a matrix version of the aforementioned algorithm.

Persistence Algorithm: The Matrix Version

We now present an easy to implement version of the persistence algorithm. It relies on a simple reduction of the matrix of the boundary operator.

Let K be a simplicial complex of dimension d and

$$\emptyset = K^0 \subset K^1 \subset \cdots \subset K^m = K$$

be a filtration of K such that for any $i = 0, \cdots, m-1$,

$$K^{i+1} = K^i \cup \sigma^{i+1} \text{ where } \sigma^{i+1} \text{ is a simplex.}$$

Let $M = (m_{i,j})_{i,j=1,\cdots m}$ be the matrix with coefficients in $\mathbb{Z}/2\mathbb{Z}$ of the boundary operator defined by:

$$m_{i,j} = 1 \text{ if } \sigma^i \text{ is a face of } \sigma^j \quad \text{and} \quad m_{i,j} = 0 \text{ otherwise.}$$

Hence, if σ^j is a $(k+1)$-simplex the jth column of M represents the set of the k-dimensional faces of the boundary of σ^j. Since the simplices of K are ordered according to the filtration, the matrix M is upper triangular. For any column C_j of M, we denote by $l(j)$ the index of the lowest line of M containing a nonzero term in the column C_j:

$$(i = l(j)) \Leftrightarrow (m_{i,j} = 1 \text{ and } m_{i',j} = 0 \; \forall i' > i)$$

Notice that $l(j)$ is not defined when the column C_j does not contain any non zero term. We then have the following very simple algorithm to compute the persistent pairs.

Algorithm 12: Persistent computation—Matrix version

Input: A filtration of a d-dimensional simplicial complex K containing m simplices and the matrix M of the boundary operator.
for $j = 0$ to m **do**
    while there exists $j' < j$ such that $l(j') == l(j)$ **do**
        $C_j = C_j + C_{j'} \; mod(2)$;
Output: Return the pairs $(l(j), j)$;

Proposition 11.16 *The previous algorithm computes the persistent pairs of the filtration* $\emptyset = K^0 \subset K^1 \subset \cdots \subset K^m = K$.

Proof   The result immediately follows from a sequence of elementary facts.

Fact 1: At each step of the algorithm, the column C_j represents a chain of the following form

$$\partial\left(\sigma^j + \sum_{i<j} \varepsilon_i \sigma^i\right) \quad \text{with} \quad \varepsilon_i \in \{0, 1\}.$$

This is proven by an immediate induction.

Fact 2: At the end of the algorithm, if j is such that $l(j)$ is defined, then $\sigma^{l(j)}$ is a positive simplex.

Indeed, the column C_j represents a chain of the form

$$\sigma^{l(j)} + \sum_{p<l(j)} \eta_p \sigma^p \quad \text{with} \quad \eta_p \in \{0, 1\},$$

but according to Fact 1, C_j also represents a boundary in K^j. So the previous chain is a cycle (since $\partial \circ \partial = 0$) in $K^{l(j)}$ containing $\sigma^{l(j)}$. The simplex $\sigma^{l(j)}$ is thus positive.

Fact 3: If at the end of the algorithm the column C_j only contains zero terms, then σ^j is positive.

Indeed, according to Fact 1, we have

$$\partial\left(\sigma^j + \sum_{i<j} \varepsilon_i \sigma^i\right) = 0,$$

so σ^j is contained in a cycle of K^j.

Fact 4: If at the end of the algorithm, the column C_j contains non zero terms, then $(\sigma^{l(j)}, \sigma^j)$ is a persistence pair.

Combining Facts 1 and 2, the boundary of σ^j can be written as

$$\partial\sigma^j = \sigma^{l(j)} + \sum_{p<l(j)} \eta_p \sigma^p + \partial\left(\sum_{i<j} \varepsilon_i \sigma^i\right)$$

Moreover $\sigma^{l(j)}$ is positive and thus was added to the persistent homology basis at time $l(j)$ and has not been paired before time j. Remarking that at the end of the algorithm a line of the matrix cannot contain more than one lowest nonzero term of a column, we deduce that $(\sigma^{l(j)}, \sigma^j)$ is a persistence pair. $\qquad\square$

Remark 11.17 Notice that the time complexity of the above algorithm is $O(m^3)$ in the worst case. However in practical applications it usually happens to be much faster ($O(m)$ or $O(m \log m)$).

11.5.3 Persistence Diagrams and Bottleneck Distance

For a fixed k, the persistent pairs of simplices of respective dimensions k and $k + 1$ are conveniently represented as a diagram in the plane $\mathbb{R}^2$: each pair $(\sigma^{l(j)}, \sigma^j)$ is represented by the point of coordinates $(l(j), j)$. For each positive simplex σ^i which is not paired to any negative simplex in the filtration, we associate the pair $(\sigma^i, +\infty)$. For technical reasons that will become clear in the next section, we add to this finite set the diagonal $\{y = x\}$ of $\mathbb{R}^2$ to get the *k-dimensional persistence diagram* of the filtration. More generally, if the filtration is indexed by a non decreasing sequence of real numbers, as, e.g., in the case of a filtration associated to the sublevel sets of a function,

$$\emptyset = K^{\alpha_0} \subset K^{\alpha_1} \subset \cdots \subset K^{\alpha_m} = K \text{ with } \alpha_0 \leq \alpha_1 \cdots \leq \alpha_m$$

a persistent pair of simplices (σ_i, σ_j) is represented in the diagram as the point of coordinates (α_i, α_j). In this later case, we have to take care that, since the sequence (α_i) is non decreasing, several pairs can be associated to the same point in the plane. A persistence diagram is thus a multiset and the *multiplicity* of a point is defined as the number of pairs associated to this point. By convention, the points on the diagonal have infinite multiplicity. By convention, if a simplex σ_i is not paired, we then add the point of coordinates $(\alpha_i, +\infty)$ to the persistence diagram. Notice that, as a consequence, the persistence diagram is a multiset in $\overline{\mathbb{R}}^2$ where $\overline{\mathbb{R}} = \mathbb{R} \cup +\infty$.

Persistence diagrams can be compared using a matching distance called the *bottleneck distance*.

Definition 11.18 (Bottleneck distance) Let D_1 and D_2 be two persistence diagrams The bottleneck distance between D_1 and D_2 is defined as

$$d_B(D_1, D_2) = \inf_{\gamma} \sup_{p \in D_1} \|p - \gamma(p)\|_\infty$$

where γ is the set of bijections between the multisets D_1 and D_2 (a point with multiplicity $m > 1$ is considered as m disjoint copies) and $\|p - q\|_\infty = \max (|x_p - x_q|, |y_p - y_q|)$. By convention, if $y_p = y_q = +\infty$, then $\|p - q\|_\infty = |x_p - x_q|$.

The above definition motivates the inclusion of the diagonal of $\mathbb{R}^2$ in the definition of persistence diagram: it allows to compare diagrams that do not

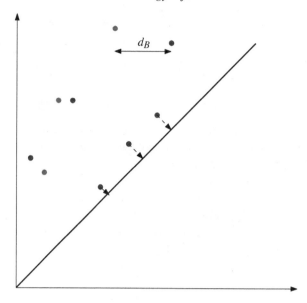

Figure 11.9 The bottleneck distance between two diagrams

have the same numbers of off-diagonal points by matching them with points on the diagonal (see Figure 11.9).

11.5.4 Persistence Modules, Interleaving, and Stability

Persistence can be defined in a purely algebraic way that turns out to be particularly useful and powerful in many settings. The proofs of the results presented in this section are beyond the scope of this book but the algebraic framework introduced in this section allows to efficiently prove the results of the next sections.

The notion of persistence can be extended to more general sequences of vector spaces in the following way.

Definition 11.19 (Persistence modules) A persistence module $\mathbb{V}$ over a subset I of the real numbers $\mathbb{R}$ is an indexed family of vector spaces ($V_a \mid a \in I$) and a doubly-indexed family of linear maps ($v_a^b : V_a \to V_b \mid a \leq b$) which satisfy the composition law $v_b^c \circ v_a^b = v_a^c$ whenever $a \leq b \leq c$, and where v_a^a is the identity map on V_a.

Definition 11.20 (q-tameness) The persistence module $\mathbb{V}$ is said to be q-tame if $rk(v_a^b) < +\infty$ whenever $a < b$.

The sequence of homology groups of the filtration of K considered in the previous section together with the homomorphisms induced by the inclusion maps is a persistence module indexed over the set $I = \{0, 1, \cdots, m\}$. It can be shown that the persistence diagram of a filtration $\{\emptyset = K^{\alpha_0} \subset K^{\alpha_1} \subset \cdots \subset K^{\alpha_m} = K\}$ is completely determined by the rank of the homomorphisms $H_k(K^{\alpha_i}) \to H_k(K^{\alpha_j})$ for any $i < j$. This property extends to q-tame modules.

Theorem 11.21 *If a persistence module $\mathbb{V}$ is q-tame, then it has a well-defined persistence diagram $\mathsf{dgm}(\mathbb{V}) \subset \overline{\mathbb{R}}^2$. When $\mathbb{V}$ is the persistence module defined by a filtration of a finite simplicial complex, this diagram coincides with the one defined in Section 11.5.3.*

To avoid technical difficulties in the sequel of this section, we assume that all the considered persistence modules are indexed by $\mathbb{R}$. This is not a restrictive assumption in our setting: if $\mathbb{V}$ is a persistence module indexed by a finite set $\alpha_1 < \alpha_2 < \cdots < \alpha_m$ it can be extended to a piecewise constant module indexed by $\mathbb{R}$ by defining $V_\alpha = V_{\alpha_j}$ for $\alpha \in [\alpha_j, \alpha_{j+1})$ with the convention $\alpha_0 = -\infty$ and $\alpha_{m+1} = +\infty$. The linear maps are then defined in an obvious way by letting $v_a^b = Id$ whenever $\alpha_j \le a \le b < \alpha_{j+1}$.

Let $\mathbb{U}, \mathbb{V}$ be persistence modules over $\mathbb{R}$, and let ε be any real number. A *homomorphism of degree ε* is a collection Φ of linear maps

$$(\phi_a : U_a \to V_{a+\varepsilon} \mid a \in \mathbb{R})$$

such that $v_{a+\varepsilon}^{b+\varepsilon} \circ \phi_a = \phi_b \circ u_a^b$ for all $a \le b$. We write

$$\mathrm{Hom}^\varepsilon(\mathbb{U}, \mathbb{V}) = \{\text{homomorphisms } \mathbb{U} \to \mathbb{V} \text{ of degree } \varepsilon\},$$

$$\mathrm{End}^\varepsilon(\mathbb{V}) = \{\text{homomorphisms } \mathbb{V} \to \mathbb{V} \text{ of degree } \varepsilon\}.$$

Composition is defined in the obvious way. For $\varepsilon \ge 0$, the most important degree-ε endomorphism is the shift map

$$1_\mathbb{V}^\varepsilon \in \mathrm{End}^\varepsilon(\mathbb{V}),$$

which is the collection of maps $(v_a^{a+\varepsilon})$ from the persistence structure on $\mathbb{V}$.

If Φ is a homomorphism $\mathbb{U} \to \mathbb{V}$ of any degree, then by definition $\Phi 1_\mathbb{U}^\varepsilon = 1_\mathbb{V}^\varepsilon \Phi$ for all $\varepsilon \ge 0$.

Definition 11.22 (Interleaving of persistence modules) Two persistence modules $\mathbb{U}, \mathbb{V}$ are said to be ε-interleaved if there are maps

$$\Phi \in \mathrm{Hom}^\varepsilon(\mathbb{U}, \mathbb{V}), \qquad \Psi \in \mathrm{Hom}^\varepsilon(\mathbb{V}, \mathbb{U})$$

such that $\Psi\Phi = 1_\mathbb{U}^{2\varepsilon}$ and $\Phi\Psi = 1_\mathbb{V}^{2\varepsilon}$.

The notion of interleaving allows to state the fundamental stability theorem for persistence diagrams.

Theorem 11.23 (Stability of persistence diagrams)   *Let* $\mathbb{U}, \mathbb{V}$ *be two q-tame persistent modules that are ε-interleaved for some $\varepsilon \geq 0$. Denoting by* $\mathsf{dgm}(\mathbb{U})$ *and* $\mathsf{dgm}(\mathbb{V})$ *their persistence diagrams, we have*

$$d_B(\mathsf{dgm}(\mathbb{U}), \mathsf{dgm}(\mathbb{V})) \leq \varepsilon.$$

In the next sections, we apply the stability to different settings.

11.5.5 Persistence Stability for Functions

Let $f : X \to \mathbb{R}$ be a real-valued function defined on a topological space X. Let consider the *sublevel set filtration* $\{F_\alpha = f^{-1}((-\infty, \alpha])\}_{\alpha \in \mathbb{R}}$ and consider the (singular) homology groups $H_k(F_\alpha)$ of these sublevel sets. Notice that the canonical inclusion $F_\alpha \subseteq F_\beta$ whenever $\alpha \leq \beta$ induces an homeomorphism $H_k(F_\alpha) \to H_k(F_\beta)$. So, the sublevel sets filtration of f induces a persistence module $\mathbb{F}_k$.

Definition 11.24   A real-valued function f defined on a topological space X is said to be q-tame if its associated persistence modules $\mathbb{F}_k$ are q-tame for any non-negative integer k.

The following result provides sufficient conditions for f and g to be q-tame.

Proposition 11.25   *If X is homeomorphic to a finite simplicial complex and $f : X \to \mathbb{R}$ is continuous, then f is q-tame. In particular,* $\mathsf{dgm}(\mathbb{F}_k)$ *is well-defined.*

Proposition 11.26   *Let $f, g : X \to \mathbb{R}$ be two functions defined on a topological space X such that $\|f - g\|_\infty = \sup_{x \in X} |f(x) - g(x)| < \varepsilon$. Then the persistence modules $\mathbb{F}_k$ and $\mathbb{G}_k$ induced by the sublevel sets filtrations of f and g are ε-interleaved.*

Proof   Since $\|f - g\|_\infty < \varepsilon$, we have, for any $\alpha \in \mathbb{R}$, $F_\alpha \subseteq G_{\alpha+\varepsilon} \subseteq F_{\alpha+2\varepsilon} \subseteq G_{\alpha+3\varepsilon} \subseteq \cdots$ These inclusions induce homomorphisms $H_k(F_\alpha) \to H_k(G_{\alpha+\varepsilon})$ and $H_k(G_\alpha) \to H_k(F_{\alpha+\varepsilon})$ for all $\alpha \in \mathbb{R}$. The sets of these homomorphisms define an ε-interleaving between $\mathbb{F}_k$ and $\mathbb{G}_k$. $\square$

In the sequel, when there is no ambiguity, the notation $\mathsf{dgm}(f)$ denotes the persistence diagram of $\mathbb{F}_k$, for any k. Applying the Persistence Stability Theorem 11.23, we immediately obtain the following stability result for functions.

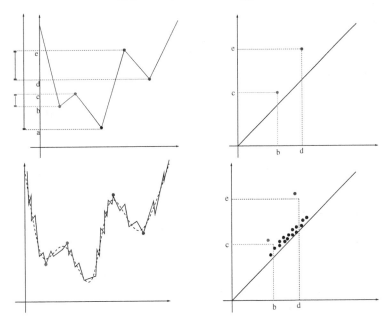

Figure 11.10 Comparing the persistence diagrams of two close functions defined on a segment

Theorem 11.27 *Let X be a topological space and let $f, g : X \to \mathbb{R}$ be two q-tame functions. Then*

$$d_B(\mathsf{dgm}(\mathbb{F}_k), \mathsf{dgm}(\mathbb{G}_k)) \le \|f - g\|_\infty.$$

From a practical point of view, the above theorem provides a rigorous way to approximate the persistence diagrams of continuous functions defined on a triangulated space. For example, assume that X is a triangulated manifold in $\mathbb{R}^d$ where the diameter of each simplex is upper bounded by some $\delta > 0$ and assume $f : X \to \mathbb{R}$ to be c-Lipschitz for some $c > 0$, i.e. $|f(x) - f(x')| \le c\|x - x'\|$. Then, given a non-negative integer k, one can easily check that the bottleneck distance between the persistence diagram of f and the persistence diagram of the filtered complex induced by the values of f at the vertices of the triangulation is upper bounded by $c\delta$ (see Exercise 11.8).

11.5.6 Persistence Stability for Compact Sets and Complexes Built on Top of Point Clouds

Proposition 11.28 *Let $X \subset \mathbb{R}^d$ be a compact set. The distance function $d_X : \mathbb{R}^d \to \mathbb{R}$ is q-tame.*

Proof   Given $0 \le \alpha < \beta$ and a non-negative integer k, we just need to prove that the homomorphism $H_k(X^\alpha) \to H_k(X^\beta)$ induced by the inclusion of the offsets, $X^\alpha \subset X^\beta$, has finite rank. Denoting $\varepsilon = (\beta - \alpha)/2 > 0$, because X is compact, there exists a finite subset $P \subseteq X$ of X such that $d_H(X, P) < \varepsilon$. As a consequence, we have the following inclusion

$$X^\alpha \subseteq P^{\alpha+\varepsilon} \subseteq X^\beta$$

that induces the following sequence of homomorphisms

$$H_k(X^\alpha) \to H_k(P^{\alpha+\varepsilon}) \to H_k(X^\beta).$$

Now, it follows from the nerve Lemma that $P^{\alpha+\varepsilon}$ is a finite union of balls homotopy equivalent to $\check{C}ech(P, \alpha + \varepsilon)$, which is a finite simplicial complex. As a consequence $\dim H_k(P^{\alpha+\varepsilon}) < +\infty$ and $rk(H_k(X^\alpha) \to H_k(X^\beta)) \le \dim H_k(P^{\alpha+\varepsilon}) < +\infty$. $\square$

The aforementioned proposition implies that distance functions to compact subsets of $\mathbb{R}^d$ have well-defined persistence diagrams. Recalling that if $X, Y \subset \mathbb{R}^d$ are compact, then $d_H(X, Y) = \|d_X - d_Y\|_\infty$, we immediately obtain the following corollary.

Corollary 11.29   *Let $X, Y \subset \mathbb{R}^d$ be compact. Then*

$$d_B(\mathrm{dgm}(d_X), \mathrm{dgm}(d_Y)) \le d_H(X, Y).$$

In particular, if $P, Q \subset \mathbb{R}^d$ are finite point clouds, then for any non-negative integer k,

$$d_B(\mathrm{dgm}(H_k(\check{C}ech(P))), \mathrm{dgm}(H_k(\check{C}ech(Q)))) \le d_H(P, Q)$$

where $\check{C}ech(.)$ denotes the $\check{C}ech$ filtration.

The second part of the corollary follows from the nerve Lemma 2.8 and the paragraph before Proposition 11.10 showing that P^α and $\check{C}ech(P, \alpha)$ are homotopy equivalent for any α and the homotopy equivalences can be chosen to commute with the inclusion maps at the homology level. As a consequence the persistence modules induced by the sublevel sets of d_P and the $\check{C}ech$ filtration are 0-interleaved. Using that P^α is also homotopy equivalent to the alpha-complex $\mathcal{A}(P, \alpha)$ the same result also holds when $\check{C}ech(P)$ is replaced by the alpha-complex filtration $\mathcal{A}(P)$.

Application: Topological Signatures for Shapes.   The same kind of result can be also established for the Vietoris-Rips complex and, thanks to these stability properties, the obtained persistence diagrams can be considered as robust multiscale topological signatures associated to point clouds. They can thus be used to compare the topological structure of points clouds sampled from different shapes. Notice that if the finite point cloud P is transformed by an isometry of $\mathbb{R}^d$ into another point cloud P', then the Čech, the Vietoris-Rips and alpha-shape filtrations of P and P' are the same. However, $d_H(P', Q)$ can become much larger than $d_H(P, Q)$ while the bottleneck distance between persistence diagrams remains unchanged, making the second inequality of Corollary 11.29 less interesting. To overcome this issue one can consider the *Gromov-Hausdorff distance* defined in the following way.

Definition 11.30 Let $X, Y \subset \mathbb{R}^d$ be two compact sets and let $\varepsilon \geq 0$. An ε-correspondence between X and Y is a subset $C \subseteq X \times Y$ such that

(i) for any $x \in X$, there exists $y \in Y$ such that $(x, y) \in C$;
(ii) for any $y \in Y$, there exists $x \in X$ such that $(x, y) \in C$;
(iii) for any $(x, y), (x', y') \in C$, $|d(x, x') - d(y, y')| \leq \varepsilon$, where $d(x, x') = \|x - x'\|$ is the Euclidean distance.

The Gromov-Hausdorff distance between X and Y is defined by

$$d_{GH}(X, Y) = \inf\{\varepsilon \geq 0 : \text{there exists an } \varepsilon\text{-correspondence between } X \text{ and } Y\}.$$

Notice that the aforementioned definition can be extended verbatim to any pair of compact metric spaces. Indeed the Gromov-Hausdorff distance allows to compare compact metric spaces, up to isometry, independently of any embedding. Coming back to the point clouds P, P', and Q where P' is the image of P by an ambient isometry of $\mathbb{R}^d$, we have that $d_{GH}(P, Q) = d_{GH}(P', Q)$. Moreover, Corollary 11.29 has the following generalization.

Theorem 11.31 *Let $P, Q \subset \mathbb{R}^d$ be finite point clouds and let* Filt(.) *be any of the* Čech *, Vietoris-Rips or alpha-shape filtered complexes. Then for any non-negative integer k,*

$$d_B(\mathsf{dgm}(H_k(\mathrm{Filt}(P))), \mathsf{dgm}(H_k(\mathrm{Filt}(Q)))) \leq d_{GH}(P, Q).$$

This theorem can be extended to point clouds in non-Euclidean metric spaces, except for the alpha-shape filtration which is no longer defined. In particular, to define the Vietoris-Rips complex, one just needs to know the pairwise distances between the points. As the computation of the Gromov-Hausdorff distance is usually intractable in practice, we can thus use the persistence diagrams of the Vietoris-Rips filtrations to compare the topological structure of finite data sets coming with pairwise distance information. Thanks to Theorem 11.31, the bottleneck distance provides a discriminative comparison tool: if the bottleneck distance between the diagrams is large, the two corresponding sets are far away from each other with respect to d_{GH}. The reverse is not true.

11.6 Exercises

Exercise 11.1　Let K be a finite simplicial complex. Prove that $\beta_0(K)$ is equal to the number of connected components of K.
Hint: Use the result of Exercise 2.1.

Exercise 11.2　Compute the Betti numbers of the simplicial complexes of Figure 11.3.

Exercise 11.3 (Difficult)　Let P be a finite set of points in $\mathbb{R}^2$. Prove that for any $\alpha \geq 0$

$$\text{Rips}(P,\alpha) \subseteq \check{\text{C}}\text{ech}(P,\alpha\sqrt{\frac{d}{2(d+1)}}) \subseteq \text{Rips}(P,2\alpha\sqrt{\frac{d}{2(d+1)}})$$

Hint: see [63], Theorem 2.5.

Exercise 11.4　Chains with coefficient in $\mathbb{Z}/2\mathbb{Z}$ have an obvious geometric interpretation: because any k-chain can be uniquely written as $c = \sigma_{i_1} + \sigma_{i_2} + \cdots \sigma_{i_m}$ where the σ_{i_j} are k-simplices, c can be considered as the union of the simplices σ_{i_j}. Show that the sum of two k-chains is equal to their symetric difference [1].

Exercise 11.5　Let $P \subset \mathbb{R}^d$ be a finite set of points. Prove that, for any $r \geq 0$, the Betti numbers $\beta_k(P^r)$ of the r-offset P^r are finite.
Hint: Use the Nerve theorem.

Exercise 11.6　Let $\mathbb{F}$ be a filtration of a simplicial complex K. Prove that all the vertices of K are positive and that an edge σ^i is positive if and only if the two ends (vertices) of σ^i are in the same connected component of K^{i-1}.

Exercise 11.7　Let $\mathbb{F}$ be a filtration of a simplicial complex K.

1. Prove that any cycle in K contains at least one positive simplex.
2. Prove that the cycle associated to a positive simplex in lemma 11.14 is uniquely defined.

Exercise 11.8　Let X be a (finitely) triangulated subset of $\mathbb{R}^d$ and let $f : X \to \mathbb{R}$ be a c-Lipschitz function, $c > 0$. Let K_f be the filtration induced by f on the

---

[1]　The symetric difference of two sets A and B is defined by $A \triangle B = (A \cup B)\backslash(A \cap B)$.

triangulation of X. Denoting by $\delta > 0$ the largest diameter of the simplices of the triangulation of X, prove that,

$$d_B(\mathsf{dgm}(K_f), \mathsf{dgm}(f)) \le c\delta.$$

11.7 Bibliographical Notes

A detailed introduction to algebraic topology and simplicial and singular homology can be found [110, 96].

The results of Section 11.4 are derived from [50] where complete proofs are given.

Persistent homology has been independently introduced by different authors [74, 83, 118] and has know important developments during the last decade. The stability of persistence diagrams has been initially proven by [60] for tame continuous functions defined on triangulable spaces. It was then extended and generalized by [36] and [51] to a more algebraic framework that appeared of fundamental importance in topological data analysis. An introductory course to computational topology is provided in [72] and a recent and general presentation of persistent homology theory is given in [114].

Theorem 11.31 is a particular case of a result proven in [43] and it has found various applications in shape classification [37] and in statistical analysis of data; see, e.g., [53, 79, 10, 44].

Bibliography

[1] N. Alon and J. H. Spencer. *The Probabilistic Method.* Wiley-Interscience, New York, 2nd edition, 2008.

[2] N. Amenta and M. Bern. Surface reconstruction by Voronoi filtering. *Discrete Comp. Geom.,* 22(4):481–504, 1999.

[3] D. Attali, J.-D. Boissonnat, and H. Edelsbrunner. Stability and computation of the medial axes. A State-of-the-Art Report. In T. Möller, B. Hamann, and R. Russell, editors, *Math. Foundations of Scientific Visualization, Comp. Graphics, and Massive Data Exploration,* volume 555 of *Mathematics and Vizualization,* pages 109–125. Springer-Verlag, Berlin, Germany, 2009.

[4] D. Attali, H. Edelsbrunner, and Y. Mileyko. Weak witnesses for Delaunay triangulations of submanifolds. In *Proc. ACM Symp. Solid and Physical Modeling,* pages 143–150, 2007.

[5] D. Attali, A. Lieutier, and D. Salinas. Efficient data structure for representing and simplifying simplicial complexes in high dimensions. *Int. J. Comp. Geom. Appl.,* 22(4):279–304, 2012.

[6] F. Aurenhammer. Power diagrams: Properties, algorithms and applications. *SIAM J. Comp.,* 16:78–96, 1987.

[7] F. Aurenhammer, R. Klein, and D.-T. Lee. *Voronoi Diagrams and Delaunay Triangulations.* World Scientific, Singapore, 2013.

[8] M. Berger. *Géométrie (vols. 1-5).* Fernand Nathan, Paris, 1977.

[9] G. Biau, F. Chazal, D. Cohen-Steiner, L. Devroye, and C. Rodriguez. A weighted *k*-nearest neighbor density estimate for geometric inference. *Electronic J. Stat.,* 5:204–237, 2011.

[10] A. J. Blumberg, I. Gal, M. A. Mandell, and M. Pancia. Robust statistics, hypothesis testing, and confidence intervals for persistent homology on metric measure spaces. *Found. Comp. Math.,* 14(4):745–789, 2014.

[11] J.-D. Boissonnat, C. S. Karthik, and S. Tavenas. Building efficient and compact data structures for simplicial complexes. Algorithmica, Vol. 79, No 2, 2017.

[12] J.-D. Boissonnat, O. Devillers, S. Pion, M. Teillaud, and M. Yvinec. Triangulations in CGAL. *Comp. Geom. Theory Appl.,* 22:5–19, 2002.

[13] J.-D. Boissonnat, R. Dyer, and A. Ghosh. Delaunay stability via perturbations. *Int. J. Comp. Geom. Appl.,* 24(2):125–152, 2014.

[14] J.-D. Boissonnat, R. Dyer, and A. Ghosh. The Stability of Delaunay Triangulations. *Int. J. Comp. Geom. Appl.*, 23(4 & 5):303–333, 2014.

[15] J.-D. Boissonnat, R. Dyer, and A. Ghosh. A probabilistic approach to reducing algebraic complexity of Delaunay triangulations. In *Proc. 23rd European Symp. on Algorithms*, Patras, Greece, pages 595–606, September 2015.

[16] J.-D. Boissonnat, R. Dyer, A. Ghosh, and M. Wintraecken. Local criteria for triangulation of manifolds. In *Proc. 34st Symp. Comp. Geom.*, Budapest, Hungary, June 2018.

[17] J.-D. Boissonnat and J. Flötotto. A coordinate system associated with points scattered on a surface. *Comp.-Aid. Des.*, 36:161–174, 2004.

[18] J-D. Boissonnat and A. Ghosh. Manifold reconstruction using tangential Delaunay complexes. *Discrete & Comp. Geom.*, 51(1):221–267, 2014.

[19] J.-D. Boissonnat, A. Lieutier, and M. Wintraecken. The reach, metric distortion, geodesic convexity and the variation of tangent spaces. In *Proc. 34st Symp. Comp. Geom.*, Budapest, Hungary, June 2018.

[20] J.-D. Boissonnat and C. Maria. The simplex tree: An efficient data structure for general simplicial complexes. *Algorithmica*, 70(3):406–427, November 2014.

[21] J.-D. Boissonnat, F. Nielsen, and R. Nock. Bregman Voronoi diagrams. *Discrete Comp. Geom.*, 44(2), 2010.

[22] J.-D. Boissonnat and S. Oudot. Provably good sampling and meshing of surfaces. *Graphical Models*, 67:405–451, 2005.

[23] J.-D. Boissonnat, C. Wormser, and M. Yvinec. Curved Voronoi diagrams. In J.-D. Boissonnat and M. Teillaud, editors, *Effective Computational Geometry for Curves and Surfaces*, pages 67–116. Mathematics and Visualization. Springer-Verlag, Berlin, 2006.

[24] J.-D. Boissonnat, C. Wormser, and M. Yvinec. Anisotropic Delaunay mesh generation. *SIAM J. Comput.*, 44(2):467–512, 2015.

[25] J.-D. Boissonnat and M. Yvinec. *Algorithmic Geometry*. Cambridge University Press, New York, NY, 1998. Translated by Hervé Brönnimann.

[26] J.-D. Boissonnat, O. Devillers, K. Dutta, and M. Glisse. Delaunay triangulation of a random sample of a good sample has linear size. Technical report, Inria, 2018.

[27] J.-D. Boissonnat, R. Dyer, and A. Ghosh. Delaunay triangulation of manifolds. *Found. Comp. Math.*, 18(2):399–431, 2018.

[28] F. Bolley, A. Guillin, and C. Villani. Quantitative concentration inequalities for empirical measures on non-compact spaces. *Probab. Theory Rel.*, 137(3): 541–593, 2007.

[29] M. Buchet, F. Chazal, S. Y. Oudot, and D. R. Sheehy. Efficient and robust persistent homology for measures. In *Proc. 36th ACM-SIAM Symp. on Discrete Algorithms*, pages 168–180. SIAM, 2015.

[30] D. Burago, Y. Burago, and S. Ivanov. *A Course in Metric Geometry*, Volume 33 of *Grad. Studies in Math.* American Mathematical Society, Providence, RI, 2001.

[31] C. Caillerie, F. Chazal, J. Dedecker, and B. Michel. Deconvolution for the Wasserstein metric and geometric inference. *Electron. J. Stat.*, 5:1394–1423, 2011.

Bibliography

[32] S. S. Cairns. A simple triangulation method for smooth maniolds. *Bull. Amer. Math. Soc.*, 67:380–390, 1961.

[33] P. B. Callahan and S. R. Kosaraju. A decomposition of multidimensional point sets with applications to k-nearest-neighbors and n-body potential fields. *J. ACM*, 42(1):67–90, 1995.

[34] P. Cannarsa and C. Cinestrari. *Semiconcave Functions, Hamilton-Jacobi Equations, and Optimal Control*, volume 58. Brikhauser, Boston, 2004.

[35] R. Chaine. A geometric convection approach of 3d-reconstruction. In *1st Symp. Geom. Processing*, pages 218–229, 2003.

[36] F. Chazal, D. Cohen-Steiner, M. Glisse, L. J. Guibas, and S. Y. Oudot. Proximity of persistence modules and their diagrams. In *Proc. Comp. Geom.*, Aarhus, Denmark, pages 237–246, 2009.

[37] F. Chazal, D. Cohen-Steiner, L. J. Guibas, F. Memoli, and S. Y. Oudot. Gromov-Hausdorff stable signatures for shapes using persistence. *Comp. Graph. Forum*, pages 1393–1403, 2009.

[38] F. Chazal, D. Cohen-Steiner, and A. Lieutier. Normal cone approximation and offset shape isotopy. *Comp. Geom. Theory Appl.*, 42(6–7):566–581, 2009.

[39] F. Chazal, D. Cohen-Steiner, and A. Lieutier. A sampling theory for compact sets in euclidean space. *Discrete Comp. Geom.*, 41(3):461–479, 2009.

[40] F. Chazal, D. Cohen-Steiner, A. Lieutier, and B. Thibert. Shape smoothing using double offsets. In *Proc. ACM Solid Phy. Model.*, Beijing, China, pages 183–192, 2007.

[41] F. Chazal, D. Cohen-Steiner, A. Lieutier, and B. Thibert. Stability of curvature measures. *Comp. Graph. Forum*, pages 1485–1496, 2009.

[42] F. Chazal, D. Cohen-Steiner, and Q. Mérigot. Geometric inference for probability measures. *Found. Comp. Math.*, 11(6):733–751, 2011.

[43] F. Chazal, V. de Silva, and S. Oudot. Persistence stability for geometric complexes. *Geometriae Dedicata*, 173(1):193–214, 2014.

[44] F. Chazal, B. Fasy, F. Lecci, B. Michel, A. Rinaldo, and L. Wasserman. Subsampling methods for persistent homology. In D. Blei and F. Bach, editors, *Proc. 32nd Int. Conf. on Machine Learning*, pages 2143–2151. JMLR Workshop and Conference Proceedings, Lille, France, 2015.

[45] F. Chazal, B. T. Fasy, F. Lecci, B. Michel, A. Rinaldo, and L. Wasserman. Robust topological inference: Distance to a measure and kernel distance. *arXiv preprint arXiv:1412.7197 (to appear in JMLR)*, 2014.

[46] F. Chazal and A. Lieutier. The λ-medial axis. *Graphical Models*, 67(4):304–331, July 2005.

[47] F. Chazal and A. Lieutier. Weak feature size and persistent homology: Computing homology of solids in $\mathbb{R}^n$ from noisy data samples. In *Proc. 21st Symp. Comp. Geom.*, Pisa, Italy, pages 255–262, 2005.

[48] F. Chazal and A. Lieutier. Stability and computation of topological invariants of solids in $\mathbb{R}^n$. *Discrete Comp. Geom.*, 37(4):601–617, 2007.

[49] F. Chazal, P. Massart, and B. Michel. Rates of convergence for robust geometric inference. *Electron. J. Stat.*, 10(2):2243–2286, 2016.

[50] F. Chazal and S. Y. Oudot. Towards persistence-based reconstruction in Euclidean spaces. In *Proc. 24th Sympos. Comp. Geom.*, pages 232–241, 2008.

[51] Frédéric Chazal, Vin de Silva, Marc Glisse, and Steve Oudot. *The structure and stability of persistence modules*. Springer Briefs in Mathematics. Springer, Basel, 2016.

[52] B. Chazelle. An optimal convex hull algorithm in any fixed dimension. *Discrete Comp. Geom.*, 10:377–409, 1993.

[53] F. Chazal, M. Glisse, C. Labruère, and B. Michel. Convergence rates for persistence diagram estimation in topological data analysis. *J. Mach. Learn. Res.*, 16:3603–3635, 2015.

[54] J. Cheeger. Critical points of distance functions and applications to geometry. In *Geometric Topology: Recent developments, Montecani Terme*, volume 1504 of *Lecture Notes in Math.*, pages 1–38. Springer, Basel, 1990.

[55] J. Cheeger, W. Müller, and R. Schrader. On the curvature of piecewise flat spaces. *Comm. Math. Phys.*, 92:405–454, 1984.

[56] S.-W. Cheng, T. K. Dey, H. Edelsbrunner, M. A. Facello, and S.-H. Teng. Sliver Exudation. *J. ACM*, 47:883–904, 2000.

[57] S.-W. Cheng, T. K. Dey, and E. A. Ramos. Manifold Reconstruction from Point Samples. In *Proc. 16th ACM-SIAM Symp. Discrete Algorithms*, Vancouver, Canada, pages 1018–1027, 2005.

[58] F. H. Clarke. *Optimization and Nonsmooth Analysis*. Wiley-Interscience, New-York, 1983.

[59] K. L. Clarkson and P. W. Shor. Applications of random sampling in computational geometry, II. *Discrete Comp. Geom.*, 4:387–421, 1989.

[60] D. Cohen-Steiner, H. Edelsbrunner, and J. Harer. Stability of persistence diagrams. *Discrete Comp. Geom.*, 37(1):103–120, 2007.

[61] M. de Berg, M. van Kreveld, M. Overmars, and O. Schwarzkopf. *Computational Geometry: Algorithms and Applications*, 2nd edition. Springer-Verlag, Berlin, Germany, 2000.

[62] V. de Silva. A weak characterisation of the Delaunay triangulation. *Geometriae Dedicata*, 135(1):39–64, 2008.

[63] V. de Silva and R. Ghrist. Coverage in sensor networks via persistent homology. *Algebraic & Geom. Topol.*, 7:339–358, 2007.

[64] B. Delaunay. Sur la sphère vide. *Izv. Akad. Nauk SSSR, Otdelenie Matematicheskii i Estestvennyka Nauk*, 7:793–800, 1934.

[65] T. K. Dey. *Curve and Surface Reconstruction: Algorithms with Mathematical Analysis*. Cambridge University Press, New York NY, 2007.

[66] R. Dyer, G. Vegter, and M. Wintraecken. Riemannian simplices and triangulations. *Geometriae Dedicata*, 179:91–138, 2015.

[67] H. Edelsbrunner. *Algorithms in Combinatorial Geometry*, volume 10 of *EATCS Monographs on Theoretical Comp. Science*. Springer-Verlag, Heidelberg, West Germany, 1987.

[68] H. Edelsbrunner. The union of balls and its dual shape. *Discrete Comp. Geom.*, 13(1):415–440, 1995.

[69] H. Edelsbrunner. *Geometry and Topology for Mesh Generation*. Cambridge University Press, Cambridge, 2001.

[70] H. Edelsbrunner. Surface reconstruction by wrapping finite point sets in space. In B. Aronov, S. Basu, J. Pach, M. Sharir (Eds.), *Ricky Pollack and Eli Goodman Festschrift*, pages 379–404. Springer-Verlag, Berlin, 2003.

[71] H. Edelsbrunner, M. Facello, and J. Liang. On the definition and the construction of pockets in macromolecules. *Discrete Appl. Math.*, 88(1-3):83–102, 1998.

[72] H. Edelsbrunner and J. L. Harer. *Computational Topology: An Introduction.* American Mathematical Soc., Providence, RI, 2010.

[73] H. Edelsbrunner, D. Kirkpatrick, and R. Seidel. On the shape of a set of points in the plane. *IEEE Trans. on Inform. Theory*, 29(4):551–559, 1983.

[74] H. Edelsbrunner, D. Letscher, and A. Zomorodian. Topological persistence and simplification. *Discrete Comp. Geom.*, 28:511–533, 2002.

[75] H. Edelsbrunner, X.-Y. Li, G. L. Miller, A. Stathopoulos, D. Talmor, S.-H. Teng, A. Üngör, and N. Walkington. Smoothing and cleaning up slivers. In *Proc. 32nd ACM Symp. on Theory of Comput., May 21–23, 2000*, Portland, OR, pages 273–277, 2000.

[76] H. Edelsbrunner and E. P. Mücke. Three-dimensional alpha shapes. *ACM Trans. Graph.*, 13(1):43–72, 1994.

[77] H. Edelsbrunner and H. Wagner. Topological data analysis with Bregman divergences. In *33rd Symp. Comp. Geom*, pages 39:1–39:16, Brisbane, Australia, July 2017.

[78] D. Eppstein, M. Löffler, and D. Strash. Listing all maximal cliques in sparse graphs in near-optimal time. In *Proc. 21st Int. Symp. on Algorithms and Computation*, Jeju Island, Korea, December 15–17, pages 403–414, 2010.

[79] B. T. Fasy, F. Lecci, A. Rinaldo, L. Wasserman, S. Balakrishnan, A. Singh, et al. Confidence sets for persistence diagrams. *Ann. Stat.*, 42(6):2301–2339, 2014.

[80] T. Feder and D. Greene. Optimal algorithms for approximate clustering. In *Proc. of 20th ACM Sympos. Theory of Computing*, pages 434–444, New York, NY, 1988. ACM.

[81] H. Federer. Curvature measures. *Trans. American Math. Society*, 93(3):418–491, 1959.

[82] D. Freedman. Efficient simplicial reconstructions of manifolds from their samples. *IEEE Trans. on Pattern Analysis and Machine Intelligence*, 24(10): 1349–1357, 2002.

[83] P. Frosini and C. Landi. Size theory as a topological tool for computer vision. *Pattern Recognition and Image Analysis*, 9:596–603, 1999.

[84] J. H. G. Fu. Convergence of curvatures in secant approximations. *J. Diff. Geom.*, 37:177–190, 1993.

[85] J. H. G. Fu. Tubular neighborhoods in Euclidean spaces. *Duke Math. J.*, 52(4):1025–1046, 1985.

[86] W. Fulton. *Algebraic Topology: A First Course.* Springer-Verlag, New York, 1995.

[87] J. Gallier. Notes on convex sets, polytopes, polyhedra combinatorial topology, Voronoi diagrams and Delaunay triangulations. Research Report RR-6379, Inria, 2007.

[88] S. Gallot, D. Hulin, and J. Lafontaine. *Riemannian Geometry.* Springer-Verlag, Berlin Heidelberg, 1990.

[89] J. Giesen and M. John. The flow complex: a data structure for geometric modeling. In *Proc. 14th ACM-SIAM Symp. Discrete Algorithms (SODA)*, pages 285–294, 2003.

[90] J. Giesen and U. Wagner. Shape dimension and intrinsic metric from samples of manifolds. *Discrete Comp. Geom.*, 32:245–267, 2004.

[91] T. F. Gonzales. Clustering to minimize the maximaum intercluster distance. *Theoretical Comp. Science*, 38(2-3):293–306, 1985.

[92] K. Grove. Critical point theory for distance functions. In *Proceedings of Symposia in Pure Mathematics*, American Mathematical Society, Providence, RI, volume 54, 1993. Part 3.

[93] L. Guibas, D. Morozov, and Q. Mérigot. Witnessed k-distance. *Discrete Comp. Geom.*, 49(1):22–45, 2013.

[94] S. Har-Peled. *Geometric approximation algorithms*, volume 173. American Mathematical Society, Providence, RI, 2011.

[95] S. Har-Peled and M. Mendel. Fast construction of nets in low-dimensional metrics and their applications. *SIAM J. Comp.*, 35(5):1148–1184, 2006.

[96] A. Hatcher. *Algebraic Topology*. Cambridge University Press, Cambridge, UK, 2002.

[97] M. W. Hirsch. *Differential Topology*. Springer-Verlag, New York, NY, 1976.

[98] I. T. Jolliffe. *Principal Component Analysis*. Springer, New York, 2002.

[99] X.-Y. Li. Generating well-shaped d-dimensional Delaunay meshes. *Theor. Comp. Science*, 296(1):145–165, 2003.

[100] J. Liang, H. Edelsbrunner, and C. Woodward. Anatomy of protein pockets and cavities: Measurement of binding site geometry and implications for ligand design. *Prot. Sci.*, 7:1884–1897, 1998.

[101] A. Lieutier. Any open bounded subset of $\mathbb{R}^n$ has the same homotopy type as it medial axis. *Comp.-Aid. Design*, 36(11):1029–1046, September 2004.

[102] Y. Ma, P. Niyogi, G. Sapiro, and R. Vidal Ed. Dimensionality reduction via subspace and submanifold learning. *IEEE Sig. Process. Mag.*, 28(2), 2011.

[103] C. Maria, J.-D. Boissonnat, M. Glisse, and M. Yvinec. The Gudhi Library: Simplicial complexes and persistent homology. In *The 4th Int. Congress on Math. Software*, Hanyang University, Seoul, Korea, France, August 2014.

[104] T. Martinetz and K. Schulten. Topology representing networks. *Neural Networks*, 7(3):507–522, 1994.

[105] J. Milnor. *Morse Theory*. Princeton University Press, Princeton, NJ, 2006.

[106] R. A. Moser and G. Tardos. A constructive proof of the generalized Lovász lemma. *J. ACM*, 57(2), 2010.

[107] R. Motwani and P. Raghavan. *Randomized Algorithms*. Cambridge University Press, New York, NY, 1995.

[108] K. Mulmuley. *Computational Geometry: An Introduction through Randomized Algorithms*. Prentice Hall, Englewood Cliffs, NJ, 1994.

[109] J. R. Munkres. *Elementary Differential Topology*. Princeton University Press, Princeton, NJ, 1966.

[110] J. R. Munkres. *Elements of Algebraic Topology*. Addison-Wesley, Redwood City, CA, 1984.

[111] J. R. Munkres. *Topology*. Prentice Hall, Upper Saddle River, NJ, 2000.

[112] P. Niyogi, S. Smale, and S. Weinberger. Finding the homology of submanifolds with high confidence from random samples. *Discrete Comp. Geom.*, 39(1): 419–441, 2008.

[113]   A. Okabe, B. Boots, and K. Sugihara. *Spatial Tessellations: Concepts and Applications of Voronoi Diagrams*. John Wiley & Sons, Chichester, UK, 1992.

[114]   S. Y. Oudot. *Persistence Theory: From Quiver Representations to Data Analysis*, volume 209 of *AMS Mathematical Surveys and Monographs*. American Mathematical Society, Providence, RI, 2015.

[115]   D. Pedoe. *Geometry, A Comprehensive Course*. Dover Publications, New York, 1970.

[116]   S. Peleg, M. Werman, and H. Rom. A unified approach to the change of resolution: Space and gray-level. *IEEE Trans. Pattern Anal. Mach. Intell.*, 11(7):739–742, 1989.

[117]   A. Petrunin. Semiconcave functions in alexandrov's geometry. In *Surveys in Differential Geometry: Metric and Comparison Geometry, volume XI*, Boston, 2007. Internationational Press of Boston.

[118]   V. Robins. Towards computing homology from finite approximations. *Topol. Proceed.*, 24:503–532, 1999.

[119]   R. T. Rockafellar. *Convex Analysis*. Princeton University Press, Princeton, NJ, 1970.

[120]   Y. Rubner, C. Tomasi, and L. J. Guibas. The earth mover's distance as a metric for image retrieval. *Int. J. Comp. Vision*, 40(2):99–121, 2000.

[121]   R. Seidel. The upper bound theorem for polytopes: An easy proof of its asymptotic version. *Comp. Geom. Theory Appl.*, 5:115–116, 1995.

[122]   J. Shewchuk. Star splaying: An algorithm for repairing delaunay triangulations and convex hulls. In *Proc. 21st Symp. on Comp. Geom.*, pages 237–246, 2005.

[123]   R. Sibson. A vector identity for the Dirichlet tesselation. *Math. Proc. Camb. Phil. Soc.*, 87:151–155, 1980.

[124]   R. Sibson. A brief description of natural neighbour interpolation. In Vic Barnet, editor, *Interpreting Multivariate Data*, pages 21–36. John Wiley & Sons, Chichester, 1981.

[125]   J. Spencer. Robin Moser makes Lovász Local Lemma Algorithmic! https://www.cs.nyu.edu/spencer/moserlovasz1.pdf, 2009.

[126]   The GUDHI Project. *GUDHI User and Reference Manual*. GUDHI Editorial Board, 2015.

[127]   L. N. Trefethen and D. Bau. *Numerical Linear Algebra*. Society for Industrial and Applied Mathematics, 1997.

[128]   C. Villani. *Topics in Optimal Transportation*. American Mathematical Society, Providence, RI, 2003.

[129]   E. Welzl. Smallest enclosing disks (balls and ellipsoids). In H. Maurer, editor, *New Results and New Trends in Comp. Science*, volume 555 of *Lecture Notes Comp. Sci.*, pages 359–370. Springer-Verlag, Berlin, 1991.

[130]   J. H. C. Whitehead. On C^1-complexes. *Ann. Math.*, 41:809–824, 1940.

[131]   H. Whitney. *Geometric Integration Theory*. Princeton University Press, Princeton, NJ, 1957.

[132]   G. M. Ziegler. *Lectures on Polytopes*, volume 152 of *Graduate Texts in Mathematics*. Springer-Verlag, Heidelberg, 1994.

Index

231